Univ

Subje

ht

Transforming Public Enterprise in Europe and North America

Transforming Public Enterprise in Europe and North America

Networks, Integration and Transnationalisation

Edited by

Judith Clifton
Francisco Comín

and

Daniel Díaz-Fuentes

First published 2007 by
PALGRAVE MACMILLAN
Houndmills, Basingstoke, Hampshire RG21 6XS and
175 Fifth Avenue, New York, N.Y. 10010
Companies and representatives throughout the world

PALGRAVE MACMILLAN is the global academic imprint of the Palgrave Macmillan division of St. Martin's Press, LLC and of Palgrave Macmillan Ltd. Macmillan® is a registered trademark in the United States, United Kingdom and other countries. Palgrave is a registered trademark in the European Union and other countries.

ISBN-13: 978-1-4039-9162-1   hardback
ISBN-10:1-4039-9162-6   hardback

This book is printed on paper suitable for recycling and made from fully managed and sustained forest sources.

A catalogue record for this book is available from the British Library.

Library of Congress Cataloging-in-Publication Data

Transforming public enterprise in Europe and North America : networks, integration and transnationalization / edited by Judith Clifton, Francisco Comín and Daniel Díaz-Fuentes.
     p. cm.
Includes bibliographical references and index.
ISBN-13: 978-1-4039-9162-1 (cloth)
ISBN-10: 1-4039-9162-6 (cloth)
     1. Public utilities—Europe. 2. Public utilities—North America. 3. Privatisation—Europe. 4. Privatisation—North America. I. Clifton, Judith, 1967– II. Comín, Francisco, 1950– III. Díaz-Fuentes, Daniel.

HD2768.E8514T73 2007
338.94'05—dc22

2006043016

10   9   8   7   6   5   4   3   2   1
16   15   14   13   12   11   10   09   08   07

Printed and bound in Great Britain by
Antony Rowe Ltd, Chippenham and Eastbourne

Contents

List of Figures and Tables

Tables

Figures

Acknowledgements

We acknowledge the help, support and inspiration of many individuals and institutions in the writing of this book. We would particularly like to thank all the authors of these chapters who made our work with them so stimulating, especially Pierre Lanthier, who organised sessions at the University of Québec at Trois-Rivières in 2001 and Buenos Aires in 2002 with future collaborators Pier Angelo Toninelli, Era Belabed and Nuno Valerio, Patrick Fridenson who encouraged us from the start, and Robert Millward who helped throughout. We are also indebted to William Megginson and Privatization Barometer. Harm Schröter must also be thanked for organising the related sessions in Milan 2005 and Helsinki 2006. Thanks also are due to conference organisers of the CEEP in Leipzig 2004, the Spanish Institute of Fiscal Studies for sponsoring our IEHA pre-session in 2003 at the University of Cantabria, UNU-CRIS, especially Mary Farrell, UACES 2005 and 2006, REM Madrid 2005 and Alicante in 2006.

In terms of institutional support, we acknowledge financing from the Spanish Ministry of Education and Science Plan Nacional (2002–2005, and 2005–2008). Judith Clifton was Ramón y Cajal Research Fellow supported by the European Social Fund and Daniel Díaz-Fuentes was awarded the Spanish Ministry's Salvador de Madariaga for 2006–8. We are also grateful for the facilities provided by the Universities of Alcalá de Henares, Cantabria and Oviedo, our home universities, as well as universities we have visited, especially the Open University in the UK (particular thanks to Janet Newman and John Clarke) and the European University Institute in Florence (thanks particularly to Helen Wallace and Adrienne Héritier). Finally, thanks to Michael Mortimore and the ECLAC team.

List of Abbreviations

ABSU	Accenture Business Services for Utilities
AGIP	Azienda Generale Italia Petroli
BCHIL	British Columbia Hydro International Ltd
BCTC	British Columbia Transmission Corporation
BOO	Build, Own, Operate
BP	British Petroleum
CAA	Civil Aviation Authority
CEE	Central and Eastern European countries
CFE	Comisión Federal de Electricidad
CGT	Confédération Générale du Travail
COFETEL	Comisión Federal de Telecomunicaciones
CPTA	County Public Transport Administration
DGT	Directorate General for Telecommunications
DNS	Domain Name System
DP	Deutsche Post
DSB	Danske Statsbaner
EADS	European Aeronautic Defence and Space Company
EBIDTDA	Earnings before Interest, Depreciation and Amortisation
EC	European Commission
ECLAC	Economic Commission for Latin America and the Caribbean
ECSC	European Coal and Steel Community
EDF	Electricité de France
EDP	Electricidade de Portugal
EEC	European Economic Community
ESAM	Energy Services Alliance of Manitoba
ESI	Electricity supply industry
ETCS	European Train Control System
ETO	Unified Tariff Organ
EU	European Union
FAA	Federal Aviation Authority
FAS	Federal Antimonopoly Service
FDI	Foreign Direct Investment
FEC	Federal Energy Commission
FERC	Federal Energy Regulatory Commission
FHLMC	Federal Home Loan Mortgage Corporation
FIF	Fonds de l'infrastructure Ferroviaire
FNMA	Federal National Mortgage Association
FT	France Télécom
IFB	Interferry Boats

GATS	General Agreement on Trade in Services
GATT	General Agreement on Tariffs and Trade
GDF	Gaz de France
GDI	Gross Domestic Investment
GDP	Gross Domestic Product
HEP	Hydro-Electric Power
HQI	Hydro-Québec International
HVDC	High Voltage Direct Current
IATA	International Air Transport Association
IMEMO RAN	Institute of World Economy and International Relations of the Russian Academy of Sciences
IMF	International Monetary Fund
INI	Instituto Nacional de Industria
INH	National Hydrocarbons Institute (Instituto Nacional de Hidrocarburos)
IOU	Investor-Owned Utility
IPO	International Public Offering
IREQ	Institute of Electricity Research (Institut de recherche d'Hydro-Québec)
IRI	Industrial Reconstruction Institute
MAPP	Mid-Continent Area Power Pool
MISO	Midwest Independent System Operator
NAFTA	North American Free Trade Agreement
NMBS	Nationale Maatschapij der Belgische Spoorwegen (Belgian National Railway Company)
NERC	North American Electric Reliability Council
NPCC	Northeast Power Coordinating Council
NSB	Norske Statsbaner
OECD	Organisation for Economic Cooperation and Development
PEMEX	Petróleos Mexicanos
PO	Public Offering
PP	Partido Popular
PT	Portugal Telecom
PTO	Public Telephone Network Operator
PTT	Post, Telegraph and Telephone
PSOE	Partido Socialista Obrero Español
R&D	Research and Development
RJSC UES	Russian Joint-Stock Company for Unified Energy System
ROE	Return on Equity
RTO	Regional Transmission Operators
SAS	Scandinavian Airlines
SBC	Southwestern Bell
SEBJ	Société d'énergie de la Baie James

SEPCOL	Southern Electric Power Co. Ltd
SEPI	State Society of Industrial Participations (Sociedad Estatal de Participaciones Industriales)
SEPPA	State Society for Property Participations that hold State Shares in Enterprises (Sociedad Estatal de Participaciones Patrimoniales)
SJ	Statens Järnvägar
SNCF	Société Nationale des Chemins de Fer
SOE	State-Owned Enterprise
STRM	Sindicato de Telefonistas de la Republica Mexicana
TAP	Transportes Aéreos Portugueses
TELMEX	Teléfonos de México
TENP	Trans-Europa-Naturgas-Pipeline
TLAC	Trans Latin American Corporation
TNC	Transnational Corporation
UK	United Kingdom
UNCTAD	United Nations Conference on Trade and Development
USA	United States of America
USPS	United States Postal Service
URGE	Uniform Rating of Generating Equipment
WECC	Western Electricity Coordinating Council

Notes on the Contributors

Lena Andersson-Skog is Professor of Economic History at the University of Umeå. She is a member of the editorial board of the *Journal of Transport History*, the Swedish National Council for Nuclear Waste and the Swedish Research Council. Research interests include infrastructure development and the welfare state in Scandinavia.

Sean D. Barrett is Senior Lecturer in Economics and Fellow of Trinity College, Dublin. He is Government of Ireland nominee to the National Economic and Social Council of Ireland and a member of the Electronic Communications Appeal Panel. He is a member of the editorial board of the *Journal of Air Transport Management*. Barrett has published on deregulation, airport economics and taxi services through the European Conference of Ministers of Transport and the European Science Foundation.

Carlos Bastien is Professor of Economic History at the Institute of Economics and Management (ISEG) of the Technical University of Lisbon, where he received his doctorate. His research has focused mainly on business history and the history of economic thought.

Frans Buelens is Professor of Economics at HIVT and Senior Researcher at the University of Antwerp. After receiving his doctorate from the University of Antwerp he conducted research on the economic history of companies, the stock exchange and the performance of companies in Belgium, industry and geographical investment clusters.

Candra S. Chahyadi is a PhD candidate at the University of Oklahoma. His research interests include privatisation, corporate finance, international finance and corporate governance.

Judith Clifton is Ramón y Cajal Research Fellow at the University of Oviedo, and Visiting Researcher at the Open University and the European University Institute. Since receiving her doctorate from Oxford, she has researched on public enterprises and public policy, particularly the network services. Her approach focuses on the social and political consequences of change in both Europe and Latin America.

Francisco Comín is Professor of Economic History at the University of Alcalá de Henares and winner of the National Prize for History in 1990. He is a member of the Royal Academy for Moral and Political Science and a former General Secretary of the Spanish Economic History Association. Comín has published extensively on public enterprises, fiscal systems and welfare states.

Daniel Díaz-Fuentes is Professor of Economics at the University of Cantabria and Salvador de Madariaga Visiting Researcher at the European University Institute. His research interests include public enterprises, economic development, fiscal systems and welfare states in Europe and Latin America.

Patrick Fridenson is Professor of History and Director of Studies at the École des Hautes Études en Sciences Sociales. He is also editor of the journals *Le Mouvement Social* and *Enterprise et Histoire*. His publications focus on business history, labour history and the economic functions of the state in contemporary Europe, North America and Japan (nineteenth and twentieth centuries).

Marina Klinova is Senior Research Associate at the Centre for European Studies of the Institute of World Economy and International Relations (IMEMO), Russian Academy of Sciences, and Lecturer at the Moscow International High School of Business (MIRBIS). After receiving her doctorate from IMEMO she has researched on public enterprises, privatisation and public economic policy. Her approach focuses on both the EU and the Russian context.

Pierre Lanthier is Professor at the Université du Québec à Trois-Rivières and a member of the Centre interuniversitaire d'études québécoises. After receiving his state doctorate from the Université de Paris X (Nanterre), he has conducted research on electricity and electrical manufacturing in Europe and in North America, as well as on social history in twentieth-century Québec.

Carlos Marichal is Professor of Economic History at the Colegio de México and received his doctorate from Harvard in 1977. He has published extensively on economic thought, business history, intellectual history and banking history in Latin America and Europe.

William L. Megginson is Professor and Rainbolt Chair in Finance at the University of Oklahoma's Michael F. Price College of Business. He is also a voting member of the Italian Ministry of Economics and Finance's Global Advisory Committee on Privatization, Scientific Advisor for the Privatization Barometer and privatisation consultant for the NYSE, OECD, IMF and World Bank. He has published extensively in top journals and also co-authored seven textbooks.

Robert Millward has been Professor of Economic History at the Department of History, University of Manchester, since 1989. He was previously Professor of Economics at the University of Salford, UK, and Secretary-General of the European Historical Economics Society. He has published extensively on industrial history and on the history and economics of the public sector, including the development of public health programmes and their impact on population trends.

Ana Bela Nunes is Professor of Economic History at the Institute of Economics and Management (ISEG) of the Technical University of Lisbon, where she received her doctorate. Her research has focused mainly on structural aspects of modern economic growth linked to education and urbanisation.

Thomas Pettersson is Assistant Professor of Economic History at Umeå University. He has published on transport history and regional policy, with a focus on decision-making processes and the effects of institutional path dependence.

Jesus M. Salas is a PhD candidate at the University of Oklahoma. Research interests include corporate governance, dividend policy and risk management. Salas is also treasurer of the 'Two Brothers Foundation', a non-profit organisation in Brazil.

Harm G. Schröter is Professor of Economic History at the University of Bergen. He received his doctorate in 1981 and has lectured at several German universities. He is Secretary of the European Business History Association and member of several editorial boards. Research interests include the role and character of Europe and, most recently, whether the European Enterprise exists?

Pier Angelo Toninelli is Professor of History and Business History at the Faculty of Economics of the University of Milan-Bicocca. He is currently doing research on the boundaries of private and public and performance of state-owned enterprise in Italy. He edited *The Rise and Fall of State-Owned Enterprise in the Western World* (2000).

Nuno Valério is Professor of Economic History at the Institute of Economics and Mangement (ISEG) of the Technical University of Lisbon, where he received his doctorate. His research has focused mainly on monetary and financial history and the theory of economic systems.

Michelangelo Vasta graduated cum laude at the University of Florence and received his DPhil from the University of Oxford. He is Professor of Economic History at the University of Siena (Department of Economics). Research interests include technical change in historical perspective, business history, ownership structure and industrial economics. Recent publications include (edited with R. Giannetti) *Evolution of Italian Enterprises in the Twentieth Century* (2006).

Julien van den Broeck is Professor of Economics at the University of Antwerp and honorary Doctor of the National Technical University of Kharkov, Ukraine. He is past President of the Belgian–Dutch Association of Institutional and Political Economy. His publications mainly focus on the measurement and determinants of efficiency.

Hans Willems recently finished his doctoral dissertation on the institutional history of the stock exchanges in the nineteenth century at the University of Antwerp. In 2001 he was awarded a scholarship by the Fund of Scientific Research Flanders and is involved in an interdisciplinary project on the history and structure of the Brussels Stock Exchange (1830–2000).

Part I
Network Services in Context

1

Transforming Network Services in Europe and the Americas: From Ugly Ducklings to Swans?

Judith Clifton, Francisco Comín and Daniel Díaz-Fuentes

Introduction

People have long grown accustomed to the fact that the water running through their taps, the electricity and gas heating their houses and cooking their food, the buses, trains, trams or ferries they use to move or get to work, their telephone and postal services for communication, and the radio and television programmes they tune into are nationally or locally owned and run. These services, basic and fundamental to human and organisational activity, are 'public network services' in the sense that they have a *network structure* that serves in the *public interest* and tend to be *subject to regulation that takes this into consideration*. Thus, their 'publicness' is connected to their important role in society rather than meaning that they are necessarily publicly owned or managed, though sometimes their public role, ownership and management have been confused and merged into one. For most of the twentieth century and in most countries – with the important exception of the United States of America (USA) – the nationally bound ownership of these network services has usually been accompanied by public ownership in the form of Public or State-Owned Enterprises (SOEs). Of course, private networks have sometimes accompanied public networks in the twentieth century, such as broadcasting in the UK, where the British Broadcasting Corporation was rivalled by private operators as early as the mid-1950s, or in Belgium and Spain, where electricity was partially privately owned for much of the century. In general, however, even private network services were nationally bound and exposed to similar regulation to the other SOEs.[1] Moreover, justifications for public and national or local ownership and management of these services included: their having natural monopoly characteristics; territorial considerations such as national defence (physical in the case of the railways, ports and roads, and psychological in the case of radio or television); the need to integrate infrastructure to establish a national market; the will to avoid dependency on foreigners by attaining self-sufficiency of basic inputs (oil, foods and basic materials); and plans to attain industrial development via the 'Industrial State'. Public network services were also associated with the Welfare State, and their organisation often included the application of redistributive policies, such as the cross-subsidisation of local and national networks against international ones in the cases of, say, telecommunications and railways.

Now, the increasingly deep cross-border integration of markets both in the European Union (EU) and the North American Free Trade Agreement (NAFTA) on the one hand and policy reform towards deregulation, liberalisation and privatisation on the other hand, may be signalling at least a partial rupture between public network services and national or local government. Firstly, there may be spatial reconfiguration policies, such as the Trans European Networks (TENs) project for energy, telecommunications and transport which aims to forge common networks across the Member States and their borders. Secondly, the logic of common markets means that there is little economic rationale to prioritise national or local over foreign ownership and management. This, in itself, is not new: Foreign Direct Investment (FDI) has been present in economies for centuries and, in the case of industrial Multinational or Transnational Corporations (TNCs), this may cause little alarm. What is new, however, and far more controversial, is the question of foreign ownership and management of FDI in public network services, in particular after society has become accustomed to decades of nationally-bound ownership and management during which time these services have come to play a key role in society and political life. For example, the provision of gas has been and still is critical in economic, social and geopolitical terms in Europe and Asia. The Russian government's decision to take control over the gas giant GAZPROM by putting government allies in key managerial positions and launching an aggressive campaign to seek out markets as changing borders reshape and redefine markets in network infrastructure, poses challenges to the international relations regime. Looking at European investment in public services abroad, social protest has mobilised over foreign ownership and management of basic resources such as water, energy and communications in Latin America.[2] US neighbours Canada and Mexico have historically been sensitive to its economic power. Have liberalisation, deregulation and integration policies eroded older questions of national or local protection of national or local network infrastructure? Even without histories of centuries-old geopolitical questions, 'friendly' nations struggle to answer these questions. In Europe, the mass media are, at the time of writing, covering developments arising from the German energy giant E.ON's bid to take over Spain's Endesa to create what could constitute Europe's largest energy TNC (which the Catalonian Gas Natural had already planned to take over). This is resulting in debates as to what is and what is not in the national (Spanish) or indeed local (Catalonian) public interest. In the telecommunications and electricity sectors, even after years of EU deregulation and liberalisation policies that have had direct consequences for privatisation and FDI, it seems that effects on competition have been limited.[3] For instance, the telecommunications market share of new entrants was below 20 per cent in the EU15 countries even by 2004, and below 5 per cent in 11 EU countries. Despite the Merger and Acquisition (M&A) 'mania', the dominance of the former PTO of the five largest economies is still unrivalled. Electricity liberalisation has been less ambitious and more delayed than that for telecommunications. In December 1996 the Electricity Directive was drawn up by the European Commission requiring each Member State to gradually open its market to competition, to a minimum of 33 per cent by 2003, and restricting electricity generation by a single company to 50 per cent. Some countries agreed, reluctantly, to a partial liberalisation (Italy, Portugal and the Netherlands). Others (Finland, Germany, Sweden and the UK) had already liberalised before the Directive was passed. France has powerfully resisted liberalisation to date. Despite this resistance, however, many of Europe's electricity companies have transformed themselves quite dramatically in recent years through internationalisation strategies and M&As, including France's EDF. Moreover, some governments have promoted the policy of creating 'national champions' to protect their domestic markets whilst also expanding their market shares abroad. In the EU electricity market, new TNC leaders emerged in the 1990s, such as EDF in France, RWE and E.ON in Germany, ENEL in Italy, Vattenfall in Sweden and Endesa and Iberdrola in Spain. As a result of market liberalisation and corporate transnationalisation many companies have opted to relocate abroad: EDF is London's main electricity supplier and Vattenfall is Germany's third most important electricity supplier.

These developments concerning the foreign ownership and/or management of public services may test the political will of integration processes, precisely because network services differ fundamentally from the average manufactured commodity. Their development interests society because it depends on them on a daily basis, guaranteeing it welfare and living standards. To put it more boldly, if, from the 1980s, the overarching question dominating public enterprise, including network services, was whether private or public ownership and management were superior (in financial and economic efficiency terms), could this debate (still unresolved and disputed) be transformed into one concerning whether nationally or locally-bound ownership and management are superior to foreign ownership and management? Superior for whom? Do foreign ownership and management actually matter?

Services did not play a leading role in FDI flows during the second half of the twentieth century: rather, it was the industrial sector which dominated these flows. Dunning's eclectic paradigm (1977, 1988), an important point of reference for FDI and TNC analysis, tended to assume enterprises were both private and industrial, logically, given the context from the 1950s was that most FDI was due to US industrial enterprise internationalisation. From the mid-1990s, there has been a new trend in FDI flows, with the rise of a service-based TNC. Though services cover a vast range of business activity, an important part can be explained by public network service internationalisation in sectors such as telecommunications, energy, transport and water. This trend is the focus of this book, with the intention of trying to understand this development as well as some of its consequences from a long-term perspective.

The title of this chapter reveals the paradox and a major inspiration for writing. From the 1980s, starting in the UK during the Thatcher administration and spreading to continental Europe during the 1990s, former SOEs were privatised rather dramatically (though there had been other instances of privatisation previously, including in Pinochet's Chile and Adenauer's and, before that, Nazi Germany.[4] Although, particularly with the benefit of hindsight, pro-market ideology was not the only, or necessarily the main, reason for privatisation across Europe,[5] there was certainly a diffusion of ideas and economic theories used to promote private ownership. Privatisation seemed to be a cure for all SOE ills and a blueprint to enhanced economic efficiency. As private and public ownership and management were dichotomised, the belief became fashionable that public ownership and management of enterprises were inherently inferior to private ownership and management: hence public enterprises were cast as 'ugly ducklings' that needed transformation through exposure to the 'cold winds' of the market in order to become privatised economic 'swans'. Some scholars forecast the 'death' of the public enterprise.[6]

By 2006, however, the privatisation process was still uneven by country and sector, and there was resistance to privatisation in certain sectors, particularly the network services – telecoms, transport, energy and water. Moreover, by the beginning of the twenty-first century, some of the same public network services – France Telecom, E.ON, RWE, Suez–Gaz de France, Telefonica, Deutsche Post, Endesa, Deutsche Telekom, Enel, Telecom Italia, National Grid Tasco, and so on – emerged as the world's leading TNCs. Some of these were privatised, whilst others remained in state hands, at least partially. Their privatisation, therefore, cannot be the cause – or, at least, the only cause – of public enterprise transformation. How, then, can this development be explained? Was the decline of public enterprises exaggerated? Have some 'risen from the ashes' like the phoenix? Were market regulatory reform and competition policies at least as important or more important than ownership, as Newbury argued?[7] What role did technological change play? Is this best explained by regional (European or North American) or global integration processes? Of course, not all public service networks have internationalised. Many have not internationalised at all, others have internationalised only recently, whilst others embarked on internationalisation strategies over a century ago. Why did some networks internationalise and not others? Moreover, different degrees of success have been obtained through internationalisation. Perhaps paradoxically, some enterprises with significant state ownership and a near monopoly at home have been successful in their exploitation of open, competitive markets abroad, such as EDF. Is EDF a public or private TNC in this regard? Do public enterprises behave as private enterprises abroad? How does this affect their managerial culture at home? If network services were owned and run nationally or locally with their function as a public service in a given territory and public service obligations in mind, how will this change once ownership and/or management is internationalised? For example, Deutsche Post, privatised from 1995, aspires to become Europe's FedEX. What consequences does this have for public service provision to citizens and organisations (at home and abroad)?

This transformation of public services into transnational operators poses a multitude of questions. Since this trend is relatively recent, or, put more accurately, since this 'second wave' of network transnationalisation is still recent (since the first wave of transnationalisation occurred during the nineteenth century, as Millward shows in Chapter 2) there has been little research to date on these questions and, given the importance of public services to daily life, we think serious attention is now due. This book was written with the aim of coming to grips with this development by placing it in historical context and by starting to formulate some important questions and, where possible, provide answers. This book thus proposes to take a first step in the analysis of the transformation of network services in Europe and North America with the aim of understanding what has happened and why. Before the organisation of the book is explained, some time is dedicated to the question of enterprise ownership.

I. Enterprise Ownership – Unlocking a Dead-End Debate?

The role of government and private investors and management in business has been an enduring, sometimes contentious and highly politicised topic worldwide, particularly during the twentieth century, which witnessed dramatic changes in enterprise ownership and management patterns. In the case of public service networks, private capital and enterpreneurialism tended to dominate the setting up of much public infrastructure during the nineteenth century.[8] Yet a generalised shift occurred in the twentieth century whereby these networks came under government ownership and control in most countries worldwide, perhaps the most important exception being the USA.[9] The era of privatisation from the 1980s brought full circle this ownership trend, bringing many public enterprises (though by no means all, and not always 100 per cent) back into the private sector.

Ownership has been politicised by the left (Karl Marx's insistence on the need for collective ownership of the means of production) and the right (so-called neoliberal theories that defend the unquestionable virtues of private property: World Bank economist Mary Shirley labelled public ownership a 'deadly disease').[10] On both sides, stereotypes have been created. This has had important consequences for the debate about enterprise. In particular from the 1980s, public–private ownership of enterprise has been dichotomised, to the extent that the behaviour – even the identity and culture – of enterprises are often reduced to whether they are publicly or privately owned. This dichotomy tends to oversimplify enterprise reality at best and, at worst, deadlock the debate. Ownership is only one factor that needs consideration alongside other, often more important issues. Competition is a key factor used to explain performance and behaviour, which has been recognised by many analysts,[11] and yet has been continually overshadowed by the seemingly more seductive, simpler (and more lucrative?) notion of ownership. Management capabilities are another. Recently, research has been pointing to the need to pay attention to the relationship between business and government and, in particular, between the new network services regulation and emerging TNCs.[12]

At the institutional level of the EU there has been a change in focus since the 1990s: because the EU has no competence in ownership matters, it must show itself indifferent to private or public ownership preferences: what it does have (partial) competence in is the regulatory environment in which an enterprise operates. The EU has introduced a range of overlapping discourses and policies from the mid 1990s which aim to protect citizen access to public services in the face of change. According to EU discourse, therefore, it is unimportant whether a train service is owned by a private or public enterprise: what matters is that the citizen is guaranteed a reliable service – including accessibility, affordability, reliability and security, in getting from A to B, and means to redress this if this is not the case. What matters is that citizens are entitled to specific and agreed standards of service, possibly in the form of a charter, backed up by regulation and monitoring – whether this be a train journey, electricity or water consumption.[13]

Since the 1980s, the view that private enterprise is the inherently and unquestionably superior option for enterprise has come to dominate much thinking and policy-making within major international economic institutions such as the World Bank, the International Monetary Fund (IMF) and the Organisation for Economic Cooperation and Development (OECD). This view has become diffused around universities, think tanks, policy-making bodies and so on.[14] Ask a room full of students to signal, out of public and private enterprise, which is the most dynamic, efficient and modern, and which is the most bureaucratic, centralised and inefficient, and the test usually works. Of course, the importance of this is enormous: developing countries have witnessed wide-scale privatisation programmes from the 1980s, which were largely justified on these grounds, a view which crystallised as the so-called 'Washington Consensus'.

The public/private dichotomy has become so prevalent that public enterprises are understood to inhabit different, even antagonistic worlds to private enterprise. The literature on the behaviour of TNCs tends to assume that enterprises are privately owned (and this despite the fact that there have been important publicly-owned TNCs).[15] The worlds of private enterprise expanding and operating on a dizzying international scale are perceived as remote from the more 'humdrum' world of public enterprises which are associated with national or local government ownership and bureaucratic management techniques. For some authors, state monopolies and internationalised firms are as incompatible as oil and water. One of the reasons may be that American privately owned TNCs, especially in the manufacturing sector, led the trend to internationalise enterprise in the 1950s. Moreover publicly owned and managed enterprises have been exceptionally weak in the USA, in contrast to many other countries[16] and the literature reflects this bias. Challenging this perception is one of the points of departure of this book.

There are many problems with dichotomising public–private ownership and/or management. For one thing, there still remains a lack of consensus about the relative merits of public or private ownership–management, and these differences are reflected in the diverse perspectives in this book. Among the most recent scholarship, Megginson and Netter come out in full support of the comparative virtues of private ownership,[17] whilst Millward remains much more sceptical.[18] Other authors claim many comparisons of public and private enterprise performance are falsely presented: authors such as Parker and Héritier claim that the criteria selected to compare public and private enterprises are biased, so that private enterprise always ends up coming up trumps.[19] Once a broader definition of efficiency is used, taking in, for instance, safety criteria, private firms are not always more efficient than their public equivalents. Another approach focuses on the need for good corporate governance rather than ownership questions. Even before the collapse of Enron and WorldCom the Nordic countries were pressurising from within the OECD[20] to establish and diffuse internationally rules, norms and recommendations for good corporate governance in the face of failures and mismanagement in business activity. The aim of this book, however, is not to add another volume to the evidence on the ownership–performance question. Another problem concerns definitions. 'Public' in the sense of 'public service' has historically had a dual meaning: enterprises were 'public', firstly because they were owned and run by the government, and second because they were services required for the public interest.[21] The debate on public goods, whether at the national, regional or global levels, has to resolve a similar issue: Kaul claims that the traditional concept of public goods should be renamed 'Samuelson goods',[22] since the concept desperately needs updating. A different approach would be to label all those network services that function for the public interest – communications, transport, energy and water – as public services, despite their being owned and run by public or private bodies.

The public–private dichotomy lags behind the reality of what is happening to enterprises in the twenty-first century. When does an enterprise become 'private', for instance? Does private ownership have to exceed 50 per cent or with only 1 per cent private ownership does behaviour start to change? The public–private dichotomy does not help us better understand an SOE network at home that invests heavily in privatised services in other countries, such as many ports across Europe or airport authorities such as AENA of Spain that operates in South America, exporting its know-how and expertise in Latin American airport management and so on.

The UNCTAD *World Investment Report* (2004) signalled the change at the beginning of the twenty-first century with the title of the report *The Shift to Services*. In 1997 only two public service TNCs were among the top 100. By 2003, this had increased to 22, as can be seen from Table 1.1. Some of these enterprises have been recently wholly, or nearly wholly, privatised, such as Telefonica, Endesa, Telecom Italia, National Grid Transco or Scottish Power. Others, such as Vodafone, are private greenfield FDI companies. Others have been partially privatised, such as Deutsche Telecom, France Telecom, E.ON, Deutsche Post or SingTel. With the exception of the latter, most of the new actors and the transformed TNCs were former SOEs from the five largest EU15

Table 1.1   Public Services TNCs in World Top 100 Non-Financial TNCs, Ranked by Foreign Assets, 1997–2003

	Home	*Main activity*	*Ranked position in*		*Best*	*TNI in 2003*
			1997	*2003*		
Vodafone Group Plc	UK	Telecom		2	1	84.5
Vivendi Universal-Générale des Eaux	FR	E.G.W./media	80	20	4	65.7
Deutsche Telekom	GE	Telecom		14	5	15.9
France Télécom	FR	Telecom		10	9	49.5
Telefónica	SP	Telecom		36	9	50.0
Suez-Lyonnaise des Eaux	FR	E.G.W.		11	11	78.1
E.ON	GE	E.G.W.		13	12	40.2
Electricité de France	FR	E.G.W.		12	12	29.3
RWE Group	GE	E.G.W.		15	13	43.4
Telecom Italia	IT	Telecom		24	24	20.3
Cable & Wireless	UK	Telecom	34		34	69.4
Veolia Environnement SA	FR	E.G.W.		37	37	62.9
AES Co.	US	E.G.W.		60	38	70.2
Deutsche Post World Net	GE	Logistic		42	41	35.1
Texas Utility	US	E.G.W.			41	44.7
Endesa	SP	E.G.W.		53	45	41.7
National Grid Transco	UK	E.G.W.		68	50	42.9
Verizon Communications	US	Telecom		82	58	7.3
SBC	US	Telecom			60	9.3
NTL Inc	US	Telecom			61	99.1
Singtel Ltd	SI	Telecom		66	66	61.4
Bertelsmann	GE	Media		98	75	63.4
Scottish Power	UK	E.G.W.		87	76	52.8
Duke Energy Co.	US	E.G.W.		77	77	23.8

Notes: FR: France; GE: Germany; IT: Italy; SI: Singapore; SP: Spain; UK: United Kingdom; US: United States; E.G.W.: electricity, gas and water; Telecom: telecommunications; TNI: Transnationality Index is calculated by UNCTAD as the average of the following three ratios: foreign assets to total assets; foreign sales to total sales; and foreign employment to total employment.
Source: Elaborated by the authors based on UNCTAD *World Investment Report* (1998–2005).

economies, which could be an indicator that market size mattered for the transnationalisation. Moreover all these new public service actors have reached significant levels of internationalisation, as indicated by the TNI for 2003.

These trends complicate simplistic public–private categories of enterprise. This is not just because of conscious efforts to introduce public–private partnerships in some countries, but because SOEs may be highly active in private businesses abroad whilst remaining public at home.

II. Questions Asked and Book Organisation

To resume, in recent years we have seen a 'second wave' of network internationalisation (the first wave occurring principally in the second half of the nineteenth century) affecting basic services such as energy, transport, communications and water. Some of these were established originally as private enterprises, some were established as public enterprises and then privatised, whilst others are still public enterprises or have mixed capital. In recent years, some of these enterprises have taken up the top positions as the world's leading TNCs. How and why has this happened? Why did this transformation affect some enterprises and not others? If the public enterprise was the 'ugly duckling' of the 1980s, how can we explain their rise as top TNCs competing with world private actors? Ownership change must surely be only a partial explanation and even a consequence of other ongoing changes such as technological change and policy reform. How important are national and international policies to deregulate and introduce competition? Thus, the idea of this book is to explain the recent second wave and the perhaps unexpected phenomenon of the 'rise' or 'resurrection' of public enterprises as TNCs in the network service sector from a long-term perspective.

To do so, this book is organised in the following way. Part 1 comprises three other chapters that revisit crucial ground in order to set the scene. In Chapter 2, FDI flows in the network services across Europe from 1830 to 1980 are surveyed by Robert Millward. He shows how the recent wave of FDI in the services is a 'second wave', the first FDI wave being concentrated in the nineteenth century, triggered by governments' intentions to ensure adequate private investment in constructing public infrastructure such as railways, telecommunications systems, gas and electricity distribution and so on. Chapter 3 revisits the reasons why ownership of network services has undergone a general shift from public to private hands in Britain compared to the rest of Western Europe. Millward argues that, even in the case of Britain, where ideology was arguably more important than on the continent, the role of ideology has been exaggerated and instead observes that we have to fully understand the importance of technological, socio-political and economic characteristics of networks. Finally, in Chapter 4, the role of public network services in economic growth and the rise of the service sector is analysed in the Italian case by Pier Angelo Toninelli and Michelangelo Vasta. The authors also tackle the question of the relation between public and private ownership and performance and demonstrate there are no fixed answers since the relationship very much depends on the time period in question. Part 2 contains a range of country or regional studies that focus on the shifting ownership preferences in different contexts and, in particular, examine cases of network service transnationalisation. In Chapter 5 Patrick Fridenson analyses the internationalisation experiences of EDF, Suez and France Télécom in the historical context of changing ownership and management patterns. Leading German energy, transport and telecommunications utility TNCs are analysed in Chapter 6 by Harm G. Schröter who explains the way in which E.ON, REW, Deutsche Post and Deutsche Telekom became quite aggressive players, particularly in European markets, though some with more success than others. Judith Clifton, Francisco Comín and Daniel Díaz-Fuentes in Chapter 7 classify phases in the transnationalisation of the Spanish economy, providing some examples of network internationalisation, in particular Telefonica and Endesa. In Chapter 8, Ana Bela Nunes, Carlos Bastien and Nuno Valério, analyse the relationship between privatisation and transnationalisation and emphasise the importance of Spain and Portuguese-speaking countries in the developing world in this development. Sean Barrett, in Chapter 9, examines the emergence of Ryanair, Europe's first 'low-cost airline', as well as the simultaneous transformation of Aer Lingus in the face of market deregulation and the Ryanair threat. In Chapter 10, Lena Andersson-Skog and Thomas Pettersson analyse the different patterns of the internationalisation of SAS and the Scandinavian railways, signalling the importance attached to the welfare aspect of public services. In Chapter 11 the case of Belgian railways is analysed by Frans Buelens, Julien van den Broek and Hans Willems who show how problems regarding ownership and management that are centuries old still have relevance to questions surrounding the future of the railways in the face of the Trans European Networks (TENs). Chapter 12, by Marina Klinova, takes us through ownership in Russia before the Revolution to the transition to a market economy, particularly from the point of view of the gas sector, above all the transnational gas giant GAZPROM, where Soviet plans to extend gas to COMECON are still strategically relevant in projects in Europe and Asia. In the last three chapters, NAFTA member countries are considered. In Chapter 13, Judith Clifton, Daniel Díaz-Fuentes and Carlos Marichal consider ownership and transnationalisation in Mexico from the Porfiriato through to the 'golden age', debt and the era of the 'Washington Consensus'. TELMEX, the main telecommunications enterprise, linked to billionaire Carlos Slim, is the main case study here. Pierre Lanthier, in Chapter 14, comparatively analyses the internationalised activities of three Canadian hydro-electric companies, showing how enterprises of different sizes with various markets have responded in similar ways to the challenges of integration. Finally, privatisation 'guru' William Megginson, with Candra Chahyadi and Jesus Salas, argue that privatisation has taken a different course in the USA, partly because it is understood in a different way, and partly because, given that the public enterprise sector has been historically small, there has been little to sell. Rather than transformation, the key word here would be 'non-transformation'. Finally, in the Conclusion, Judith Clifton, Francisco Comín and Daniel Díaz-Fuentes synthesise the main findings of all the chapters and, in doing so, try to answer their original questions, as well as formulating new questions for future research.

A final word for the sake of clarity: this research has received funding from scientific and academic national councils over the last few years. No funding has been sought – or accepted – from the business sector. When dealing with the future of public services, neutrality and freedom to think and write are of paramount importance to all three editors.

Notes

1   See Millward (2005) for a comprehensive historical treatment of public and private network ownership in Europe from the nineteenth century.
2   Castro (2006); Grugel (2006); Clifton and Díaz-Fuentes forthcoming in Farrell (2007), Hall (2006).
3   Newbury (2004).
4   Bel (2006).
5   Clifton, Comín and Díaz-Fuentes (2006).
6   Toninelli (2000); Tracey (1998).
7   Newbury (2004).
8   Millward (2005); Aharoni and Vernon (1981).
9   Galambos (2000).
10   Kikeri, Nellis and Shirley (1992).
11   Newbury (2004) and Motta (2004).
12   Grosse (2005) and Meyer (2004).
13   Clifton, Comín and Díaz-Fuentes (2005).
14   Arnt Arne (2001).
15   See Wilkins (1970 and 1974).
16   See Galambos (2000); Megginson this volume (Chapter 15).
17   Megginson and Netter (2003).
18   Millward (2005).
19   Parker (1998 and 2004) and Héritier (2002).
20   OECD (2003, 2004 and 2005).
21   According to official EU thinking since the mid-1990s this 'confusion' should be avoided by replacing the term 'public service' by the term 'service of general interest'. Although in theory the EU was motivated to de-politicise the question of ownership critics point out that the neutralisation of the new terminology helps soften the path towards privatisation. See Clifton, Comín and Díaz-Fuentes (2005).
22   Kaul (2003).

References

Aharoni, Y., and R. Vernon (1981) *State-Owned Enterprises in the Western Economies* (London: Croom Helm).

Arnt Arne, J. (2000) *Selling the Free Market. The Rhetoric of Economic Correctness* (The Guildford Press).

Bel, G. (2006) 'Against the Mainstream: Nazi Privatization in 1930s Germany', working paper, http://www.ub.es/graap/nazi.pdf

Castro, E. (2006) *Water, Power and Citizenship: Social Struggle in the Basin of Mexico* (Basingstoke and New York: Palgrave Macmillan).

Clifton, J., F. Comín and D. Díaz-Fuentes (2005) 'Empowering Europe's Citizens? Towards a Charter for Services of General Interest', *Public Management Review*: Special issue on customer satisfaction and service quality (fall 2005).

Clifton, J., F. Comín and D. Díaz-Fuentes (2006) Privatising Public Enterprises in the European Union 1960–2002: Ideological, Pragmatic, Inevitable? *Journal of European Public Policy* (September).

Clifton, J., and D. Díaz-Fuentes (forthcoming 2007) 'Regional Public Goods in Latin America', in M. Farrell (ed.), *Regional Public Goods* (Oxford University Press).

Dunning, J. H. (1977) 'Trade, Location of Economic Activity and the Multinational Enterprise: The Search for an Eclectic Approach', in B. Ohlin, P.O. Hessleborn and P.M. Wijkman (eds), *The International Allocation of Economic Activity* (London: Macmillan).

Dunning, J. H. (1988) 'The Eclectic Paradigm of International Production: A Restatement and Possible Extensions', *Journal of International Business Studies*, 19, pp. 1–32.

Galambos, L. (2000) 'State-Owned Enterprises in a Hostile Environment', in Pier Angelo Toninelli (ed.), *The Rise and Fall of State-Owned Enterprise* (Cambridge University Press), pp. 273–302.

Grosse, R. (ed.) (2005) *International Business and Government Relations in the 21st Century* (Cambridge University Press).

Grugel, J. (2006) 'Regionalist Governance and Transnational Collective Action in Latin America', *Economy and Society*, 35 (2) pp. 209–231.

Hall, D. (2006) 'Evaluating Network Services in Europe', PSIRU Report, http://www.psiru.org/reports/2006-03-EU-EPNIcrit.doc.

Héritier, A. (2002) 'Public-Interest Services Revisited', *Journal of European Public Policy*, 9 (6 December) pp. 995–1019.

Kaul, I. (2003) *Global Public Goods: A Key to Achieving the Millennium Development Goals* (New York: Office of Development Studies).

Kikeri, S., J. Nellis and Mary Shirley (1992) 'Policy Views from the Country Economics Department', *Outreach 3, Privatization: Eight Lessons of Experience* (World Bank).

Megginson, W., and J. Netter (2001) 'From State to Market: A Survey of Empirical Studies on Privatisation', *Journal of Economic Literature*, 39 (2) (June).

Meyer, L. (2004) 'Perspectives on Multinational Enterprises in Emerging Economies', *Journal of International Business Studies*, 35, pp. 259–276.

Millward, R. (2005) *Public and Private Enterprise in Europe* (Cambridge University Press).

Motta, M. (2004) *Competition Policy: Theory and Practice* (Cambridge University Press).

Newbery, D. M. (2004) 'Privatizing Network Industries', CESIFO Working Paper No. 1132, Category 9: Industrial Organisation (CESIFO, February).

OECD (2003) *Corporate Governance of State-Owned Enterprises: A Survey of OECD Countries* (OECD: Paris).

OECD (2004) *OECD Principles of Corporate Governance* (OECD: Paris).

OECD (2005) *OECD Guidelines on Corporate Governance of State-Owned Enterprises* (OECD: Paris).

Parker, D. (1998) *Privatization – the European Union: Theory and Policy Perspectives* (Guildford/ New York: Routledge).

Parker, D. (2004) 'The UK's Privatization Experiment: The Passage of Time Permits a Sober Assessment', CESIFO Working Paper No 1126 (CESIFO).

Toninelli, P. A. (2000) *The Rise and Fall of State-Owned Enterprise in the Western World* (Cambridge University Press).

Tracey, M. (1998) *The Decline and Fall of Public Service Broadcasting* (Oxford University Press).

Wilkins, M. (1970) *The Emergence of Multinational Enterprise: American Business Abroad from the Colonial Era to 1914* (Harvard University Press).

Wilkins, M. (1974) *The Maturing of Multinational Enterprise: American Business Abroad from 1914 to 1970* (Harvard University Press).

2
Cross-Border Investment and Service Flows in Networks within Western Europe, c.1830–1980

Robert Millward

Introduction

The 1990s witnessed a massive expansion of cross-border share and debt acquisition (portfolio investment) and of cross-border investment where individuals and companies exercised an element of entrepreneurial control (foreign direct investment, FDI). The staff of UNCTAD have attempted to capture the transnational nature of much modern investment by measuring, for each host country, various dimensions of its size: the ratio of FDI inflow to total investment and of FDI stock to GDP; for foreign affiliates, their value added relative to GDP and their employment relative to total employment. These four dimensions are converted into a 'transnational index' which averaged 18 per cent in 1999, ranging from highs of 30–40 per cent in countries like Singapore, Ireland, Sweden and Nigeria, to lows of less than 10 per cent in USA, Belarus, Italy and Japan.[1] Much of this, however, was in manufacturing while the focus of this chapter is energy, telecommunications and transport where, up until recently, they have constituted only a small element. By the early 1990s FDI in 'infrastructure sectors' accounted for less than 5 per cent of the total inflows and outflows, despite the fact that infrastructure is very capital intensive and likely to make demands of capital beyond the means of many current developing countries. There were some significant exceptions: the outflows from Japan (7 per cent) and USA (8 per cent) and the inflows in particular years to Denmark (25 per cent), Romania (65 per cent) and Algeria (50 per cent). There are signs moreover that the position is changing. The trend in infrastructure FDI inflows in the 1990s was upwards and in the early 2000s public network services were starting to appear more prominently in the lists of top 100 non-financial transnational corporations.[2]

Two factors explain why FDI infrastructure started at low levels, and as we shall see, they find echoes in earlier periods. The first is that these are sectors which display natural monopoly characteristics that inevitably draw in government regulation which may not be a stable variable from the point of view of the foreign investor. Secondly, the services which flow from these investments – railways, telecommunications, airlines, electricity supplies – invariably have a strategic significance for national security or a welfare impact wider than that of the average manufactured commodity. Hence host governments tend to take a close interest in these sectors and often want close control. The questions we pose in this chapter with respect to flows within Western Europe are, firstly, to what extent did these factors operate in the nineteenth and twentieth centuries and, secondly, what accounted for variations in the strength of these factors and hence caused changes in service and investment flows?[3]

Although we do not have the same detailed quantitative information about FDI flows for the nineteenth century, one part of the story is well known, the export of capital for railways both within and outside Western Europe. Less well known is the cross-border activity in other network industries within Western Europe. Here we attempt to describe and analyse the broad patterns of such cross-border activity in energy, telecommunications and transport from the early 1800s to the 1980s – from the arrival of gas supplies (from coking coal) and railways to the era of the information revolution and privatisation. We shall show how there were extensive private investment flows across borders in the nineteenth century which, because of the nature of the services, gradually led to control by the host countries' local and central government agencies. As technology changed in the late twentieth century the scope for more liberal regimes emerged, at least within Western Europe.

I. Electricity, Gas and Water Supplies and Tramways

A strong feature of the nineteenth century patterns was the role of the leading industrial nations – Britain initially, to be followed almost immediately by Belgium, and later Germany and France. Here we see a pattern echoed in the modern era where the developing world occupies a similar role to that of Spain, Italy and parts of Scandinavia in the nineteenth century. New technologies of the early nineteenth century were developed mainly in the leading nations (including the United States) and the other countries, initially, did not have the skilled manpower to operate the new systems, let alone build them, and did not have project inputs like water and gas pipes. Nor did the initial technologies often facilitate cross-border service flows (shipping being the classic exception). In the stage of construction also host governments were less concerned about national security and regulatory issues than about encouraging investment and the influx of trained personnel. Characteristically the initial schemes were build/own/operate (BOO in modern terminology). By the end of the nineteenth century the regulatory, fiscal and public service issues were to lead to some transfers to indigenous companies and government agencies, a trend which accelerated in the twentieth century. In all cases it was, however, technology rather than ideology which was the driving force.

Gas supplied from plants using coking coal was the first of the new infrastructure industries. Its birth is associated with the classic early industrialisation of Britain, blessed as that country was with excellent coking coal for gas, such that, even by the First World War, Britain's production was many times larger than the rest of Europe. Those countries, like Denmark, which were able and willing to draw on British coal exports also raced ahead and Germany was not far behind when its coal reserves were brought into play. At the same time the limited size of economies of scale in production and the high transport costs meant that the natural monopoly advantages of a single supplier had a limited range. Everywhere the introduction of gas supply was initiated by private enterprise and municipal ownership seems to have flourished only when the technology and systems had settled down.

The Gas, Light and Coke Company started public lighting in London in 1814; Brussels opened in 1819, Rotterdam and Berlin in 1826, Amsterdam in 1833 and Lyons in 1834. British equipment, engineers and coal were exported wholesale with English companies, like the Imperial Continental Gas Association, heavily involved in the construction of gas works in Hanover, Berlin, Ghent and Rotterdam. The process was spread over the whole of the first half of the nineteenth century. The other 'first towns' were Barcelona 1841, Vienna 1842, Gothenburg 1845 and Oslo 1846, while in 1853 Odense was the first town in Denmark with a public lighting system, built by an English company, 'The Danish Gas Company'.[4] Spain and Italy also relied on foreign companies like the Credit Mobilier in Madrid and entrepreneurs like Charles Lebrun who was extensively involved in Barcelona.[5] A similar pattern could be seen in the companies involved in water supply in Spain, like Sociedad Generale de Aguas de Barcelona (owned by Société Générale des Eaux de Barcelone, with headquarters in Paris) and Aguas de Santander (mixed British, French and Spanish ownership). The foreign companies were often manufacturers of water pipes and, in conjunction with banks, like the Belgian Crédit Général Liégois, took over water concessions and contracts which small Spanish companies were unable to complete.[6]

The main initial spurt in the development of electricity supplies came in the 1880s and 1890s. Most undertakings that were selling electricity were vertically integrated concerns engaged in generation, transmission and distribution. The capacity of coal-fired generating stations was determined largely by peak demand during the year, since electricity could not be stored and with, initially, transport limited to small distances the networks were essentially local rather than regional or national. This was also true of the early hydroelectricity schemes. The private sector was dominant in most countries in the initial stages for two reasons. The first was a repeat of the experience of all nineteenth-century utilities, namely that initial uncertainties persuaded most governments to leave development to the private sector. It was a new product but with competing interests in town councils with municipal gas supply.[7] Publicly available supplies of electricity spread very rapidly in the 1880s and 1890s. Even in Spain and Italy where consumption per head was relatively low, in part because of very high tariffs, the number of connections was large. The first public supply in Italy was by the Edison company in Milan in 1883 and in Spain it was in Barcelona by the Sociedad Espanol de Electricidad.[8] By the 1890s all Andalusian towns had public electric lighting.[9] Electrification of tramways started in Spain in 1896 and the undertakings were financially controlled by foreign, often Belgian, companies.[10] The very high level of self-consumption reinforced this early role for the private sector. In 1898 there were 2286 electricity 'installations' in Italy of which 80 per cent were for self-consumption by manufacturing firms.[11] In France firms like Thomas Houston found the manufacture of equipment more profitable than distributing electricity supply and operating trams but the strategic position of such firms made for heavy involvement of the private sector.

In the case of hydroelectricity a thorny issue was property rights over watercourses, and government attitudes often affected the pace of development. The regulatory regime was very loose in Spain. Private enterprise was dominant and most supplies came from a small number of regionally based companies. The firms who gained concessions were often those with a licence to import electrical equipment or to manufacture foreign company models in Spain. Spanish banks and entrepreneurs were heavily involved – as in the company Hydroelectrica Iberia – except for Catalonia where there were many foreign companies. Government regulation was so light that companies did not have any 'obligation to supply' so that capacity was often less than the demand emanating from connected consumers.[12] Although the number of connected consumers was high, consumption per head of population was amongst the lowest in Europe. In Italy 16 hydroelectric power (HEP) plants were built in the period 1900–4 and a further 27 in 1905–9 in the Alps and the Apennines. Banks were often involved with large private undertakings.[13]

In Denmark it was the municipalities and cooperatives which, through their shareholdings, facilitated the development of two large regional networks. Nordsjaellands Elektricitet Selskab, a mixed electricity enterprise, based in the northeast of the country, developed a submarine cable which allowed HEP from the Sydkraft Company in Sweden to pass from Halsingburg across the Sound to Helsinger in Denmark. From 1915 HEP flowed from Sweden and thermal power flowed in the other direction from Denmark. It triggered off the interconnection of the whole of Zealand with power emanating mainly from a large Copenhagen thermal plant and the submarine cable. Another big regional network emerged in western Denmark (Jutland) following the construction of an HEP plant in the River Gudernia in 1920.[14]

Gas, water, electricity supply and tramways had no particular relevance for national security nor for national unification since the networks were essentially local. Because of natural monopoly features, however, each company tended to finish up with a local monopoly which thereby attracted regulation from central and local government. Ownership was also an issue and the decisive factor was fiscal considerations. Here there was a big difference between urban and rural areas. The former faced mounting public health problems in the nineteenth century requiring expenditure programmes which put a strain on local taxes. Many municipalities in growing industrial towns were therefore attracted to the idea of taking over the local utilities and using the profits to relieve income and property taxes paid by local elites.[15] The major initial surge in municipalisation was for gas and water in the period 1850–80, followed by electricity and tramways in the next 40 years. It was strongest in the new industrial towns of Britain and Germany and weakest in rural areas and where local government units were weak or too small – hence it was not common in France, Belgium, Spain and Italy and even London before the 1890s local government reforms. From the 1920s it spread more extensively across Europe.

II. Railways and Telecommunications

Following their apparent success in Britain, railways were perceived in parts of Continental Europe (rightly or wrongly) as engines of economic growth. Spain and Italy were the recipients of much FDI in railways but because of the difficult terrain and uncertain market, government guarantees of returns were needed. In Sweden and Norway early investments were quite risky and several British and Swedish companies failed. The state then stepped in to develop the trunk networks (and secured foreign loans) which were seen also as important instruments of national unification of disparate regions, as in Italy. In Spain a scanty population and difficult terrain made railways problematic even with government guarantees but the central government had continuous budget problems of its own so that foreign capital was essential.[16]

It is worth looking at the cases of Spain and Italy in more detail. Traditional transport was very costly because of the limited development of waterways and roads (the Po Valley excepted).[17] Yet railways made little headway until the late 1850s. By then state governments were keen to promote railway expansion – the Progressives in Spain and the new national government in Italy from 1860. State initiatives took the form of special privileges for private rail companies, the granting of subsidies, guaranteeing financial returns and direct state ownership, though the last was used only in Italy. The 1855 railway law in Spain permitted the government to grant subsidies to foreign owned companies who were allowed to import rails, rolling stock and other equipment free of duty.[18] Sections of projected track were offered for franchise bidding, with the lowest bidder getting the concession. In some cases a direct subsidy was seen to be a better incentive than an interest guarantee. Thus in 1860, for the Manzana–Cordoba line, 40 per cent of the annual costs were met by the government – a method which Cameron felt promoted cost escalation and generally unscrupulous behaviour.[19] In the case of the North

Spain Company a cash subsidy was raised by the Credito Mobiliano Espanol in 1858 on the credit of the Spanish government.[20] In Italy the governments (state and later national) guaranteed interest (for example for the Livourian Railway Company) and in other cases, to avoid paying too many cash subsidies 'up front', guaranteed revenue returns per kilometre of completed track.[21] In addition to state ownership in Piedmont the central government subsidised the Mediterranean network and bought out the Sicily/Calabria network in 1868 – construction was then sub-contracted to the Vitali Company and railway operations to the Meridionale Company.

These inducements were enough to allow considerable expansion of the railway systems in the 1860s with the basic trunk network complete in Spain and a four-network plan in place in Italy. By the end of the decade there were 5000 kilometres open in Spain and 6000 in Italy. The whole venture was, however, financially disastrous and provided, in the short term, only modest economic benefits. The causes have been well discussed in the literature.[22] Of more relevance here is to note that backward economic linkages were limited because, initially at least, rails, rolling stock and other equipment were all imported whilst engineers and even relatively unskilled imported labour ran the systems.[23] The contrast is with 1830s Belgium where, after a short infusion of English capital, local finance and industry took over – Belgium was, in other words, already industrialising. Foreign companies in Spain and Italy had links with expatriate and indigenous engineers in government and with engineering companies in north-western Europe. Domestic industry seems to have been limited in the 1860s and 1870s to producing sleepers and wagons. Indeed several writers have suggested that the railway systems were over-expanded since the imports of railway equipment created balance of payment problems – certainly an issue in Spain, less so in Italy because of emigrant repatriated earnings – whilst capital funds were diverted from manufacturing industry, especially from Catalonian manufacturing.[24] On the other hand it does not seem that Spanish industry could have supplied railway equipment in this period so that, in so far as calculations do suggest there were some social returns to railway investment, a protectionist policy might have been damaging.[25]

The overall outcome was that by the late 1860s many networks were running into financial difficulties and sought loans from government. Indeed the creditworthiness of railway companies was linked closely to that of their governments so that when Italian government bonds fell on the Paris Bourse in 1866 both Spanish and Italian rail bonds also fell and the Credito Mobilario Espanol collapsed.[26]

The railways in Britain were run by private companies throughout the nineteenth century but the Continental powers, faced as they were by hostile neighbours on their borders, were very conscious of the military significance of railways. This was especially true of Prussia where the system was nationalised in 1879 and in France where the military ensured that where a network was unprofitable but had military significance it would be sub-sidised by the state or taken over – the Western Network in 1906 and the Alsace-Lorraine network after the First World War. In Italy, Belgium and the Scandinavian countries the importance of national unity prompted their governments to take over the trunk networks so that overall, by 1914, large parts of the railway systems of Western Europe were in the hands of central governments and foreign influences were rapidly disappearing.

In telecommunications, security issues were even more important and accounted for the limited role of foreign investment (excluding of course the supply of equipment). Symptomatic of whose interests were at stake was the way in which the visual telegraph by arms and flags (the Chappe Telegraph) was established in France in 1797. It was incorporated into the government administration and financed through the budgets of the army and the navy and from the proceeds of the national lottery. In Sweden the Televerket was set up in 1856 and financed by the Merchant and Shipping Foundations as well as by Parliamentary subventions.[27] All systems were nationalised by 1913 with the exception of the Great Northern Telegraph Company estab-lished in Denmark in 1869 with a concession to operate international telegrams from western to eastern Europe. Submarine cables to locations outside Europe were another matter.

All these state systems claimed property rights over the telephone. Foreign involvement could be seen in some early developments. In Britain the first tele-phone exchanges had opened in 1879 in Glasgow and in London, where the Edison Company was given a concession. The market was, however, fairly chaotic, with disagreements about whether competition should be encouraged, and in 1912 all the UK systems were absorbed by the Post Office.[28] Elsewhere the response to outsiders was more guarded. In Germany telephone subscriber networks were developed from the 1880s but strictly by the Reichspost only. The Rathenau and Bell companies were refused concessions.[29] In France the telegraph had always been seen by some as a symbol of Bonapartism, so the Third Republic regarded it and the telephone as one of its key instruments of social control, along with railways and schools.[30] In Norway, the Telegrafslret, the National Telephone Authority, rather disingenuously claimed it alone had the technical personnel to develop the system even though the skills of com-panies like Edison were available throughout Europe.[31] By the interwar period most systems were fully state-owned or, as in Scandinavia and Italy, the state owned at least the trunk networks. The exception was Spain where ITT owned Telefónica.

III. Shipping

There was actually one part of the infrastructure, merchant shipping, where gov-ernments were not so directly involved and where cross-border service flows remained at a high level for much of the nineteenth and twentieth centuries.

Here there were no economies of scale from lumpy track investments, as in gas and railways, and no spillover effects in the form of congestion and health as in tramways and water supply. Even by the late twentieth century use of the sea involved no major congestion problems (contrast fishing) and few environmental effects apart from oil spills. Economies from increases in ship size were present but in relation to the size of the market were small and shipping could and did operate like a classic competitive industry. The key resource was coal, and Britain's coal resources, its early industrialisation and the development of its shipbuilding industry proved decisive. By the 1860s it had nearly 3000 steam ships – more than twice as many as the rest of Europe put together – and accounted for one third of the world's merchant shipping tonnage. It faced rising competition from Sweden, Norway and Germany in the latter part of the nineteenth century. Many British contemporaries thought these other countries benefited from state subsidies. Certainly in countries like Spain the central government in the late nineteenth century supported shipping and the navy programme such that its merchant fleet tonnage, relative to population, grew to the level of France and Germany by 1913, if not to those of Britain and the Scandinavian countries. The Danish government subsidised shipping services to Britain to promote its growing export trade in butter and bacon. In Britain shipping subsidies were restricted to support for postal services and for aiding the admiralty. Aldcroft's study of Anglo-German rivalry suggests that the impact of subsidies by the imperial German government was small and any gains that Germany achieved were genuinely competitive gains. In France there were huge subsidies which, however, favoured the building of inexpensive sailing vessels and the growth of France's mercantile marine was consequently quite modest.[32] By 1913 the British steam ship fleet had risen to 12,602 – still more than the rest of Europe put together. Its tonnage was still one third of the world total and, relative to population, was in Europe exceeded only by Norway. British ship-owners (as well as shipbuilders) clearly held their own in this period.

Denmark and Sweden had long traditions of shipbuilding and the former developed shipping services to its colonies as well as other European countries and their colonies. Shipping tonnage in Denmark increased rapidly from the 1860s to the First World War and the associated earnings were important ingredients of the balance of payments. Whilst the period up to 1880 saw a large growth in the number of steam ships in Denmark a significant part of the total fleet was sail and so by 1913 its tonnage per head of population was, like Sweden, higher than France but much less than Norway. In the latter, tramp shipping and fishing had for long been part-time complementary occupations to self-subsistent farming. Much timber was exported and as trade regimes liberalised in the nineteenth century Norway came to be heavily engaged in shipping grain, timber and coal all over Europe and largely independent of its own transport needs. Norway's strengths were in tramping and it lost out in the development of tanker fleets. Nevertheless by the end of the nineteenth century it had the third largest fleet in the world, generating one half of its export earnings and, relative to population, was way ahead of the rest of Europe in its total tonnage, even in 1913.[33]

IV. The Twentieth Century

Cross-border investment flows were much less in the twentieth century, prior to the privatisation era. Two basic factors were at work. One was that the nineteenth century was the era of construction of basic infrastructures, much of which had a very long expected life. After the First World War there were only limited extensions to the railway track, now facing growing competition from road transport. The heyday of coal gas was past and in electricity supply network integration dominated the first half of the twentieth century. This was very much a matter of national development of national electricity networks so foreign influence was minimal. The same was true of telephone networks (except Telefónica in Spain) with the additional factor that security considerations were ever dominant and the telecom enterprises were invariably integral parts of government departments (PTT, the PO, Reichspost, Televerket, and so on). Moreover Italy and Spain were developing their own industrial base so that whatever investment was needed could increasingly come from home industry.

Secondly, by the end of the 1930s the central governments in each country had taken a strong grip on most of the infrastructure industries and municipalities for water supply and the process was finalised in the 1940s. By 1950 railways, gas, electricity, coal mines and the central banks had been nationalised in France and Britain. The railways and telephone systems were virtually or actually nationalised in Sweden, Spain and Norway, as were airlines in all countries. The central governments of Spain, Italy and the Federal Republic of Germany owned undertakings with extensive and often dominant holdings in electricity and gas supply, coal and manufacturing companies, while the state electricity power boards in Sweden and Norway were dominant institutions in their sector. Central governments had complete or partial ownership of the major companies supplying oil. New investment was therefore invariably under the control of government departments, public corporations or companies with significant government shareholdings. Of the few examples of cross-border network investment before the 1980s one was for electricity supply, where western Denmark (Jutland) was connected in the 1960s to Sweden via the Konti-Scan cable through Germany. Of course there was much cross-border activity in infrastructure industries like oil and airlines but these sectors did not carry the same natural monopoly characteristics as the classic network industries. For oil the main investment flows in the first half of the twentieth century were of course to the Middle East and North Africa. Governments were involved for strategic reasons – in the form of part ownership of BP, AGIP and CFP. With the growth of indigenous supplies in the second half of the twentieth century, especially in the North Sea, taxation was also important. As far as airlines are concerned, by the early 1950s Europe was dominated by the national flag fliers so that whilst cross-border services were large, the amount of cross-border investment was probably small.

Conclusions

In sum, the scale of cross-border investment and service flows within Europe which followed privatisation, deregulation and pressures for closer European integration from the 1980s represented a large break from the earlier twentieth century experience. It had its counterpart, however, in the cross-border private investment which characterised the initial development of railways, gas and electricity networks in the nineteenth century. Many of the flows then were from the advanced industrial nations like Britain and Belgium to the less industrialised parts of Europe. The role of the developed countries at the turn of the twenty-first century vis-à-vis developing countries is a mirror image of Britain and Belgium facing the rest of Europe in the nineteenth century. How far this trend continues will depend crucially on two factors. For each nation state the instruments for safeguarding national security and ensuring political and social cohesion reflect changing technology and the energy, telecommunications and transport sectors may not play, in the future, the central role they had in the past. Network integration and cross-border investment in these sectors will also depend on whether regional groupings like the EU start to dominate in the military/strategic fields.

Notes

1 See UNCTAD (2002), pp. 20–1.
2 UNCTAD (1996 and 2004).
3 More details may be found in Millward (2005).
4 Hyldtoft (1995) pp. 76–99; see also Hyldtoft (1994); Duchene (1995) p. 21; and Peterson (1990).
5 Sudria (1983); Antolin (1991); Tortella (2000).
6 Matés Barco (2000).
7 Fernández (1996) and (1999); Magee (1899).
8 Antolin (1992).
9 Núñez (1990).
10 Nuñez (forthcoming) p. 7.
11 Conti (1990).
12 Ibid. See also Nuñez (forthcoming); Motes (1987); Balbin (1999) pp. 235, 245–6.
13 Fenoaltea (1982) pp. 615–16; Giannetti (1987); Bruno (1987) p. 44.
14 Kaijser (1995).
15 See Dawson (1916); Hennock (1963).
16 Nadal (1973); Tortella (2000) chapter 5.
17 Giuntini (1995); Gomez-Mendoza (1995).
18 Nadal (1973); see also Harrison (1978).

19   Cameron (1961) p. 258.
20   Ibid. p. 251.
21   Ibid. p. 297.
22   Mitchell (1964); Nadal (1973); Fenoaltea (1983).
23   Cafagna (1973).
24   Nadal (1973) and Milward and Saul (1977), chapter 4. For a pessimistic view of railways in Portugal see Confraria (1999).
25   Gomez-Mendoza (1983).
26   Cameron (1961) p. 297.
27   Bauer and Latzer (1988); Andersson-Skog (1996 and 1999).
28   Holcombe (1906); Perry (1977); Foreman-Peck (1985); Foreman-Peck and Millward (1994) pp. 97–111.
29   Thomas (1978); see also Wengenroth (2000) p. 105.
30   Attali and Stowdze (1977). See also Dormois (1999) p. 65 for the view that the desire for government control was important in the move to nationalisation.
31   Espeli (2002) p. 2.
32   Aldcroft (1974). For France see Dormois (1999).
33   See the three articles by Fritz, Gjolberg, and Hornby and Nilsson in the 1980 issue of *Scandinavian Economic History Review*.

References

Aldcroft, D. (1974) 'British Shipping and Foreign Competition: The Anglo-German Rivalry, 1880–1914', in D. Aldcroft, *Studies in British Transport History* (Newton Abbott: David and Charles) pp. 53–99.

Andersson-Skog, L. (1996) 'The Making of the National Telephone Networks in Scandinavia: the State and the Emergence of National Regulatory Patterns 1880–1920', in L. Magnusson and J. Ottoson (eds), *Evolutionary Economics and Path Dependence* (Cheltenham: Edward Elgar) pp. 138–54.

Andersson-Skog, L. (1999) 'Political Economy and Institutional Diffusion: The Case of the Swedish Railways and Telecommunications up to 1950, in L. Andersson-Skog and O. Krantz (eds), *Institutions and the Transport and Communications Industries* (Canton, MA: Science History Publications, Watson) pp. 245–66.

Antolin, F. (1991) 'Las empresas de servicos publicos municipales', in F. Comín and P. M. Aceña (eds), *Historia de la empresa publica en Espana* (Madrid: Espasa Calpe) pp. 283–330.

Antolin, F. (1992) 'Public Policy in the Development of the Spanish Electric Utility Industry', paper presented at the European Historical Economics Society Conference 'A Century of Industrial Policy in Europe', Oxford, Worcester College, 1992.

Attali, J., and Y. Stowdze (1977) 'The Birth of the Telephone and Economic Crisis: The Slow Development of Monologue in French Society', in I. de Sola Pool (ed.), *The Social Impact of the Telephone* (Cambridge, MA: MIT Press) pp. 97–111.

Balbin, P.F. (1999) 'Spain: Industrial Policy under Authoritarian Politics', in J. Foreman-Peck and G. Federico (eds), *European Industrial Policy: The Twentieth-Century Experience* (Oxford University Press) pp. 233–67.

Bauer, J.M., and M. Latzer (1988) 'Telecommunications in Austria', in J. Foreman-Peck and J. Mueller (eds), *European Telecommunications Organisation* (Baden-Baden: Nomosverlagsgesellschaft) pp. 53–85.

Bruno, G. (1987) 'L'utilisation des resources hydroliques pour la production d'énergie électrique en Italie du Sud: 1895–1915', in F. Cardot (ed.), *1880–1980: une siècle de l'électricité dans le monde* (Paris: Presses Universitaires de France) pp. 253–67.

Cafagna, L. (1973) 'Italy 1830–1914', in C. Cipolla (ed.), *Fontana Economic History of Europe: The Emergence of Industrial Societies: Part 1* (Glasgow: Fontana-Collins) pp. 279–328.

Cameron, R.E. (1961) *France and the Economic Development of Europe 1880–1914: Conquests of Peace and Seeds of War* (Princeton University Press).

Confraria, J. (1999) 'Portugal: Industrialisation and Backwardness', in J. Foreman-Peck and G. Federico (eds), *European Industrial Policy: The Twentieth Century Experience* (Oxford University Press) pp. 268–94.

Conti, F. (1990) 'The Creation of a Regional Electrical System: Selt Valdarno Group and the Electrification of Tuscany', in M. Trédé (ed.), *Éléctricité et électrification dans le monde 1880–1980* (Paris: Association pour l'histoire de l' éléctricité en France/Press Universitaires de France).

Dawson, W.H. (1916) *Municipal Life and Local Government in Germany* (London: Longmans, Green and Co.).

Dormois, J.-P. (1999) 'France: The Idiosyncracies of Voluntarisme', in J. Foreman-Peck and G. Federico (eds), *European Industrial Policy: The Twentieth Century Experience* (Oxford University Press) pp. 58–97.

Duchene, V. (1995) *150 jaar stadsgas te Leuven. Een episode ust de geschiedernis van de Belgische energie esctoru* (Deurne).

Espeli, H. (2002) 'From Dual Structure to State Monopoly in Norwegian Telephones, 1880–1924', working paper, Norwegian School of Management, Scandvika, Norway (January).

Fenoaltea, S. (1982) 'The Growth of the Utility Industries in Italy 1861–1913', *Journal of Economic History*, 42, pp. 601–28.

Fenoaltea, S. (1983) 'Italy', in P. O'Brien (ed.), *Railways and the Economic Development of Europe* (London: Macmillan) pp. 48–120.

Fernandez, A. (1996) 'Production and Distribution of Electricity in Bordeaux, 1887–1956: Private and Public Operation', *Contemporary European History*, 5, pp. 159–70.

Fernandez, A. (1999) 'Les lumières de la ville: l'administration municipale à l'épreuve de l'électrification', *Vingtième Siècle Revue d'Histoire*, 62, pp. 107–22.

Foreman-Peck, J. (1985) 'Competition and Performance in the UK Telecommunications Industry', *Telecommunications Policy*, 9, pp. 215–27.

Foreman-Peck, J., and R. Millward (1994) *Public and Private Ownership of British Industry 1820–1990* (Oxford University Press).

Fritz, M. (1980) 'Shipping in Sweden, 1850–1913', *Scandinavian Economic History Review*, 28, pp. 147–60.

Giannetti, R. (1987) 'Resources, Firms and Public Policy in the Growth of the Italian Electrical Industry from the Beginnings to the 1930s', in F. Cardot (ed.), *1880–1980: une siècle de l'électricité dans le monde* (Paris: Presses Universitaires de France) pp. 41–50.

Giuntini, A. (1995) 'Inland Navigation in Italy in the 19th Century', in A. Kunz and J. Armstrong (eds), *Inland Navigation and Economic Development in 19th Century Europe* (Mainz: Verlag Philipp von Zabem) pp. 147–57.

Gjolberg, O. (1980) 'The Substitution of Steam for Sail in Norwegian Ocean Shipping, 1866–1914: A Study in the Economics of Diffusion', *Scandinavian Economic History Review*, 28, pp. 135–46.

Gomez-Mendoza, A. (1983) 'Spain', in P. O'Brien (ed.), *Railways and the Economic Development of Europe* (London: Macmillan) pp. 148–69.

Gomez-Mendoza, A. (1995) 'Europe's Cinderella: Inland Navigation in 19th Century Spain', in A. Kunz and J. Armstrong (eds), *Inland Navigation and Economic Development in 19th Century Europe* (Mainz: Verlag Philipp von Zabem) pp. 131–45.

Harrison, R.J. (1978) *An Economic History of Modern Spain* (Manchester University Press).

Hennock, E.P. (1963) 'Finance and Politics in Urban Local Government in England 1835–1900', *Historical Journal*, 6 (2), pp. 212–25.

Holcombe, A.N. (1906) 'The Telephone in Britain', *Quarterly Journal of Economics*, 21, pp. 96–135.

Hornby, O., and C.A. Nilsson (1980) 'The Transition from Sail to Steam in the Danish Merchant Fleet, 1865–1910', *Scandinavian Economic History Review*, 28, pp. 109–34.

Hyldtoft, O. (1994) *Den Lysende Gas: Etablerinjen af det danske gassystem 1800–1890* (Herning, Denmark: Systimes Teknologihistorie, European Educational Publishers Group) (English summary pp. 173–190).

Hyldtoft, O. (1995) 'Making Gas: The Establishment of the Nordic Gas systems, 1800–1870', in A. Kaijser and M. Hedin (eds), *Nordic Energy Systems: Historical Perspectives and Current Issues* (Canton, MA: Science History Publications) pp. 76–99.

Kaijser, A. (1995) 'Controlling the Grid: The Development of High Tension Power Lines in the Nordic Countries', in A. Kaijser and M. Hedin (eds), *Nordic Energy Systems: Historical Perspectives and Current Issues* (Canton, MA: Science History Publications) pp. 31–53.

Magee, L. (1899) 'Electricity Railway Practice in Germany', *Street Railway Journal*, 19, pp. 647–62.

Matés Barco, J.M. (2000) 'Strategy of Foreign Firms in the Sector of Water Supply in Spain (1850–1990)', paper presented at IV European Business History Conference, 2000.

Millward, R. (2005) *Private and Public Enterprise in Europe: Energy, Telecommunications and Transport c. 1830–1990* (Cambridge University Press).

Milward, A.S., and S.B. Saul (1977) *The Development of the Economies of Continental Europe 1850–1914* (Harvard University Press).

Mitchell, B.R. (1964) 'The Coming of the Railway and UK Economic Growth', *Journal of Economic History*, XXIV, pp. 315–336.

Motes, M. de (1987) 'L'électricité, facteur de développement économique en Espagne: 1930–36', in F. Cardot (ed.), *1880–1980: une siècle de l'électricité dans le monde* (Paris: Presses Universitaires de France) pp. 57–67.

Nadal, J. (1973) 'Spain 1830–1914', in C. Cipolla (ed.), *Fontana Economic History of Europe: The Emergence of Industrial Societies: Part 2* (Glasgow: Fontana-Collins) pp. 532–626.

Nuñez, G. (1990) 'Devéloppement et integration regionale de l'industrie électrique en Andalousie jusqu'en 1935', in M. Trédé (ed.), *Éléctricité et électrification dans le monde 1880–1980* (Paris: Association pour l'histoire de l' éléctricité en France/Presses Universitaires de France) pp. 169–201.

Nuñez, G. (forthcoming) 'Spanish Cities in a Forgotten Modernising Process', in M. Morner and G. Tortella (eds), *Different Paths to Modernisation* (University of Lund).

Perry, C.R. (1977) 'The British Experience 1876–1912: The Impact of the Telephone during the Years of Delay', in I. de Sola Pool (ed.), *The Social Impact of the Telephone* (Cambridge, MA: MIT Press) pp. 69–96.

Peterson, H.J.S. (1990) 'Diffusion of Coal Gas Technology in Denmark 1850–1920', *Technological Forecasting and Social Change*, 38, pp. 37–48.

Sudria, C. (1983) 'Notas sobre la implantacion y el desarrollo de la industria del gas en España 1840–1901', *Revista de Historia Economica*, 1 (2), pp. 97–118.

Thomas, F. (1978) 'The Politics of Growth: the German Telephone System', in R. Maintz and T.P. Hughes (eds), *The Development of Large Technical Systems* (Boulder, Colorado: Frankfurt and Westview Press) pp. 179–213.

Tortella, G. (2000) *The Development of Modern Spain* (Harvard University Press).

United Nations Conference on Trade and Development (UNCTAD) (1996) *World Investment 1996: Investment, Trade and International Policy Arrangement* (New York and Geneva: United Nations).

United Nations Conference on Trade and Development (UNCTAD) (2002) *World Investment Report 2002: Transnational Corporations and Export Competitiveness* (New York and Geneva: United Nations).

United Nations Conference on Trade and Development (UNCTAD) (2004) *World Investment Report 2004* (New York and Geneva: United Nations).

Wengenroth, U. (2000) 'The Rise and Fall of State-Owned Enterprise in Germany', in P.A. Toninelli (ed.), *The Rise and Fall of State-Owned Enterprise in the Western World* (Cambridge University Press) pp. 103–27.

3
Explaining Institutional Change in the Networks: Britain in Comparative Perspective, 1945–90

Robert Millward

Introduction

The years since the Second World War witnessed two dramatic changes in the ownership and control of British industry and in particular of the infrastructure industries in energy, telecommunications and transport, on which this chapter focuses.[1] The late 1940s saw the nationalisation of coal, gas, electricity, steel and railways by the Attlee Labour government. The 1980s and early 1990s saw a great wave of privatisations by the Thatcher Conservative governments. These acts are perceived as having been strongly motivated by ideologies – socialism for the Labour Party and free enterprise capitalism for the Conservatives.[2] Whilst the 1940s experience in Britain had some similarities to what transpired in France it has been seen by many observers as rather different from the rest of Western Europe: Germany, Italy, Spain and Scandinavia never experienced the same socialist-inspired policies. As for privatisation the British pattern was not followed simplistically elsewhere in Europe. In the 1980s it was largely concentrated in Britain alone, with the other countries of Western Europe following in a more cautious way in the 1990s.

Close examination of the historical record, however, suggests that ideologies of socialism and capitalism played a much smaller role in explaining the phases of nationalisation and privatisation. The purpose of this chapter is to set out an alternative explanation with more emphasis on technological and economic forces. There are basically two questions:

a) How far was state enterprise in Britain different from the rest of Europe?
b) How far was institutional change, including nationalisation and privatisation, prompted more by economic and technological forces than ideologies of socialism and capitalism?

I. The Origins of State Enterprise

In the literature on the history of state enterprise there are two themes which are questionable. One is that undertakings like the National Coal Board and the Central Electricity Generating Board in Britain were established as state-owned monopolies in the 1940s in the wake of the economic depression of the 1930s, the rise of the Labour Party and the success of administrative planning in the Second World War. A similar line of argument applies to Électricité de France and Charbonnages de France with the resistance movement (Conseil de Résistance) playing a strong role. However, the socialist nature of state enterprises in France and the UK has been exaggerated. Socialism seemed to stop at the gates of manufacturing industry (apart from steel in Britain which was nationalised in 1951 and the Renault car company in France, the latter deemed to have collaborated during the war) and left land and commerce in the private sector. It was not a takeover of the means of production as some socialists had wanted. Moreover the central governments of France and Britain had a strong grip on all the infrastructure industries by the end of the 1930s, before the electoral success of social democratic parties in the 1940s. By the end of the 1940s it was clear that the outcome was not fundamental socialism and socialist views on the way state enterprises should be organised and administered were not widely accepted – the boards were headed not by trade union leaders but by specialists in finance, engineering and management.[3]

A second theme in the literature seeks to emphasise the smaller scale and very different origins of state ownership in other Western European countries.[4] The argument is that the former fascist regimes in Italy, Germany and Spain never experienced the process of socialist-inspired nationalisations seen in France and the UK in the 1940s, nor did Sweden where public enterprises, so the argument goes, were set up over a long period dating from the middle of the nineteenth century in a fairly pragmatic way. The problem with this argument is that, whatever their origins, most of the infrastructure industries in Western Europe were under the control of the state by the end of the 1940s. By 1948 British Railways, the General Post Office (embracing telecommunications) and the British Overseas Airways Corporation had been established as state enterprises but railways, telecommunications and airlines were in complete or near complete state ownership also in the other countries on which this paper focuses – France, Germany, Italy, Scandinavia and Spain. Coal, electricity and gas supply were nationalised in France and Britain in 1946–8 and Italy followed suit for electricity supply in 1962. The central state exerted strong control over electricity networks in Scandinavia and Germany too, however. The Swedish trunk network in rails and telegraph, together with the major part of the electricity and gas industries, were in the hands of state or municipal bodies before the war and there was no coal industry to nationalise.

II. The Origins and Objectives of Government Policy in the Network Industries

If the extent of state ownership did not differ much across Europe and was not predominantly socialist-inspired what accounts for its existence and its institutional form? History is absolutely central here and we have to look at the whole nineteenth- and twentieth-century experiences though considerations of space allow only a brief indication of these issues in this section.[5]

The origins of government involvement in the infrastructure industries date back to the early nineteenth century, which prompts a key question: why in a period when free enterprise and free trade were dominant philosophies did governments ever get involved in these sectors? The essential issue was the need for rights of way for railway track, telegraph lines and gas and water mains. Parliaments granted compulsory expropriation rights and governments followed up the easing of rights of way by controlling prices and profits and by monitoring the engineering and financial soundness of the companies. This was a common phenomenon across Western European countries. By the end of the 1840s Britain was a major industrial country with a trunk system of railways already laid and its central government was cautious about further regulation and other interventions. The Continental states were less developed economically (especially Spain and Italy) and their governments were keen to provide some help in the development of railways. In addition, political and cultural unification was important for Sweden and Belgium and military strategy in France and Germany, but here again arm's length regulation or subsidies could be the limit of government involvement – by guaranteeing rates of return for investors in railways and providing subsidies for particular sections of track.

Public ownership came in only when speed in the introduction of a new infrastructure was deemed vital and this seems to have been the case in Belgium in the 1830s, Sweden in the 1850s and Italy in the 1860s. In addition, central governments were very sensitive to communication channels which had military potential and the desire to exercise close control seems to explain why everywhere telegraphs came into state ownership and why the Prussian state took over its railways in the 1870s. Public ownership was even more important at the local level. Municipal enterprise flourished in gas, electricity, trams and water supply in the growing industrial towns of Manchester, Nottingham, Lyons, Bilbao, Dortmund and Hamburg. The historical record suggests that this reflected a desire to control local monopolies by milking their profits. So we find little municipalisation in rural areas where there were no expensive public heath problems. Nor did it arise in towns where local government was weak.

At the end of the nineteenth century and turn of the new century the technical possibilities and economic gains from the development of national networks in telecommunications and electricity supply became apparent. This was by no means easy to achieve but, by the end of the 1930s, most central governments were committed to intervention. The collapse of capitalism in the 1930s and the perceived failure to regulate private firms generated a growing uneasiness on the part of many states in dealing with private sector regional or national monopolies – and the potential was certainly there in railways, telecommunications and electricity. The growing distrust of arm's length regulation of private monopolies whilst providing subsidies made for an additional argument for public ownership. The classic case was railways which were nationalised in France, Sweden, Spain and the UK in the period 1937–47.

III. The Core Economic Problems of State Enterprise

This accumulated set of complex objectives was not significantly disturbed in the 1950s and 1960s. State enterprise emerged by 1950 distinguished from other institutions in being required to both serve the public interest and break even financially. The guiding statements were, however, notoriously imprecise about what the public interest was. The 1947 legislation for the British Transport Commission, which had taken ownership of railways, inland waterways, ports and some road transport, required it to achieve 'an adequate, efficient, coordinated system of inland transport', with no definitions supplied about how these terms were to be interpreted.

One solution to problems of defining public interest, at least for the network industries of railways, gas, electricity and telecommunications, was to go for 'universal service' – standardising prices and service quality throughout the country and it is here that state enterprises simply continued past practice in respect of the network industries. Access to services, in the context of a nation state recovering from the devastation of the Second World War, could not be markedly different in different parts of the country. Hence the charge for electricity per kilowatt hour would be the same in remote parts of rural Wales as in the middle of large towns, irrespective of the costs of transmission. The idea of the 'universal service' became common. There would be uniform rates per kilometre, freight rates per ton kilometre for similar goods, gas rates per cubic metre and electricity tariffs per kilowatt hour in different parts of the country, irrespective of the varying costs of supply. How these requirements, even when specific, were to be reconciled with the second broad aim – to break even – was never spelled out in the legislation nor in the early guidelines, which was significant for the later shift to privatisation.[6]

What about the state enterprises in oil and coal which are not network industries and in the airline industry which was, potentially, an internationally competitive industry? The major characteristics, for our purposes, of these industries are:

(i) Governments wanted to secure some leverage on airspace and on oil and coal as key fuels to ensure their availability as a tax source (via rents and royalties) and because of their strategic value in times of war or crisis.

(ii) On the other hand, the business of producing and distributing coal and oil and operating airlines does not involve natural monopoly conditions so that it might be expected to generate competitive conditions with lots of suppliers. This is what emerged for coal, oil and airlines in the nineteenth and the first half of the twentieth century.

The nationalisations of the coal industries in 1946 (National Coal Board and Charbonnages de France) had little to do with their strategic significance but rather with poor working conditions and the emergence of a politically active labour force who demanded nationalisation (an important exception to the main argument of this chapter). Indeed the coal industries of France, Germany and Britain all declined in the latter part of the twentieth century and all were protected in various ways.[7]

When it came to oil supplies, before the Second World War the known exploitable deposits were located outside Europe and this explains why governments held shareholdings in companies like British Petroleum and Azienda Generale Italia Petroli (AGIP). For the indigenous deposits of oil and natural gas exploited from the 1960s in the North Sea the important issue was to secure clear property rights and this was achieved by various forms of a concession system. In the long term, state ownership, such as in the British National Oil Corporation, was not needed to secure tax revenues and property rights, and the privatisation of these companies from the 1980s is perhaps not surprising.

In the case of air transport governments first sought control over airspace by asserting sovereignty rights at the 1919 Paris Air Convention, so an open skies regime for Europe was blighted from the beginning. A further complicating factor was that airlines, as well as airspace, were deemed, in the 1930s and 1940s when they were first emerging, to have strategic significance. It would not be enough for a country to rely on services from any old company. Each country wanted at least one national carrier and the normal military reasons for such a transport facility were greatly enhanced by the desire of countries like Belgium, France, Italy and Britain to secure good links and supplies with their colonies in Africa and Asia. However, the finances of these airlines were rather shaky in the early embryonic days of air transport and an even greater threat was posed by the economic superiority of American airlines which had flourished in a huge land mass uncluttered by national frontiers. The result was, firstly, that, by the end of the 1930s, the combination of regulation and subsidies was proving politically unpalatable. When this was added to the inability to support some services even with subsidy the balance was tipped towards state enterprise. By the 1950s each country had its own national flag carrier (Iberia, Sabena and so on). Some of the national carriers, like Air France, British European Airways and British Overseas Airways Corporation, were 100 per cent state owned while in others, like Lufthansa, Alitalia, SAS and Iberia, central governments had a clear majority holding. Secondly, the IATA system established in 1945 ensured that fares were set at such a level as to protect even the highest cost European carriers against American competition.[8]

IV. The Road to Privatisation

Now state enterprises faced many problems, the elements of which have been described above. I wish to suggest that these problems were at the heart of the shift to privatised regimes. In Western Europe at least the process of privatisation cannot be characterised simply as a shift ushered in by a great ideological surge, notwithstanding the rhetoric and rationalisation which accompanied it.

In emphasising the problems of regulation and public enterprise which paved the way for privatisation and deregulation it is first of all relevant to reject two themes from the economics literature. The first is that state enterprise was undermined by deficiencies in productivity performance. Space precludes an extensive refutation but there is little empirical support for this proposition. Suffice to state that recent work by Florio, Iordanoglou, O'Mahony and Vecchi on the infrastructure industries confirm earlier studies by others which suggest that the nationalised regime in Britain c.1950–79 did not have an inferior productivity record to private manufacturing nor to the more private comparable infrastructure industries in USA. Nor did the privatised regime in Britain c.1979–95 show a better performance than the earlier nationalised regime nor than comparable infrastructure industries in France and Germany which remained public enterprises for much of the last quarter of the twentieth century.[9] Note the emphasis here is on ownership. Regulatory regimes are another matter.

Secondly, the marginal cost pricing policies promoted by economists for adoption by state enterprises were never, outside France, accepted by governments because they flew in the face of the objectives and guidelines which governments set for their state enterprises. There are many examples: governments were loathe in times of shortages to let prices clear markets; a true marginal cost pricing regime would have allowed coal prices to be determined at the world level but governments were not willing to expose their coal industries to the full blast of market forces. The universal service concept was a complete contrast to cost-based prices.

Historically it was not the above efficiency issues which paved the way for privatisation and deregulation but rather that the industries had come to their current position as a product of a wide ranging set of objectives, for which the current institutional format was no longer necessarily optimal. Why, for example, should telecommunications be run by a section of a government department? The origins were in questions of national security. Was the telecoms sector still the dominant instrument for security? The second central problem was that the procedures and institutions for meeting these obligations were not sufficiently planned and costed. All state enterprises were expected to break even and, for the most part, they rarely did. Thereby they failed to meet one of their few quantifiable management targets. These two issues, when allied to the technological changes of the last 30 years, provide the key to understanding the shift to deregulation and privatisation.

A brief case study of telecommunications illustrates many of the issues. The break-up of the monolithic state-owned post and telecommunications enterprises from the 1980s was a central feature of the first phase of the privatisation process. Although much has been made of the ideological lead offered by the USA and by the privatisation of British Telecom, much of the institutional change can be better understood as a product of technological and economic developments which undermined the case for publicly owned monopolies. What had emerged by the early 1950s were national networks operated by state-owned enterprises; that is, in each country there was a single state-owned PTO (public telephone network operator) like the Post Office and the Deutsche Bundespost, usually an integral part of a Ministry of Posts and Telecommunications. The switching equipment was invariably supplied by private electrical equipment manufacturers (like the General Electric Company). Terminal equipment was often supplied instead by the PTO which also set technical standards for all equipment.

Public ownership by a single enterprise of a national network was the rule by 1950 and reflected, in part, the unwillingness of governments, in the inter-war period when the national networks crystallised, to use arms' length regulation of private monopolies, especially when these monopolies might have to be subsidised to facilitate social objectives. Why, however, were the trunk operators, and indeed the state enterprises in all the other countries, invariably integral parts of government departments? This can be attributed to the importance of communications for national defence – a demand to have quick access and control or 'access in crises' as the Swedish authorities put it as late as the 1980s. These reasons for public ownership and integration with government would come under threat with the growth of new means of communication – airlines, internet, satellites, mobiles. In the first few decades after the Second World War telecommunications systems were fairly simple: voice transmission to a terminal with the one telephone handset. Given the need for technical standardisation and compatibility with the national network, not much was lost by the state enterprises installing and maintaining the telephone handset. Once terminal equipment became something more than a single handset there were likely to be pressures to open up the market, as for appliances in the other utilities.

Finally there is the question of subsidies and the spread of telephone usage. A tariff system closely related to costs would likely mean lower prices in densely populated areas and for business users with many calls to make. This would not be consistent with the one-nation approach which characterised the immediate post-war period. The typical structure of telephone tariffs was seen to provide a universal service. It comprised connection charges varying according to whether the customer was a business or not, a charge for local calls which varied little with length of call in minutes and charges for trunk calls differentiated between domestic and international. Charges for local calls were low relative to trunk calls, residential relative to business calls, rural areas relative to urban. The result, in 1987 in France for example, was that local calls generated 67 per cent of the traffic of the entire system, 56 per cent of the costs but only 15 per cent of revenues.

The technological change which more than any other threatened the current institutional regime was the emergence of new customer premises equipment and value added services. New customer premises equipment included computers, modems, multiple telephone handsets, fax and telex terminals. The pressures on governments to reduce the dominance of the PTOs in these markets were strong. By extension, if the PTOs were to face competition in these markets, there was no case for their continuing to set technical standards and licence other firms. By the end of the 1980s it was clear that changes were under way and were being reinforced by pressure from the European Union, aiming for an internal market by 1992. The expansion of the equipment and services markets generated a huge increase in demands on the transmission networks, very much business-led, and gave added momentum to the business sector's demand for more favourable tariff structures.

Tariffs became more cost based and the main problem for the PTOs and their governments was that the beneficiaries were likely to be high income and business groups who made long distance calls while the bulk of the (voting) population would suffer. Hence the speed with which these price changes were introduced varied considerably reflecting the strength of the different groups. For the main networks, despite the advent of satellite and cable, in the 1980s there were still substantial natural monopoly elements. The abandonment of public ownership in the UK in 1984, with privatisation of British Telecom, was the only major privatisation of PTOs in the 1980s.

Another process which was continuing, again at a slow pace, was the disentanglement of the PTO from the supervising Ministries, obviously a prerequisite for privatisation. The fact that the process had started in the 1980s suggests that the importance of having PTOs under close state control for reasons of national defence and security was diminishing. Telecommunications were separate from posts, as a business unit, early in the century in Norway (the National Telephone Authority), Sweden (Televerket) and Spain (Telefonica) and was clearly separately supervised in Italy. The separation in the UK occurred in 1981 with the formation of British Telecom. The Directorate General of Telecommunications had been established as a separate entity within the French Ministry of Posts and Telecommunications in 1945 but it was not until 1967 that it was allowed to borrow on the capital market and it was the 1970s before it had separate accounts.[10] From 1987 Telecom Denmark was the agency responsible for operating the trunk routes in Denmark independent of postal services. These separations of posts and telecommunications were all signs of a growing commercialisation and independence from government but it was taking even longer for the telecommunications enterprise to be an entity outside the Ministry. Clearly this had occurred early in Norway, Sweden and Spain, and in the UK in 1969, albeit then still part of the Post Office.

The other countries had to await the 1990s, when French Telecom and the Swedish Telia AB were established. Germany was the most resistant and by 1990, even though telecommunications had its separate budget, it was still part of Deutsche Bundespost operating under public law and under the direction of the Ministry of Posts and Telecommunications and the Ministry of Defence, continuing the long historical tradition which continued also in the railways.

V. The Process of Privatisation

With the background of the case study of telecommunications, let us turn finally to the general process of privatisation. In the 1960s European governments had become concerned about the finances of state enterprises as the continuing list of non-commercial obligations clashed with the explicit directive of these enterprises to break even in financial terms. The inability of state enterprises to reconcile the break-even target with the non-commercial obligations of state enterprises manifested itself in a consistently large shortfall of earnings below operating costs and capital charges. It was also, in some countries, reflected in the relatively low portion of capital investment programmes financed from internal sources. These financial results deteriorated even further in the aftermath of the 1973/4 oil price hike and the downturn of economic activity, exacerbated by the fact that public sector price increases were held below cost increases.

Governments were wrestling with rising public expenditure programmes and the deficits of public sector industries were one target. It is significant that many observers of the shift to deregulation, but especially privatisation, place much emphasis on the impetus given by rising budget deficits, that is, rising public sector borrowing requirements. The timing of the privatisations varied across Europe but closely followed financial crises, best illustrated by Spain, Portugal, Italy, Germany and the UK.[11] During the period when they were still in the public sector the increasing pressure to produce a better financial performance was a key element in the gradual shift to cost-based tariffs, fares, rates and energy prices. The tradition of universal service provision with uniform prices per kilometre travelled, or per cubic feet of gas, distance of telephone call and so on had been sustained under the hope that the unprofitable sectors would be supported by the more profitable ones. Ever since the 1920s, with the advent of road competition, that hope was misplaced for railways which, slowly and creakily, shifted to pricing structures which rewarded off-peak long-distance traffic when booked in advance and penalised short-distance, short-term bookings of peak traffic. The railway was one of the oldest examples of this phenomenon but from the 1960s a general shift to cost-based prices was occurring. The technological revolution in telecommunications was creating great opportunities for the development of terminal equipment for business users, as we have seen, yet this customer group, along with other urban-based and long-distance callers had been subsidising local, rural and residential users. The pressure from business customers and their access to alternative networks could not be resisted. However, the pattern of some customers gaining and others losing meant the political power of interest groups was important so the speed of change in different countries reflected the varying strengths of these groups across Western Europe.

The technological changes in telecommunications and airlines were also undermining the case for dominant national carriers. It was, as we have seen, no longer sensible to have customer premises equipment proliferating in the form of computers, email, mobile and fax and yet have a market solely supplied by the main network provider and regulated by the selfsame body. Hence the customer premises markets were being opened up by the sort of competition which had long characterised the switching gear market. In airlines the onward march of bigger and faster planes lowering costs in the face of fixed IATA fares led to a flourishing of charter airlines and a relaxation of entry conditions in scheduled services though the IATA system lasted to the end of the century.

One of the driving forces behind state ownership over the nineteenth and twentieth centuries, as we argued earlier, was the desire to secure social and political unification but much had been achieved by the second half of the twentieth century and it was no longer clear that the old institutions were the best. There were new means of communication (roads, airlines and telecommunications) other than railways for securing links to remote communities, the colonies had now become independent and universal provision had been closely associated with financial failure. The strategic significance of certain resources and services remained. But there was no need for each country to give one airline a monopoly of all air travel. The financial returns to government for indigenous oil and natural gas deposits, together with the necessary affirmation of sovereignty, could be achieved by asserting property rights, granting concessions and levying taxes. Neither is it clear that control of information flows required that telecommunication networks be operated from within a government department.

This still left many sectors where natural monopoly conditions apply and where there would be advantages for a single supplier, supported for non-commercial obligations by explicit subsidy schemes. Electricity transmission grids, natural gas distribution networks, water supply systems, trunk telecommunications networks, railway systems – all were still dominated by the single supplier. Despite all the claims during the privatisation debates about the importance of competition, little had emerged by the 1990s. The reservations which grew in the inter-war period about arm's length regulation of private sector monopolies had disappeared by the 1990s. On the other hand the evidence does not suggest that privately owned networks in Europe are more efficient than publicly owned networks. Nor moreover is the claim that privatisation is essential to pave the way for deregulation all that convincing, even though it did work that way in Britain. Deregulation preceded privatisation in many parts of Continental Europe. The classic case for better regulated regimes seems stronger than that for privatisation.

Conclusions

In a long-term perspective the changing institutional forms witnessed in the infrastructure industries, on which we have here focused, were strongly affected by technological and economic forces. When the nineteenth-century state governments in Europe could not secure their socio-political objectives by subsidies or interest guarantees to the private sector state ownership emerged. In the twentieth century national networks were becoming economically attractive, road competition was undermining the railways' finances and the emergence of airlines meant yet another tool for the socio-political objectives of European nation states. The inter-war depression did have one key effect in this context, that of undermining confidence in arm's length regulation of private firms. State enterprises became key features of all the economies whether the leaning of the central government was socialist, capitalist or fascist. Thus the association of state enterprise with the growth of social democratic parties, especially in Britain and France, is misleading. Similarly, to explain privatisation as the product of an ideological surge led by the 1980s Thatcher governments in Britain is also misleading. There was certainly no long-term Conservative plan which was implemented when they came to power.[12] What does emerge from a long-term perspective is the importance of certain economic and technological forces. The onset of better aircraft, more sophisticated telecommunications and competition for railways undermined the role of state monopolies which were also often regulators of technical standards. The state enterprise sector was itself very vulnerable to overthrow because it had at least one clear management target, to break even financially, but one which was never properly reconciled with public service obligations. This conclusion does leave open the whole question of the role of ideological forces. Certainly they affected the form which state enterprise took in the 1945–90 period (as giant monoliths) and the scope of public ownership (especially the unsuccessful ventures into manufacturing). Ideological forces also affected the links between privatisation and popular capitalism, the ownership of shares and the property-owning democracy. How these related to the economic and technological factors is another story.

Notes

1 Some of these arguments are explored in more depth in Millward (2005).
2 See Shackleton (1984). For a classic statement from the hard left that there was no socialism in the 1940s see Miliband (1973).
3 Moch (1953) pp. 97–8; Kelf-Cohen (1958) chapter 1; Cairncross (1985) p. 463; Kuisel (1973) p. 81 and (1981) p. 202; Ostergaard (1954).

4 Prodi (1974) p. 45; Hook (2002); Wengenroth (2000); Coombe (1972) p. 183. See also Bohlin (1999); Verney (1959) chapter II; and Fritz (1990).
5 For a fuller treatment see Millward (2004) and (2006).
6 Millward (1997) p. 229; Posner and Woolf (1967) pp. 31, 121, 172; Neumann and Wieland (1985) p. 123; Dieck (1968) p. 229; Lewis (1953) p. 171; Zanetti (1994) p. 962; Pontusson (1988) p. 130; Verney (1959) p. 37; Kuisel (1981) p. 210. See also Baum (1958) p.189.
7 For more on this see Millward and Singleton (1995), especially chapters 3 and 14.
8 Dienel and Lyth (1998); Ottosson (2001); Brooks (1967); Dobson (1994) pp. 144–64.
9 Florio (2004); Iordanoglou (2001); O'Mahony and Vecchi (2001); and Millward (1990).
10 Bertho-Lavenir (1978); Coustel (1986); Richardson (1986); Blankart (1990); Haid and Mueller (1988) p. 169; in the same volume see also Nguyen (1988), Foreman-Peck and Manning (1988) and Jeppson, Paulsen and Schneider (1988).
11 Carreras, Tafunell and Torres (2000) pp. 15–16; Pontusson (1988) p. 134; Federico and Giannetti (1999) p. 144; Wengenroth (2000) pp. 122–3; and Chick (1994) p. 323.
12 Stephens (2004).

References

Baum, W.C. (1958) *The French Economy and the State* (Princeton University Press).
Bertho-Lavenir, C. (1978) 'The Telephone in France 1879–1979: National Characteristics and International Influences', in R. Maintz and T.P. Hughes (eds), *The Development of Large Technical Systems* (Boulder, Colorado/Frankfurt: Westview Press) pp. 155–73.
Blankart, C.B. (1990) 'Strategies of Regulatory Reform: An Economic Analysis with Some Remarks on Germany', in G. Majone (ed.), *De-Regulation or Re-Regulation* (London: Pinter) pp. 211–22.
Bohlin, J. (1999) 'Sweden: The Rise and Fall of the Swedish Model', in J. Foreman-Peck and G. Federico (eds), *European Industrial Policy: The Twentieth Century Experience* (Oxford University Press), pp. 152–76.
Brooks, P.W. (1967) 'The Development of Air Transport', *Journal of Transport History*, 1 (2), pp. 164–83.
Cairncross, A. (1985) *Years of Recovery: British Economic Policy* (London: Methuen).
Carreras, A., X. Tafunell and E. Torres (2000) 'The Rise and Decline of Spanish State-Owned Firms', in P.A. Toninelli (ed.), *The Rise and Fall of State-Owned Enterprise in the Western World* (Cambridge University Press) pp. 209–36.
Chick, M. (1994) 'Nationalisation, Privatisation and Regulation', in M.W. Kirby and M.B. Rose (eds), *Business Enterprise in Modern Britain* (London: Routledge) pp. 315–38.
Coombe, D. (1972) 'State Enterprise in Sweden', in *State Enterprise: Business or Politics?* (London: Allen and Unwin).
Coustel, J-P. (1986) 'Telecommunications Services in France: The Regulatory Movement and the Challenge of Competition', *Telecommunications Policy*, 10, pp. 229–43.
Dieck, M. (1968) 'Collective Economy Undertakings in the Federal Republic of Germany', *Annals of Public and Collective Economy*, 39.
Dienel, H-L. and P. Lyth (eds) (1978) *Flying the Flag: European Commercial Air Transport since 1945* (Basingstoke, UK: Macmillan).
Dobson, A. (1994) 'Regulation or Competition? Negotiating the Anglo-American Air Services Agreement of 1977', *Journal of Transport History*, 15 (2), pp. 144–64.
Federico, G., and R. Giannetti (1999) 'Italy: Stalling and Surpassing', in J. Foreman-Peck and G. Federico (eds), *European Industrial Policy: The Twentieth Century Experience* (Oxford University Press) pp. 124–51.

Florio, M. (2004) *The Great Divestiture: Evaluating the Welfare Effects of British Privatisation* (Cambridge, MA: MIT Press).

Foreman-Peck, J., and D. Manning, (1988) 'Telecommunications Policy in the United Kingdom', in J. Foreman-Peck and J. Mueller (eds), *European Telecommunications Organisation* (Baden-Baden: Nomosverlagsgesellschaft) pp. 257–78.

Fritz, M. (1990) 'Post-War Planning in Sweden', in E. Aerts and A.S. Milward (eds), *Economic Planning in the Post-War Period* (Leuven University Press) pp. 43–51.

Haid, A., and J. Mueller (1988) 'Telecommunications in the Federal Republic of Germany', in J. Foreman-Peck and J. Mueller (eds), *European Telecommunications Organisation* (Baden-Baden: Nomosverlagsgesellschaft) pp. 155–80.

Hook, J. van (2002) 'From Socialisation to Co-Determination: The US, Britain, Germany and Public Ownership in the Ruhr', *Historical Journal*, 45, pp. 179–83.

Iordanoglou, C.F. (2001) *Public Enterprise Revisited: A Closer Look at the 1954–79 UK Labour Productivity Record* (Cheltenham, UK and Northampton USA: Edward Elgar).

Jeppson, S.E., K.G. Paulsen and F. Schneider (1988) 'Telecommunications Services in Denmark', in J. Foreman-Peck and J. Mueller (eds), *European Telecommunications Organisation* (Baden-Baden: Nomosverlagsgesellschaft) pp. 109–29.

Kelf-Cohen, R. (1958) *Nationalisation in Britain: The End of a Dogma* (London: Macmillan).

Kuisel, R.F. (1973) 'Technocrats and Public Economic Policy: From the 3rd to the 4th Republic', *Journal of European Economic History*, 2.

Kuisel, R.F. (1981) *Capitalism and the State in Modern France* (Cambridge University Press).

Lewis, E.G. (1953) 'Parliamentary Control of Nationalised Industry in France', *American Political Science Review*, 51.

Miliband, R. (1973) *The State in Capitalist Society* (London: Quartet Books).

Millward, R. (1990) 'Productivity in the UK Services Sector: Historical Trends 1856–1985 and Comparison with USA 1950–85', *Oxford Bulletin of Economics and Statistics*, 52 (4), pp. 423–36.

Millward, R. (1997) 'The 1940s Nationalisations in Britain: Means of Production or Means to an End?, *Economic History Review*, L (2), p. 229.

Millward, R. (2004) 'European Governments and the Infrastructure Industries c.1840–1914', *European Review of Economic History*, 8, pp. 1–32.

Millward, R. (2005) *Private and Public Enterprise in Europe: Energy, Telecommunications and Transport c.1830–1990* (Cambridge University Press).

Millward, R. (forthcoming 2006) 'Economic and Institutional Factors in Electricity Network Integration in Western Europe c.1900–50', *Business History*.

Millward, R., and J. Singleton (eds), (1995) *The Political Economy of Nationalisation in Britain 1920–50* (Cambridge University Press).

Moch, J. (1953) 'Nationalisation in France', *Annals of Collective Economy*, XXIV, pp. 97–8.

Neumann, K.H., and B. Wieland (1986) 'Competition and Social Objectives: The Case of West German Telecommunications', *Telecommunications Policy*, 10, p. 123.

Nguyen, G.D. (1988) 'Telecommunications in France', in J. Foreman-Peck and J. Mueller (eds), *European Telecommunications Organisation* (Baden-Baden: Nomosverlagsgesellschaft) pp. 131–54.

O'Mahony, M., and M. Vecchi (2001) 'The Electricity Supply Industry: A Study of An Industry in Transition', *National Institute Economic Review*, 177, pp. 85–99.

Ostergaard, G.N. (1954) 'Labour and the Development of the Public Corporation', *Manchester School*, 22, pp. 192–226.

Ottosson, J. (2001) 'The State and Regulatory Orders in Early European Civil Aviation', in L. Magnusson and J. Ottosson, *The State, Regulation and the Economy: An Historical Perspective* (Cheltenham: Edward Elgar), pp. 148–65.

Pontusson, J. (1988) 'The Triumph of Pragmatism: Nationalisation and Privatisation in Sweden', *West European Politics*, 11 (4).

Posner, M.V., and S.J. Woolf (1967) *Italian Public Enterprise* (London: Duckworth).

Prodi, R. (1974) 'Italy' in R. Vernon (ed.), *Big Business and the State* (Harvard University Press) pp. 45–63.

Richardson, J. (1986) 'Policy, Politics and the Communications Revolution in Sweden', in K. Dyson and P. Humphries (eds), *The Politics of the Communications Revolution in Europe* (London: Cass).

Shackleton, J.R. (1984) 'Privatisation: The Case Examined', *National Westminster Bank Review* (May) pp. 59–71.

Stephens, R. (2004) 'The Evolution of Privatisation as An Electoral Policy, c.1970–1990', *Contemporary British History*, 18 (2), pp. 47–75.

Verney, D.V. (1959) *Public Enterprise in Sweden* (Liverpool University Press).

Wengenroth, U. (2000) 'The Rise and Fall of State-Owned Enterprise in Germany', in P. A. Toninelli (ed.), *The Rise and Fall of State-Owned Enterprise in the Western World* (Cambridge University Press) pp. 103–27.

Zanetti, G. (ed.) (1994) *Storia dell'industria elettrica in Italia: 5: Gli sviluppi dell ENEL 1963–1990* (Roma-Bari: Laterza & Figli Spa).

4

Public Enterprise and the Rise of Services: Networks and Performance of Italian Big Business

Pier Angelo Toninelli and Michelangelo Vasta

Introduction

The second half of the last century witnessed the rise and fall of the public enterprise in Italy. Growth of state-owned enterprises (SOEs) was more pronounced, continuous and delayed than elsewhere in the West: in 1990 the economic weight of the public sector was still around 20 per cent of GNP.[1] Afterwards, however, the decline of the public sector was very rapid and this accelerated further in the late 1990s: between 1993 and 2001 total revenue from privatisation amounted to over 1 billion US dollars, making Italy the world's privatisation leader with regard to income generated in those years. Thereafter the process slowed down, as it did in the rest of the world. A general evaluation of the entire experience is not easy: on the one hand, there are both positive and negative features, which were often deeply entangled; on the other hand, it unavoidably reflects changes of sentiment induced by contingent political and historical circumstances.

This chapter surveys public service enterprises operating in networks such as transportation, communications, energy and water from 1952 to 2001. The size, ranking and performance of these firms will be contrasted with the overall sample of the top 200 service firms for benchmark years in order to present a dynamic profile of the behaviour of the largest Italian public service network enterprises. The chapter is organised as follows: in section one the Italian experience of public enterprise history is synthesised briefly over the long term, paying special attention to the network services in oil, gas and electricity; in section two the focus is on the rise of the service sector in Italy and the changes that affected the sectoral structure of its major private and public companies: this analysis is based on a large dataset on the top 200 Italian enterprises. In section three the weight and performance of SOEs in the service sector are highlighted by comparing them with private companies. Conclusions then follow.

I. The Transformation of Public Enterprise in Italy

In Italy the first privatisation initiatives of the 1980s de facto brought to an end a century-old experience of public enterprise. The creation of IRI in 1933 is usually considered as the official birth of the country's public enterprise sector.[2] This was a major break in the history of direct government intervention in the economy, marking a shift away from a state-monopolist to a state-entrepreneur phase; however, the previous history of the country should not be disregarded since the foundations of these experiences were laid in the seven decades following Unification.[3] The construction of the SOE system accelerated in the 1950s and 1960s, when it reached its apex: afterwards its long crisis began, ending with the privatisation wave of the 1990s.

The critical terminal phase should not obscure the reasons that led to the building of the state shareholding system or the historical role SOEs played in the Italian economy. During the most crucial phase of Italy's process of growth/convergence towards the first comers (that is, until the Second World War) the state was called upon to remedy structural, interrelated deficiencies such as capital scarcity, lack of infrastructure and weak capitalist spirit. State intervention was even more decisive when private business proved unable to compete on the free market, as in the case of IRI: in fact, the bulk of the SOE system was derived from rescue operations performed by the state. This was true also in the post-war period, as control was increased over production through what was, in short, to become an organised shareholding system. By the end of the 1950s the gross revenue of the sector amounted to over 7 per cent of GDP and gross investment averaged 8.5 per cent of total national gross investment.[4] IRI stood out as the main actor in the story as well as the pillar of the system, although soon after the War new holdings were added to the first, most importantly ENI in the hydrocarbon sector.

The 1960s and early 1970s were years of continuous growth for the entire SOE system due to an increasing emphasis on its anti-cyclical role and efforts to maintain high levels of employment, particularly in the South. New steel plants as well as automobile factories were set up there, even if this did not correspond to purely economic criteria.[5] Moreover ENI began to expand outside its core business into chemicals, heavy industry and even textiles. The most important step by far, however, was the nationalisation of nearly all the electric system with the creation of ENEL, which came at the apex of the country's economic miracle and booming energy consumption. The new public holding, together with the great number of municipal utilities companies, was to guarantee continuity of supply and fair tariffs. This needed adequate investment and the integration of a regionally fragmented industry into a national system, something that private firms seemed reluctant to do, despite the huge, oligopolistic profits realised.[6] Over the long run, however, ENI and ENEL began to quarrel over the country's energy policy and their growth strategies clashed:[7] as a consequence neither succeeded in becoming a national champion. Only Agip in the 1940s and Mattei's ENI in the 1950s had got close.[8]

Italian privatisation started later than in other European countries: until the early 1990s initiatives to denationalise public concerns were the product of contingent situations, not of organic programmes. From then onwards the process accelerated, making Italy second only to Britain in regard to total revenue generated in the period 1977–2003, when Italy earned 116,900 million current US dollars compared to 121,600 million in Britain.[9]

Privatisation required major changes in the legislative and institutional framework in order to achieve a real competitive market on which companies were contestable and shareholders and savers legally protected. However, the changes made were insufficient to solve the agency problem arising from the presence of controlling shareholders. On the contrary, the spirit behind the privatisation of the main SOEs was in line with the traditional outcome of Italian capitalism which often saw state protection leaning more towards large than small owners and acting ambiguously in regard to the promotion of national champions. Indeed, the creation of *noyau durs* through direct asset sale to a small group of qualified bidders in order to give them de facto control of the privatised company was aimed at privileging the stability of control rather than to protect small shareholders.[10]

The privatisation process in Italy is still ongoing. At the beginning of the twenty-first century the process has slowed down due to changes in a few basic conditions and crossed political vetoes of the parties forming the running coalition. In 2005 significant parts of the former Italian state shareholding system – ENI, ENEL, RAI, Finmeccanica, Alitalia – were still under public control. In the late 1990s privatisation augmented state revenue and contributed to debt reduction. The revenue generated by SOEs was primarily channeled towards a fund created specifically for the redemption of state bonds.[11] At that time it was highly convenient for the Treasury to privatise: by selling its assets the state gave up relatively negligible dividends but saved the two-digit interest paid annually on the corresponding part of public debt. The post-euro lowering of interest rates and the improved performance (and relative dividends) of SOEs quoted on the stock market made privatisation less appealing. Besides, if privatisation had previously meant usually increased efficiency for formerly unhealthy SOEs the state had disposed of most of these.[12]

Therefore, though greatly reduced the SOE sector is still quite large and dominated by services. These have already provided about three quarters of the total revenue generated by the privatisation process between 1977 and 2003: 28 per cent came from telecommunications, 20 per cent from utilities, 16 per cent from financial services, 7 per cent from transport and 3 per cent from other services.[13] On the other hand, the degree of transnationalisation of network services appears quite low in comparison to many European countries: if in 1990 just four Italian companies were registered among the world's top 100 non-financial transnational companies (TNCs), ranked by foreign assets, they were further reduced to three after the dismantling of the Ferruzzi-Montedison conglomerate group of the early 1990s; and this number did not change until 2003. Although this number equals the Spanish one, it compares poorly with other major European economies: by 2003 the number of TNCs in both France and Germany had grown to 14, while the UK registered 12 TNCs (two had a double home economy, the UK and the Netherlands).[14] In 2003 Italian TNCs included one manufacturing company, Fiat (ranked 19th), and two service enterprises, ENI (25th) and a new entry, the recently privatised Telecom Italia (67th). Of these the ENI group can still be considered a state-owned network service group because of its downstream activities: its services spread over 16 host countries.

II. The Service Sector in the Italian Economy: Rise and Structure

The big transformation of Italian service companies is indicative of a long-term general process of structural change in the national economy in a latecomer context. At the beginning of the twentieth century almost two thirds of the working population was still employed in the agricultural sector, while the employees in the industrial sector constituted almost 20 per cent of the total and those in the service sector only 17.1 per cent (or 15 per cent if we exclude employees in financial services and public services). After the Second World War the 1951 census data showed that the agricultural sector was still predominant with the largest number of employees (44.3 per cent), followed by the industrial (31 per cent) and the service sector (24.8 per cent). Services still accounted for less than a quarter of the entire labour force, but if financial and public services are excluded this is reduced to 18 per cent, only marginally more than the level reached fifty years before.

Acceleration of structural change in the Italian economy coincided with the Golden Age, the period in which the growth rate of the Italian economy was higher than that of the first comers, at least up to the end of the Italian 'economic miracle' (1963). Indeed a comparison of 1951 and 1971 census data shows that the quota of those employed in agricultural activities decreased significantly due to the growth of the industrial and service sectors. However, strong growth in the tertiary sector occurred only in the last two decades of the century in Italy. Employees in the service sector exceeded those in the industrial sector in 1981, amounting to 47.4 per cent of the total number of employees, while the number of agricultural workers decreased to about 10 per cent of the total. Because of the lack of reliable data we can only presume that the rise of employment in the service sector was primarily a consequence of the growth of big business in this sector. Our discussion now turns to such growth, starting with the presentation of the different datasets on which our analysis is based.

The different samples used in this study of the largest Italian enterprises derive mainly from Imita.db.[15] From this database the top 200 enterprises were selected (excluding financial firms in all sectors) ranked in terms of assets for the years 1952, 1960, 1971 and 1981. For the last two benchmark years, 1991 and 2001, use was made of the Mediobanca data (1992; 1993; 2002; 2003) because the previous source ceased in 1984. As in most studies on the dynamics of big business the variable used to compile the ranking of the companies is assets.[16] For Italy such a choice is optimum; moreover it is widely accepted at the international level.[17] The only other alternative is, in fact, capital, since data for turnover, employment, added value or stock exchange capitalisation are not available for the entire period. Capital was discarded because it is less adequate than assets to represent the real size of the firm, as it varied a great deal among the different sectors.

Only joint stock companies are included in the analysis; this does not substantially alter the picture even though, especially in the first benchmark years, some quite large firms adopted other company forms.[18] Furthermore, firms in the financial and insurance sectors were excluded from the analysis because their assets were not comparable to those of other firms in the sector,[19] as shown also in other studies.[20] Finally, we excluded the groups of companies for which consistent data were available only for the last two decades, when it became compulsory for firms to draw up consolidated accounts of their activities.

By analysing the long-term dynamics of the top 200 companies (excluding financial services) we can trace the general framework of the weight of service sector firms. It can been observed from Figure 4.1 that the number of companies marks a downward trend from 1921 to 1952, when services enterprises in the top 200 fell from 54 to 29, thereafter growing continuously until 2001, when they numbered 49 (24.5 per cent of the total, still inferior to the 1913 level). The behaviour of the assets of services companies in comparison with total assets of the top 200 does not show significant differences from that of the distribution number, except for the last decade when the weight of assets grew to reach 42.2 per cent of the total in 2001.

The transformation toward services of Italian large-scale enterprises therefore takes place in a peculiar manner. The number of service sector enterprises does not significantly increase within the top 200 enterprises, but their weight in terms of assets rises considerably. This is explained mainly by two phenomena: (i) enterprises in the service sector clearly increase in size vis-à-vis those in other sectors; (ii) the sectoral matrix covered by the enterprises in services does not grow significantly. Indeed the structural shift of large-scale enterprises towards the service sector was mostly determined by firms managing services in a monopolistic way.

The number of service enterprises in the top 200 is small if compared with the weight the sector has acquired within the Italian economy: this probably is explained by their low propensity to grow, as big business in services was characterised during the twentieth century by great turbulence. As in the case of manufacturing firms,[21] once large enterprises in the service sector reach the top they prove unable to consolidate their position. Each firm holds

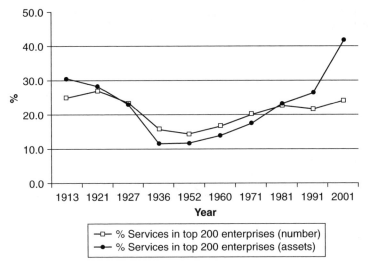

Figure 4.1   Quota of Non-Financial Services Enterprises in the Top 200 Italian Enterprises, 1913–2001
Source: Vasta (2004).

1.69 positions in the dataset of the top 200 companies for 10 benchmark years between 1912 and 2001.[22] The same operation carried out for manufacturing enterprises yields 2.3 positions.[23] Therefore enterprises in the service sector are characterised by even greater turbulence than the already considerable turbulence of Italian manufacturing enterprises. In contrast to the manufacturing sector such turbulence does not seem ascribable to the impact of technological change (except for the 1990s). Rather it was caused by changes taking place in three sectors: water transportation, wholesale trade and real estate.[24]

The structure of Italian big business – number and assets – in the service sector shows quite important changes during the Golden Age period (Table 4.1).

In the commercial sector, wholesale trade businesses remained stable, but in general there is a growing presence of commercial enterprises. This is explained mainly by two phenomena: (i) the increase of companies selling cars, spare parts and fuel; (ii) the growth of companies engaged in retail trade. In comparison the relative growth of assets is slower. The boom in this sector is likely to have increased competition.

In the transport sector the number of firms operating in land and water transportation greatly decreased; in contrast auxiliary companies significantly increased from 16 to 34, their assets growing from 3.7 per cent to 27.7 per cent of the total between 1952 and 1971.

As already observed for the commercial sector such growth was linked to the spread of the automobile, which followed the big wave of motorway construction in Italy. In 1971, in fact, four motorway companies ranked among the

Table 4.1 Distribution of Number and Percentage of Assets of Top 200 Non-Financial Services Enterprises by Sector, 1952–2001

Sector	1952 Num.	1952 Assets %	1960 Num.	1960 Assets %	1971 Num.	1971 Assets %	1981 Num.	1981 Assets %	1991 Num.	1991 Assets %	2001 Num.	2001 Assets %
Sale, maintenance and repair of motor vehicles; retail	1	1.7	1	1.8	8	2.5	14	5.4	14	2.5	15	1.8
Wholesale and commission trade, except of motor vehicles	38	5.5	31	5.6	34	4.8	49	8.9	50	8.0	18	2.3
Retail trade, except of motor vehicles and motorcycles; repair	2	1.3	4	1.9	11	4.3	18	4.2	22	5.2	18	5.5
Hotels and restaurants	7	2.1	5	1.7	6	1.1	8	1.3	5	0.9	13	1.1
Land transport; transport via pipelines	36	9.9	28	6.5	11	2.5	11	2.0	5	2.5	6	23.6
Water transport	44	30.4	66	27.3	43	13.7	20	6.4	15	3.2	11	1.6
Air transport	2	1.1	1	3.5	3	5.7	3	3.7	3	3.3	6	2.0
Supporting and auxiliary transport activities; travel agencies	16	3.7	14	9.5	34	27.7	27	13.5	27	13.5	30	7.0
Post and telecommunications	8	30.8	8	30.0	5	25.9	4	33.5	4	44.9	17	43.7
Real estate activities	29	8.6	26	6.5	22	5.5	16	3.4	2	0.6	4	0.5
Renting of machinery and equipment and of personal goods					1	0.1			1	0.2		
Computer and related activities							2	0.1	12	1.1	29	3.0
Research and development							3	0.3	4	0.3	5	0.3
Other business activities	4	0.6	8	1.3	13	3.0	19	14.8	31	9.8	18	4.5
Education					1	0.1						
Health and social work					1	0.1						
Sewage and refuse disposal, sanitation and similar activities											2	0.2
Activities of membership organisation n.e.c.											1	0.1
Recreational, cultural and sporting activities	11	4.0	4	3.7	5	2.8	4	2.2	5	4.0	7	2.8
Other service activities	2	0.3	4	0.6	2	0.2	2	0.3				
Total	200	100	200	100	200	100	200	100	200	100	200	100

Source: Authors' own elaboration of Imita.db.

top 10 enterprises in the service sector. Companies supplying services to businesses were also quite numerous, increasing from four in 1952 to 13 in 1971: however, their weight in total assets remained small, still only amounting to 3 per cent in 1971. At the time the sector was characterised by companies specialising in tolls and advertising. Therefore in the Golden Age of the world economy Italy modified its sectoral structure and experienced a general modernisation of the service sector: again the major changes depended on the rapid process of diffusion of the automobile. The diffusion of the automobile grew in Europe at a tremendous rate from 1950 to 1970: in Italy the quota of automobiles per 1000 inhabitants increased from 7 to 192 units.[25]

From the 1970s the advent of the Information Society – characterised by the diffusion of computer technology – caused a general streamlining of manufacturing to the advantage of the service sector. In Italy in this final period the service sector 'overtook' the industrial one in terms of number of employees. Structural changes in large services enterprises reflect on the one hand the discontinuity of the 'fifth technological wave',[26] which marks the movement towards the 'information society',[27] and on the other hand the process of deregulation in telecommunications. In terms of size the most relevant changes occur as an effect of the strong growth of telecommunication enterprises. Between 1981 and 1991, although constant in number, assets rose from 33.5 per cent to 44.9 per cent of the total, whilst in the following decade they grew in number while maintaining roughly the same percentage of assets. This result, however, is underestimated as a consequence of the 2001 'entry' in the sample of railroad companies.[28] The boom can be ascribed largely to the liberalisation of telephone services, in particular of mobile telephony. The magnitude of the transformations linked to technological change is also well represented by the growth of companies specialising in supplying computer services (hardware, software and integrated solutions). This sector, non-existent absent until 1971, appeared in two positions in 1981, increasing to 10 in 1991 and 29 in 2001. These were and are medium–large companies which as a whole in 2001 made up only 3 per cent of total assets. Structural change induced by the new 'technological waves' is clearly visible also in the growing number of companies specialising in research and development (R&D) (from 0 to 5) and those engaged in other business activities (from 13 to 18): in both cases, however, their weight in terms of assets remains quite small.

III. Performance of SOEs in the Service Sector

SOEs, even though at the centre of the Italian historical debate,[29] cannot be treated exhaustively without precisely mapping out their extremely changeable boundaries.[30] However, by limiting the analysis to the top 10 enterprises in all sectors (except financial) a few basic suggestions can be advanced. Already by the early 1950s four companies (marked * in Table 4.2) in the top 10 were SOEs. From 1971 onwards the presence of the state increased: eight of the

Table 4.2   Ranking of Top 10 Non-Financial Italian Enterprises, 1952–2001 (million lira)

Ranking	1952		1960		1971	
	Name	Assets	Name	Assets	Name	Assets
1	Edison	391,867	FIAT	861,964	ENEL*	8,205,602
2	FIAT	293,070	Montecatini	681,269	Montedison	2,927,956
3	Montecatini	291,421	Pirelli	556,936	FIAT	2,765,773
4	SIP	171,413	Edison	476,245	SIP*	2,574,237
5	SME	145,947	Edisonvolta	356,380	Italsider*	2,444,718
6	Terni*	140,334	SIP*	288,533	ENI*	1,369,341
7	SADE	125,087	Italsider*	273,283	Autostrade*	1,316,069
8	ILVA*	121,030	STIPEL*	267,993	AGIP*	1,217,511
9	STIPEL*	108,189	SADE	265,458	ANIC*	745,033
10	Cantieri Riuniti dell' Adriatico*	107,636	SME	259,757	SNAM*	717,974

Ranking	1981		1991		2001	
	Name	Assets	Name	Assets	Name	Assets
1	ENEL*	37,348,475	ENEL*	109,148,000	RFI – Rete Ferroviaria Italiana*	85,733,232
2	SIP*	20,550,384	SIP*	90,913,864	Telecom Italia	85,218,833
3	Italsider*	9,552,859	FIAT auto	28,831,921	Poste italiane*	74,165,409
4	AGIP*	6,907,930	SNAM*	19,264,155	ENEL*	63,529,135
5	ENI*	6,903,654	ENI*	17,345,358	ENI*	34,179,292
6	FIAT auto	6,618,637	Autostrade*	14,570,894	ENEL distribuzione*	33,136,701
7	SNAM*	5,251,381	AGIP*	14,477,605	SNAM*	27,327,942
8	FIAT veicoli industriali	3,876,609	IBM semea	12,372,988	TIM – Telecom Italia Mobile	27,319,081
9	AGIP petroli*	3,725,799	ILVA*	12,318,839	ENEL produzione*	25,527,017
10	Autostrade*	3,605,474	Fincantieri*	10,026,227	SNAM Rete Gas*	18,889,445

Note: assets in millions of current Italian lira. * State-owned enterprise.
Source: Authors' own elaboration on Imita.db.

top 10 companies were SOEs. Most of these were integrated into specialised network services: ENEL in electricity, SIP in telephony, Autostrade in running motorway systems, AGIP in gasoline distribution and SNAM in gas distribution. By 2001, despite Italy's role as one of the world's privatisation leaders during the 1990s[31] and the heavy streamlining of the main industrial enterprises eight out of the top 10 Italian companies were still SOEs. Again these were integrated network services companies: RFI in railway systems, Poste Italiane in post and telecommunications, ENEL and ENEL Distribuzione in electricity production and distribution and SNAM Rete Gas in gas distribution.

By focusing attention on the top 200 companies in the service sectors (Table 4.3) we can take a more detailed look at the relevance of SOEs. Their weight in the top 200 has always been remarkable, especially if we compare assets. In 1952 there were 27 public concerns in the top 200 Italian service companies – only 13.5 per cent of the total – but their assets constituted 47.2 per cent of the total. These increased in number continuously until 1991 when – with 65 units – they comprised 32.5 per cent of the total: their assets, however, constituted over three quarters of the total. Privatisation affected both assets and number. In 2001 these almost reverted to their initial level: there were 31 – making up 15.5 per cent of the total – while the value of their assets, amounting to about 120,000 billion lire, represented about 45 per cent of the top 200 services companies' assets.

To get a better picture of the weight of SOEs in the top 200 in the service sector we have disaggregated them by sub-sector. Those operating in transport and communication maintain an important position with regard to number and, particularly, assets: their weight constantly increases between 1952 and 1991 when their number reaches 57.4 per cent and their assets 94.4 per cent of the total of the section. In 2001 SOE weight is still remarkable (27.1 per cent and 53.5 per cent, respectively). However, this was reduced by privatisation, especially in telecommunications. Real estate and computer activities also grew until 1991: in 1952 their weight in number was three per cent (and in assets just 0.9 per cent); thereafter there were substantial increases as a consequence of the growth induced by the Third Industrial Revolution. This supports the hypothesis that in Italy – as in the cases of iron, steel and electro-mechanics during the Second Industrial Revolution – public enterprises played an important role in the diffusion of technologies related to the Third: at the beginning of the twenty-first century there are a number of public firms in computer activities (software development), particularly in the ENI group.

SOE distribution by sub-sectors leads us to two main ideas: firstly, the strength of public enterprise emerges particularly in those 'classic' sectors of state intervention such as telecommunications, social services, public utilities and transportation (Toninelli, 2000a, 2000b); secondly, it shows the significant presence of SOEs that are active in hotels, restaurants and thermal baths which were usually neglected by the state, not forgetting their role in the innovation diffusion of the Third Industrial Revolution.

We can now analyse the performance of the top 200 service sector companies by comparing SOE and private companies throughout the period. We utilise first an indicator of aggregate performance – the sum of profits divided by equities (share capital + provisions + profits) – in which larger companies have greater weight.[32] The results, as shown in Figure 4.2, reveal two different phases: the first, up to 1971, is characterised by quite a positive performance

Table 4.3 Proportion of SOEs and SOE Assets in Sector (%)

Year		Wholesale and retail trade; repair	Hotels and restaurants	Transport, storage and communications	Real estate, renting, business activities	Education	Health	Other community, social and personal services	Total
1952	No. of SOEs	2.0	–	19.0	1.0	–	–	5.0	27.0
	% no. of SOEs in total	4.9	–	17.9	3.0	–	–	38.5	13.5
	% assets SOEs in total	8.9	–	57.1	0.9	–	–	70.3	47.2
1960	No. of SOEs	1.0	–	19.0	2.0	–	–	4.0	26.0
	% no. of SOEs in total	2.8	–	16.2	5.9	–	–	50.0	13.0
	% assets SOEs in total	7.5	–	70.7	4.6	–	–	77.8	58.7
1971	No. of SOEs	2.0	1.0	23.0	7.0	–	–	3.0	36.0
	% no. of SOEs in total	3.8	16.7	24.0	19.4	–	–	42.9	18.0
	% assets SOEs in total	5.3	7.7	70.0	26.5	–	–	86.4	58.4
1981	No. of SOEs	3.0	2.0	28.0	10.0	–	–	2.0	45.0
	% no. of SOEs in total	3.7	25.0	43.1	25.0	–	–	33.3	22.5
	% assets SOEs in total	6.4	24.0	87.2	71.5	–	–	86.7	68.5
1991	No. of SOEs	10.0	1.0	31.0	22.0	–	–	1.0	65.0
	% no. of SOEs in total	11.5	20.0	57.4	44.9	–	–	20.0	32.5
	% assets SOEs in total	12.4	38.8	94.4	58.6	–	–	64.6	75.4
2001	No. of SOEs	–	–	19.0	8.0	–	–	4.0	31.0
	% no. of SOEs in total	–	–	27.1	14.3	–	–	40.0	15.5
	% assets SOEs in total	–	–	53.5	22.9	–	–	40.0	44.8

Source: Authors' own elaboration on Imita.db.

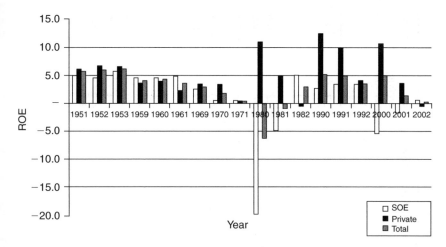

Figure 4.2 Comparison between SOEs' and Private Companies' Aggregated Performance (Profits/Equities) for Selected Years
Source: Authors' own elaboration on Imita.db.

and substantially stable and consistent behaviour on the part of both public and private companies: however, the three final years already reveal the slightly better performance of private companies. In the following period, from 1980, when SOEs' most negative performance (–19.6 per cent) was registered, the profitability of private companies was clearly superior to that of SOEs.

In order to have a more reliable proxy measure of companies' performance, we calculated the Return on Equity (ROE) for each company.[33] The mean of the ROE, disaggregated by sub-sectors, is shown in Table 4.4, the overall picture in Figure 4.3.

The comparison of the average ROEs of private and public firms emphasises again the two different phases that characterise the long-term performance of public enterprises. In the period comprising the first two benchmark years their profitability roughly corresponds to that of private enterprises. In 1960–61 it is slightly greater (1 per cent vs 0.6 per cent), while in 1952–53 it was slightly lower (3.3 per cent vs 4.3 per cent). In the central phase of the period analysed here, when Italy was hit by stagnation, the mean values of ROE were negative for both series, although the performance of the SOEs was much worse: in 1970–71 they averaged –11.1 per cent as compared to –1.7 per cent for private enterprises. Within the public sector the performance of the companies operating in transport and communications was the worst, with their ROE averaging –13 per cent as compared with –6.1 per cent for the private ones. Also in 1980–81 the returns of the public concerns were much worse than those of private companies: transport and communications were once more the critical sectors, but their performance was particularly weak also in the private sector.

Table 4.4 Comparison between SOEs' and Private Companies' Performance (ROE) for Selected Years

Year		Wholesale and retail trade; repair	Hotels and restaurants	Transport, storage and communication	Real estate, renting, business activities	Education	Health	Other community, social and personal services	Total
1952–1953	SOE	4.2	0.0	3.2	7.9			2.3	3.3
	Private	7.6	5.6	0.8	5.1			20.6	4.3
	Total	7.5	5.6	1.3	5.2			13.5	4.1
1960–1961	SOE	9.8	0.0	-0.4	13.9			-0.9	1.0
	Private	6.9	0.2	-5.1	8.6			18.2	0.6
	Total	7.0	0.2	-4.3	8.9			8.6	0.6
1970–1971	SOE	-2.8	0.3	-13.0	1.6	0.0	0.0	-35.4	-11.1
	Private	4.8	1.9	-6.1	-1.9	19.2	-84.3	11.5	-1.7
	Total	4.5	1.6	-7.7	-1.2	19.2	-84.3	-12.0	-3.4
1981–1982	SOE	31.8	19.0	-17.4	2.7			2.9	-8.0
	Private	6.3	-3.7	-19.8	-8.9			17.5	-2.9
	Total	7.0	2.0	-18.8	-5.9			12.6	-4.1
1991–1992	SOE	7.8	28.9	2.0	1.8			0.5	3.2
	Private	8.1	8.5	1.3	1.5			-3.8	5.3
	Total	8.1	12.6	1.7	1.7			-2.9	4.6
2001–2002	SOE	0.0	0.0	-7.7	16.2			-0.3	-0.5
	Private	7.6	11.2	-7.4	10.7			22.1	4.7
	Total	7.6	11.2	-7.5	11.5			13.1	3.9

Source: Authors' own elaboration on Imita.db.

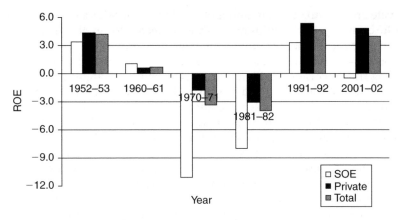

Figure 4.3   Comparison between SOEs' and Private Companies' Overall Performance (ROE) for Selected Years
Source: Authors' own elaboration on Imita.db.

In 1991 the entire service sector became profitable again, but private companies' performance still outstripped that of public ones (5.3 per cent vs 3.2 per cent); the gap, however, narrowed. Finally, in 2001–2 the performance of the public concerns turns negative once more (–0.5 per cent) and the gap in profitability with the private ones (averaging 4.7 per cent) increases. However, such a result was 'biased' by the poor performance of the three companies of the Alitalia group, Italy's flag ship airline company: if these three companies were omitted from the analysis the SOE performance would be considerably better, overtaking the private one. The ROE average of the SOE in fact would be 5.5 per cent versus 4.7 per cent for private companies. This seems to confirm that SOE profitability can at times compare well to that of private companies.

Analysis of the above set of indicators presents quite a consistent and homogenous picture that suggests that in Italy the performance of the major public enterprises of the service sector was marked by two phases. In the first phase performance was similar to that of private enterprises, sometimes even superior. However, in the second phase, from the early 1970s onwards, public performance worsened and the gap vis-à-vis private enterprises widened.

Conclusions

Until the end of the 1960s the Italian economy was characterised by backwardness in the tertiary sector – mainly small units with limited assets, often operating in local and narrow contexts. This situation was mitigated by the number of medium to large public concerns operating in particular in network services such as land and water transportation, as well as post and telecommunications. Though these were profitable – sometimes even more so than private ones, thanks to their monopoly position – the SOEs also stimulated the entire economy via the diffusion of advanced technologies, the modernisation of management and organisational structures and even the updating of accounting techniques. This critical position was somehow maintained later, during the expansion of the tertiary sector, when private firms became the main actors of the accelerated process and SOEs experienced their worst crisis. In this second period their presence was all but negligible. This was particularly true with regard to such crucial activities as those related to the Third Industrial Revolution, where the ability to monitor the technology market and integrate activities in efficient networks was likely to be a trump card. SOEs in those sectors were able to recover quite rapidly from the crisis: the taking-off of the privatisation process lessened the financial burden of a number of them through the removal of insolvent firms or divisions. Those companies quite soon became profitable again and remain so today.

As far as TNCs are concerned the dynamics of the top 100 non-financial transnational companies ranked by foreign assets prove that the Italian trend is in line with those of other major European countries: namely a shift from manufacturing to non-financial services. While in 1990 the four Italian TNCs were classified as manufacturing companies in 2003 only one (Fiat) still had its core business in manufacturing, while ENI and Telecom were by then classified as service enterprises. Of the three, ENI alone maintained significant state participation. This confirms that Italy did not develop an effective national champion policy, a failure which is likely to have a multifaceted explanation, political, institutional as well as economic: first and foremost, the presence and nature of the big conglomerate IRI, a veritable centre of political power, which was at odds with the successful establishment of national champions in specific sectors.[34]

Notes

1 Malgarini (2000).
2 Posner and Woolf (1967); Saraceno (1975); Cianci (1977); Amatori (1997, 2000).
3 Toninelli (2003).
4 Toninelli (2003) Table 2, p. 162.
5 (Amatori 2000).
6 See the essays collected in Castronovo (1994).
7 Sapelli et al. (1993).
8 Jacobini (1948).
9 Clifton, Comín and Díaz-Fuentes (2003).
10 Melis (1999) p. 129.
11 Toninelli (2003).
12 Mucchetti (2004).
13 Bortolotti (2004) p. 12, Fig. 10.
14 UNCTAD (1993) Table I.10; UNCTAD (2005) Table A.1.9.
15 Imita.db is a huge database that includes data – registry of companies, boards of directors, company balance sheets – on Italian companies from 1900 to 1982. The number of firms included varies from a minimum of 788 in 1911 to a maximum of 11,802 in 1972. The number of board directors varies from a minimum of 5904

(1911) to a maximum of 81,419 (1972). The data relative to the registry of companies and the boards of directors are available for the benchmark years, while the entire time series is available for company balance sheets. Altogether the database includes 38,182 firms, 294,335 directors and over 200,000 company balance sheets. See Giannetti and Vasta (2006), especially Appendix (see http://imitadb.unisi.it).
16 Berle and Means (1932); Chandler (1990).
17 White (2002).
18 Federico and Toninelli (2006).
19 If we had included financial intermediation (section J of NACE classification) companies in the services sample this would have distorted the picture. In the different benchmark years, in fact, banks, financial companies and insurance companies would have taken from 70 to 95 places among the top 100 enterprises in the service sector. This aspect is also discussed in Ville and Merrett (2000) p. 16.
20 Ville and Merrett (2000).
21 Vasta (2006).
22 Vasta (2004).
23 Giannetti and Vasta (2005).
24 Vasta (2004).
25 Deaton (1976).
26 Freeman and Soete (1997).
27 Castells (1996).
28 These companies in fact were transformed into joint stock companies in 2000 and 2001 in the reorganisation process of the Ferrovie dello stato group. If one does not take into consideration this phenomenon, caused by institutional changes, the telecommunications compartment would amount in 2001 to over 55 per cent of the total assets of the service sector.
29 Posner and Woolf (1967); Bonelli (1978); Barca and Trento (1997); Amatori (2000); Toninelli (2003).
30 Arrighetti, Stansfield and Virno (1982); Bognetti and Spagnolo (1992).
31 Zanetti and Alzona (1998); Affinito, de Cecco and Dringoli (2000); Bortolotti (2004); Megginson (2004).
32 The index has been calculated for 18 years: the benchmark years and the years immediately preceding and following each benchmark year (for example, for the benchmark year 1952 the values also of 1951 and 1953 were calculated). For the benchmark year 1971, however, the data for 1972 were not available so we used data for the two preceding years, 1969 and 1970.
33 By ROE we mean the ratio between profits and equity, the latter being – as usual – calculated as the mean of two years $[(E_t + E_{t-1})/2]$. Furthermore in order to avoid undesired distortions the ROE values have been normalised to a range between −100 per cent and +100 per cent.
34 For example, telecommunications. In the early 1960s the regional telephone companies – already partially in the IRI's hands – were integrated into a national system operated by SIP, a company controlled by IRI. This was counterbalanced by the empowering of its parent company STET – which stood at the top of the IRI telecommunications division – a financial holding which also controlled companies engaged in international traffic activities and in cable and plant production.

References

Affinito, M., M. de Cecco and A. Dringoli (2000) *Le privatizzazioni nell'industria manifatturiera italiana* (Rome: Donzelli).

Amatori, F. (1997) 'Italy: The Tormented Rise of Organizational Capabilities between Government and Families', in A.D. Chandler, F. Amatori and T. Hikino (eds), *Big Business and the Wealth of Nations* (Cambridge University Press) pp. 246–76.

Amatori, F. (2000) 'Beyond State and Market: Italy's Futile Search for a Third Way', in Toninelli (2000a) pp. 128–56.

Arrighetti, A., G. Stansfield and C. Virno (1982) *Le partecipazioni azionarie pubbliche. Un'analisi strutturale* (Milan: Franco Angeli-Ciriec).

Barca, F., and S. Trento (1997) 'La parabola delle partecipazioni statali: una missione tradita', in F. Barca (ed.), *Storia del capitalismo italiano dal dopoguerra ad oggi* (Roma: Donzelli) pp. 186–236.

Berle, A.A., and G.C. Means (1932) *The Modern Corporation and Private Property* (New York: Macmillan).

Bognetti, G., and C. Spagnolo (1992) *Le riforme mancate. L'intervento pubblico tra vincoli ed efficienza (1983–1988)* (Milan: Franco Angeli-Ciriec).

Bonelli, F. (1978) 'Il capitalismo italiano. Linee generali di interpretazione', in R. Romano and C. Vivanti (eds), *Storia d'Italia. Annali*, vol. I. *Dal feudalesimo al capitalismo* (Tuarin: Einaudi) pp. 1195–255.

Bortolotti, B. (2004) 'Privatisation in the EU: A Brief Historical Sketch', in *The PB Newsletter*. A Quarterly Publication of the Privatisation Barometer, www.privatisationbarometer.net, 1, pp. 9–12.

Castells, M. (1996) *The Rise of the Network Society* (Oxford: Blackwell).

Castronovo, V. (ed.) (1994) *Storia dell'industria elettrica italiana*, vol. 4. *Dal dopoguerra alla nazionalizzazione, 1945–1962* (Rome-Bari: Laterza).

Chandler, A.D. (1990) *Scale and Scope. The Dynamics of Industrial Capitalism* (Cambridge MA, Harvard University Press).

Cianci, E. (1977) *La nascita dello stato imprenditore in Italia* (Milan: Mursia).

Clifton, J., F. Comín and D. Díaz-Fuentes (2003) *Privatisation: the European Union: Public Enterprises and Integration* (Dordrecht/Boston: Kluwer Academic Publishers).

Deaton, A. (1976) 'The Structure of Demand 1920–1970', in C.M. Cipolla (ed.), *The Fontana Economic History of Europe*, vol. 5.1 (London: Collins) pp. 89–131.

Federico, G., and P.A. Toninelli (2006) 'Business Strategies from Unification up to the 1970s', in R. Giannetti and M. Vasta (eds) *Evolution of Italian Enterprises in the 20th Century* (Heidelberg–New York: Physica-Verlag) pp. 191–238.

Freeman, C., and L. Soete (1997) *The Economics of Industrial Innovation* (Cambridge, MA: MIT Press).

Giannetti, R., and M. Vasta (2005) *Storia dell'impresa industriale italiana* (Bologna: Il Mulino).

Giannetti, R., and M. Vasta (eds) (2006) *Evolution of Italian Enterprises in the 20th Century* (Heidelberg–New York, Physica-Verlag).

Imita.db, http://imitadb.unisi.it

Jacobini, O. (1948) 'La questione petrolifera mondiale e quella italiana. Nota VI. La questione petrolifera italiana' mimeo (Roma: Agip).

Malgarini, M. (2000) 'Le privatizzazioni in Italia tra il 1992 e il 1999: iter normativo e risultati quantitativi', in S. de Nardis (ed.), *Le privatizzazioni italiane* (Bologna: Il Mulino) pp. 85–117.

Mediobanca (various years), *Le principali società italiane* (Milan).

Megginson, W. (2004) 'A Hot June!', in *The PB Newsletter*. A Quarterly Publication of the Privatisation Barometer, http://www.privatisationbarometer.net 1 pp. 6–9.

Melis, A. (1999) *Corporate governance: un'analisi empirica della realtà italiana in un'ottica europea* (Turin: Giappichelli).

Mucchetti, M. (2004) 'Stato e mercato. Il capitalismo italiano e le privatizzazioni Parte 1', in *Corriere della sera*, 18 August, p. 20, 'Parte II' in idem, 20 August, p. 19.

Posner, M., and S. Woolf (1967) *Italian Public Enterprise* (London: Duckworth).

Sapelli, G., L. Orsenigo, P.A. Toninelli and C. Corduas (1992) *Nascita e trasformazione d'impresa. Storia dell'Agip Petroli* (Bologna: Il Mulino).

Saraceno, P. (1975) *Il sistema della imprese a partecipazione statale nell'esperienza italiana* (Milan: Giuffrè).

Toninelli, P.A. (ed.) (2000a) *The Rise and Fall of State-Owned Enterprises in the Western World* (Cambridge University Press).

Toninelli, P.A. (2000b) 'The Rise and Fall of Public Enterprise: The Framework', in Toninelli (ed.) (2000) pp. 3–24.

Toninelli, P.A. (2003) *Industria, impresa e stato. Tre saggi sullo sviluppo economico italiano* (Trieste: Edizioni Università di Trieste).

UNCTAD (United Nations Conference on Trade and Development) (1993) *World Investment Report 1993. Transnational Corporations and Integrated International Production* (New York and Geneva: United Nations).

UNCTAD (United Nations Conference on Trade and Development) (2005) *World Investment Report 2005, Transnational Corporations and the Internationalization of R&D* (New York and Geneva: United Nations).

Vasta, M. (2004) 'The Largest 200 Italian Firms throughout the 20th century: From Manufacturing to Services?', paper presented at the 8th EBHA Conference, Barcelona.

Vasta, M. (2006) 'The Largest 200 Manufacturing Firms (1913–2001)', in R. Giannetti and M. Vasta (eds), *Evolution of Italian Enterprises in the 20th Century* (Heidelberg–New York: Physica-Verlag) pp. 87–110.

Ville, S., and D.T. Merrett (2000) 'The Development of Large Scale Enterprise in Australia, 1910–64', *Business History*, 42 (3), pp. 13–46.

White, L.J. (2001) 'Trends in Aggregate Concentration in the United States', *Journal of Economic Perspectives*, 16 (4), pp. 137–60.

Zanetti, G., and G. Alzona (1998) *Capire le privatizzazioni* (Bologna: Il Mulino).

Part II
Transforming Network Services

5
Transforming Public Enterprise in France
Patrick Fridenson

Introduction

There is a French paradox.[1] On the one hand, by 1948 France had the largest public sector in Europe, putting the nation firmly 'on the left of Europe'.[2] The public sector included postal services and telecommunications, energy, railways, bus and subway services in Paris, a major airline, aircraft production, one automobile company (Renault), commercial banks and insurance companies, indeed, the major firms of network services. On the other hand, the initiative of the French government on 9 May 1950 which proposed the founding of a European Coal and Steel Community (ECSC) made France a key player in the creation of the European Union,[3] finally realising the idea of a large European market which some members of the French elite had been projecting from the late nineteenth century.[4] The ECSC, starting in 1952, brought together both public and private enterprises from six European nations which would exist and compete in the same market free of internal borders. When the European integration process developed into the Common Market, and then the European Union, French public firms were therefore confronted with fundamental challenges. As the word 'nationalisation' implies, would nationalised or public firms designed for the size and needs of a nation be able to thrive in foreign markets? Would they be able to keep their identity and strategy? How far should they adapt to intense competition and to internationalisation? How would foreign private firms and governments react to the arrival of French public firms in their domestic market?

Such questions became even more imperative during the early 1980s. In 1982 France's public sector was considerably enlarged with the nationalisation of 11 major private groups in industry and services.[5] Most of these were already highly internationalised. However, nationalisation was quickly followed by privatisation. The privatisation programme affected France particularly from 1986 onward and is still ongoing. This meant further pressures on the remaining public firms to adjust to competition. With their 'rent' and privileges in the domestic market curtailed by the various French governments and also by the European Commission, French public enterprises gradually came to the conclusion that their dilemma was to persist and perish or to transform and try to survive. At the same time, experienced French private firms operating in public services had to decide whether to opt for opportunities offered by deregulation and the worldwide trend of service growth and internationalisation.

This chapter focuses on the transformation of French public enterprises in different network industries such as railways, post and telecommunications, electricity, gas, water, air and space. The chapter will be organised into three main sections: firstly, their experiences of internationalisation; secondly, the evolution of their ownership; and finally, specific experiences of three of France's most important network industries: EDF, Suez and France Télécom.

I. The Internationalisation of French Network Industry

The current wave of network internationalisation is only the latest phase in what is a complex history of internationalisation, which can be divided into three stages.

Initially, all French public firms underwent a learning process in international business through cooperation with foreign counterparts across borders. The pioneer was the Post Office which became a member of the Universal Postal Union at its inception in 1874. However, for most state-owned enterprises (SOEs) internationalisation itself was not an issue, if only because they were short of cash. For many years only the airline Air France (created in 1933, but fully nationalised in 1948) carried the French flag abroad. Even some of the private French firms active in the network industry did not go beyond international cooperation and, apart from the French colonies, did not pursue export or foreign direct investment (FDI) strategies: the water and electricity utility Lyonnaise des Eaux et de l'Eclairage is a case in point (in contrast to the Compagnie Générale des Eaux) until as late as 1980.[6] In the electricity sector cooperation commenced during the 1920s in terms of agreeing technical norms and interconnections (France to Switzerland, France to Germany). This was a Europe of engineers, promoted by international associations. When, in 1946, all electricity producers were nationalised and merged into Electricité de France (EDF), EDF continued to increase cooperation between national networks in Europe in the same direction.[7]

A second stage began in the 1960s. French governments, initially bent on supporting national champions (both private and public firms) in the Common Market and beyond, came to recognise that in some branches the knowledge capabilities and financial capital required might exceed national resources. This became particularly apparent in areas involving high technology, and joint ventures thus came to the forefront. In order to run supersonic airlines between Europe and America French and British public firms jointly designed and produced the Concorde aircraft, an object of controversy from its inception.[8] In 1972 the French government initiated the European Space Agency which became efficient enough to design and operate the Ariane rocket, a successful means of launching commercial satellites thanks to the joint venture Ariane-space (established in 1980). Awareness of the shortcomings of Concorde led to the creation in 1970 of a European consortium of public and private firms in order to compete with the US firm Boeing: Airbus became a private firm, EADS, in 2000. Like Ariane in space Airbus was proof that technological and economic performance was within reach thanks to international cooperation.

The 1990s saw a dramatic change. Lured by the growing pressure of market competition and also of consultants and financial analysts advocating the opportunities of internationalisation,[9] most French SOEs in the network industry moved aggressively abroad. At first they relied on banks and financial markets to finance their expansion by debts or bonds. With the boldness of French top civil servants and the credit of the French state behind them they sent teams on missions abroad to search for local opportunities to exploit economies of scope. As had been the case from the late 1950s for the French SOE Renault,[10] this internationalisation drive led to the production within these firms of know-how in international product, service and capital markets, as well as a more customer-oriented business approach. However, this met, as it had in Renault previously, the constant opposition of the communist-led majority trade union, the Confédération Générale du Travail (CGT). CGT activists claimed the drive towards internationalisation meant neglecting the needs of national customers, putting at risk job stability and heralding privatisation. On the whole the internationalisation record was quite mixed. Only Gaz de France (GDF) fared well on most of its international ventures.[11] The need to adjust to the demands of new markets, the growth of business and the accommodation of different national cultures led to incremental changes in products, services, human resources, information systems, financial policies, top management and, finally, to revisions of the structures and strategies of these SOEs.

More or less at the same time private firms of the French network industry also moved aggressively abroad. Two examples must suffice from the water sector which remain polemical today.[12] In 1980 the water utility Lyonnaise des Eaux, when its former CEO retired (and was replaced by a new management style), decided to send 'commandos' to foreign markets, starting with Asia, in order to tap their growth opportunities. Early success brought about the generalisation of a management style based on a combination of local initiative and global resources at the disposal of local subsidiaries.[13] Its century-long competitor, the Compagnie Générale des Eaux,[14] diversified in 1994 by acquiring from Havas (a privatised SOE) the pay channel Canal Plus, born in 1984 and already a multinational. Next it further diversified on a world scale in the mass media, film and Internet industries, renaming itself Vivendi Universal. Nevertheless its eyes were bigger than its belly. On the verge of bankruptcy, the company had to be restructured, with Veolia (the new name of the water utility) being spun off and Vivendi itself divesting Universal Studios and many other assets. However, the downsized company has since returned to profitability and has been in good shape since 2004. Below we return to its competitor and counterpart Lyonnaise as it merged with Suez in 1997.

On the whole the level of internationalisation reached in a relatively short period is impressive. EDF and GDF are now among the world's most dynamic and innovative service champions. In 2001 Vivendi was fourth in UNCTAD's list of the world's 50 largest transnational corporations and Suez eleventh. The downsized Vivendi is lower down this list. But the argument holds: despite trials and errors these public enterprises have become agile international operators. How did changes in ownership impact this turnaround?

II. Ownership of French Network Industry

In France, nationalisation had never precluded internationalisation. In 1985 three academics of business administration devoted an entire book to 'French public multinationals'.[15] However, the issue of ownership puts to the test some well-known hypotheses: for the network industry was privatisation not only a political decision, but also a consequence of the financial needs arising from multinationalisation or of the cultural reluctance of foreign societies and markets in relation to French SOEs?

The percentage of the capital of SOEs in the network industry that the state controlled varied according to the wave of nationalisation and to the sector to which it belonged. State ownership was lowest in transportation: the state owned 25 per cent of Air France and 51 per cent of French Railways (SNCF) when these were founded, in 1933 and 1937 respectively. In the domestic airline Air Inter, founded by private bankers and transport companies in 1954, the state (through Air France) bought 50 per cent of the capital in 1958, while the company was finally absorbed by Air France only in 1997.[16] Transportation appears thus to be a special case. Elsewhere in the network industry the most common practice has been 100 per cent ownership of capital. Obvious exceptions have been in water, electricity and space. Public water utilities were local companies, thus in the hands of local government. Public ownership of electricity was also 100 per cent, with the exception of the Compagnie Nationale du Rhône (founded in 1933 and preserved in 1946 when all other French utilities were nationalised).[17] In the case of space a European joint venture was selected from the beginning, as already mentioned. The issue of 100 per cent control instead of a less costly 51 per cent option divided the left-wing government in 1981 when it launched the last wave of nationalisations. This was enforced on symbolic political grounds with a decision taken by the Socialist President of the Republic François Mitterrand.[18] A major caveat applies here. Never was a uniform rule of capital control demanded for the subsidiaries of the SOEs of the network industry. Accordingly, the percentage of capital held by the state in these subsidiaries varied enormously.

Two qualifications are necessary at this point. First, historical experience has shown that the percentage of public ownership has not really mattered in France as the state (as in a number of other countries) always kept full control of the companies whatever share of the capital it owned. Second, the governance of SOEs was peculiar. Their boards contained both independent administrators and representatives of the labour force. Neither, however, were able to challenge or control public management. This could behave as an autonomous technocracy without significant limitations, making international moves relatively easy.

French privatisations in general started in 1986, when the right returned to power. There were several waves, in keeping with French politics and with the condition of financial markets.[19] Consequences for the network industry at the beginning of the twenty-first century are highly differentiated. Government and Parliament have decided that, for a minority of relatively old SOEs, the status quo should remain the rule. This is true of the Post Office (allowed to run its own bank from 1 January 2006) and of French Railways. Another minority of recently nationalised SOEs have been 100-per cent privatised, good examples being Suez and the television channel TF1 in 1987. The larger SOEs of this sector have been only partly and gradually privatised. Partial privatisation ranges between 13.7 per cent of EDF and 20 per cent of GDF, both in 2005, and 46 per cent of France Télécom (privatisation increased gradually from 1997 onwards). The gradualness of this process is due mainly to three reasons: the ability of financial markets to invest the large amounts of capital required by such companies; the political caution displayed by governments towards trade unions; and the strategic character of energy supply. Relating these changes in the structure of capital back to the transformation of public enterprise it may be noted that the most influential shareholders are neither the wage earners of the companies themselves nor mainstream French small investors, but British and US companies, particularly pension funds, as elsewhere in the French economy. Thus, albeit at a lower level, network industry privatisation has meant an internationalisation of the capital structure, as in the French economy at large. The internationalisation of activities itself has been effectively invoked as a major incentive to privatise, even by left-wing CEOs of those companies concerned with the financing and local acceptance of their expansion abroad. It is not an exaggeration therefore to conclude that internationalisation weighed in favour of privatisation. Finally, the privatisation of companies operating in network industries can often be connected to a change of CEO and a reshuffling of top management. The new managers were even more prone to internationalisation, growth being the key issue as deregulation brought increased competition to the domestic market. The openness and yet uncertainty of international perspectives meant that their financial investment abroad would not always be performed 100 per cent by their foreign subsidiaries and thus would often require partners, and this would vary from country to country.

III. Three Case Studies: EDF, Suez and France Télécom

These general trends can be further explained by looking in more detail at three key firms of the network industry: the first in electricity, the second in water and other urban services and the third in telecoms.

III.i EDF

EDF is the largest producer and distributor of electricity in the industrial world. It has vast experience in technology, management, economic calculation, transmission and distribution. It has also a strong financial position and brand image. EDF structured its international policy between 1990 and 1992 with the reinforcement of its Division of International Affairs and in 1992 with the creation of a subsidiary, EDF International SA, to invest in firms abroad. It opened foreign offices, starting in Washington (1990). It aimed at moving from technical partnerships into industrial implantations. Its first industrial experience abroad was in 1991. After the unification of Germany EDF went into East German *Länder* in alliance with two German companies to build generation stations (and to finish a nuclear station in Slovakia).[20] Logically Europe was its first foray. The wider world would come later. In 1995 it took part in the building and operation of the nuclear electricity plant at Daya Bay in China. From 1999 EDF changed gear. Its socialist president François Roussely displayed the eagerness of the neophyte for transnational investment. In six years EDF became present in 20 countries. As Table 5.1 shows, its activities are dispersed across Europe, the Americas, Africa and Asia, and EDF's share of the capital of the subsidiaries varies from country to country, and even within the same country. However, predictably enough, following France's dominant pattern of internationalisation from the 1980s,[21] the largest investments were made in Europe, notably in Germany (ENBW), Great Britain (EDF Energy) and Italy (Edison). Amounts invested in Poland or Hungary are smaller.

Table 5.1 Foreign Direct Investment at EDF as a Percentage of the Subsidiaries' Capital (2005)

Europe		%
Germany:	**ENBW**	**45.01**
Austria:	ASA	100
	ESTAG	25
Great Britain:	**EDF Energy**	**100**
	EDF Trading	100
Poland:	**EC Krakow**	**66.26**
	EC Wybrzeze	77.44
	Kogeneracja	35.86
	Rybnik	78.25
	Zielona Gora	26.75
Slovakia:	SSE	45

(Continued)

Table 5.1   (Continued)

Hungary:	Demasz	60.91
	BERT	95.57
Switzerland:	Emosson	50.00
	EDF Helvetica	100
Italy:	Fenice	100
	EDF Energia Italia	100
	Edison	**15**
Spain:	Hispaelec	100
	Elcogas	31.39
Portugal:	Tejo Energia	10
Belgium:	EDF Belgium SA	
Americas		
United States:	EnXco	100
	EDF INA	100
	Easenergy Inc	100
	NuStart Energy Development	
Mexico:	Saltillo	100
	Comego	100
	Cominse	100
	Anahuac	100
	Altamira	51
	Gasoducto del Rio	100
	Valle Hermoso	100
	Lomas del Real	100
Brazil:	Light	94.79
	Norte Fluminense	90
Argentina:	Edenor	90
	Distrocuyo	10.57
	EDF Global Solución SA	99
	Hinisa-Hidisa over (via holdings)	50
Africa		
Ivory Coast:	Azito Energie	32.85
	Azito O&M	50
	Enerci	51
Morocco:	CED Tetouan	84.5
	Temasol	50
Egypt:	Port Suez	100
	Port Saïd	100
Asia		
Vietnam:	Meco	56,25
China:	Figlec	100
	Synergie	85
	SZPC	19.65

Note: The largest amounts are in bold.
Source: Compiled by the author based on EDF website information (http://www.edf.fr/1i/Accueilfr.html – accessed January 2006).

Public opinion became concerned only in relation to what happened in three of the 20 countries targeted: Italy, Argentina and Brazil. There expansion did not deliver the quick and rich harvest promised by EDF's strategists. The SOE experienced major losses in Latin America's two largest developing countries due to fragile economies and currencies. Its campaign in Italy (Edison) was blocked by the nationalist reaction of Italian government and business to being allotted only 2 per cent of voting rights. The ensuing losses, the growth of debts (25.8 billion euros) and the decline of Ebitda (earnings before interest, depreciation and amortisation), topped by the opacity of EDF's international accounts, were used as arguments by the French conservative government against the CEO, despite his stance in favour of partial privatisation. François Roussely was fired while travelling in China in September 2004. He was replaced by the CEO of sister SOE Gaz de France, who exhibited conservative leanings. But the expectations of the opponents of internationalisation were disappointed. The new CEO continued the transnational policy. Moreover in 2005 he clinched a long expected agreement with the Italians thanks to which EDF at last became a major player in Italy. The same year, EDF was partially privatised. Despite a protracted, public and heated strategic debate continuity prevailed.

III.ii Suez

Whereas EDF's history is that of a former state 'natural monopoly' turned international predator, Suez's trajectory followed another pattern. Here transnationalisation brought to the forefront the coexistence of strong national cultures within Europe.[22] Then a merger with an established water utility introduced tension between two types of internationalisation.

After the nationalisation of the Suez Canal in 1956 Suez became a cosy French financial company. Its focus was French firms and markets with a limited internationalisation activated by its banking subsidiary Indosuez. The wave of nationalisations of 1982 changed not only its ownership, but also its top management. When in 1987 a conservative majority privatised the company management decided that the new context (financial deregulation, development of the European Economic Community, globalisation) called for a bolder strategy. In 1988 Suez acquired Belgium's largest company, Société Générale de Belgique, an internationalised conglomerate of banks, mines, oil, commodities, steel and metalworking interests. But it never turned into a binational group à la Unilever or Royal Dutch-Shell. The compromises made with Belgian capital and government prevented real economies of scope, a reshaping of the portfolio and a dynamic management. Losses in some activities and new regulatory constraints on finance led to a major departure in 1995. The general assembly of shareholders ousted the CEO, electing a new CEO, Gérard Mestrallet, in his place. The option to become a full bank and finance group was discarded, notably because of the deadlock between the Belgians and the French, and Suez chose to exit banking and finance.

Instead it opted to become a multi-utilities European leader, focusing on water, garbage, power and gas by competing with European first movers in these profitable fields. The key decision was in 1997 with the merger with the highly transnational French water utility Lyonnaise des Eaux.[23] In the early 1990s Lyonnaise began to design a new type of organisation which combined an active centre and the operation of many different services in a large number of countries. After the 1997 merger its characteristics were refined and extended to the whole group. It relies on four features: a central role played by local units, procedures for reporting toward a compact centre, assistance from the centre and direct exchanges between local units according to a 'principle of connectivity'. The structure was reorganised by core businesses, with energy located in Belgium. But such a local–global management puts to task the Belgian influence in the new group and fosters a new strategic dilemma: to become either a binational group or an integrated multinational on a global scale. So far the excellent financial results have shown the soundness of Gérard Mestrallet's persistent rejection of the hybris into which several other French corporations fell during the process of internationalisation of the 1990s and the effectiveness of the strategy of refocusing which in 2003 involved major divestments and reinforcements of internal controls. But in 2006, thwarting a Suez bid from ENEL of Italy, Suez and Gaz de France have launched a merger project, which would create the biggest gas company in Europe, and one of the largest electricity producers.

III.iii France Télécom

The sequel of stages here is quite different. Revolution happened first in the domestic market. Between 1974 and 1981 the Directorate General for Telecommunications (DGT), under the leadership of engineer Gérard Théry, was at last empowered to make individual telephone equipment for everyone and to convert the French to the use of computers thanks to Minitel. In the mid-1980s the conservative government allowed competition among private entrants for a new technology: the mobile phone. Then, in 1990, the

Table 5.2 The Internationalisation of R&D at FT: Laboratories Abroad

Asia
Tokyo
Beijing
[another Asian site in preparation]
America
San Francisco
Boston
Europe
London
Warsaw

Source: Compiled by the author based on France Télécom website information (http://www.francetelecom.com/fr/ – accessed January 2006).

left converted the DGT from an administration into an SOE, France Télécom (FT), which kept growing and innovating. Internationalisation itself was the decision of Michel Bon, the CEO appointed in 1995 by a conservative government.[24] A finance technocrat with a career in mass distribution he embarked on partial privatisation. Then he moved to a strategy of external growth and massive technological investment.

The fruits of the strategy varied according to the type of business. In wired telephony FT attained control of only three historical operators: Poland (TPSA), where FT transferred technologies, methods and capital, Jordan and Senegal. In mobile phones the performance was mixed. FT bought the British mobile phone network Orange, which went on to be successful. But FT also bought the German firm Mobilkom, which resulted in huge losses (20.7 billion euros in 2002). Debts climbed from 14.6 billion euros in 1999 to 68 billion euros in 2002. The government fired Michel Bon in 2002. The new CEO, Thierry Breton, spread the debt, divested not only the unprofitable Mobilkom but also the participation in the profitable Italian fixed and mobile phone firm Wind, and reduced costs. In 2005 his successor returned to the international drive, and FT, calling itself a 'European integrated operator', bought Amena, the third mobile operator and second ADSL provider in Spain (where FT was only present in wired telephony, with Unidos). In this 'more selective and cautious approach' FT decided not to buy the Turkish operator, deemed too expensive, but is currently applying to buy Tunisie Télécom. In 2005, 50 per cent of FT's turnover came from abroad. The business in wired telephony is bound to decline. Internationalisation achieved in the mobile sector via Orange is limited. The real growth sector is the Internet and IP subsidiary Wanadoo, one of the three leading European service providers (and the first for IP in Britain). Three specialised subsidiaries – Equant (services to enterprises), Etrabi (financial telecom networks) and Globecast (diffusion of events by satellite) – are also very competitive.

Conclusions

Why have certain French network industries been so successful in their internationalisation activities and others much less so? Is this related to their size, sector or management? How does France compare with other countries in this regard? The reasons for success certainly lie in the size acquired on the domestic market, but not just size: the specific experience gained in urban services in the domestic market, the practice of international technical cooperation, the readiness for joint ventures in order to save capital, the readiness to move abroad without the caution displayed by Japanese firms, technological capabilities and state support of national champions also matter. Weaknesses lie in the domination of management by the alumni of the *grandes écoles*, and hence the usually limited intercultural management, the lack of corporate governance when foreign risks emerge suddenly and the sophisticated financial engineering without adequate ceilings on risks and debts.

Comparisons with other countries need to be specified by sector. Water and other urban services are clearly where France enjoys the main competitive advantage, acquired through the culture of concession. The most complex case is that of telecoms. The international experience of FT so far differs both from the pure player in mobile phones, Vodafone (which then diversified by acquiring Mannesmann), and from moderate diversifiers Telecom Italia and Telefonica. FT has had much in common with the problems other European historical operators encountered in internationalising mobile services, especially British Telecom, Deutsche Telekom and KPN. However, FT is in relatively better shape than the three latter companies. Its trump cards are now in ASP and specialised services. Airlines are a different issue. After many failures caused by an excessive variety of planes and routes, the merger with the domestic airline Air Inter and numerous strikes, Air France turned around from 1993 and is now one of the most profitable airlines in the world. In 2005 it took over the Dutch airline KLM and is building a binational firm patterned after the Renault–Nissan alliance.

Therefore in the constantly changing legal environment of network industry the key issue for French public enterprise is becoming combining institutional flexibility and product and service adaptability, whilst bearing in mind long-term technological and societal trends.

Notes

1 I would like to thank Yves Bouvier, Eric-Gilles Fridenson and Dominique Lorrain for their data and comments on the third part of this chapter.
2 Andrieu (1986) pp. 131–53.
3 Kipping (2002).
4 Bussière (2003) pp. 12–24.
5 Hamdouch (1989).
6 Lorrain (2005) pp. 340–61.
7 Barrère and Bouvier (2003) pp. 112–14.
8 Sarre (2002); Quennouëlle-Corre (2000).
9 Tetreau (2005).
10 Fridenson (1993) pp. 583–92.
11 Beltran (2002) pp. 389–97.
12 Lenglet and Touly (2006).
13 Lorrain (2005) pp. 340–61.
14 The CGE was founded in 1853 and the Lyonnaise in 1880. See also Chick and Lanthier (eds) (2004) pp. 135–66.
15 Anastossopoulos, Blanc and Dussauge (1985).
16 Thibault (2005).
17 Giandou (1999).
18 Delors (2004).
19 Clifton, Comín and Díaz-Fuentes (2003).
20 Hamdouch (1989); Tixier and Mauchamp (2000); Varaschin (2002) pp. 377–87.
21 Mucchielli and Puech (2003) pp. 129–44.
22 Bonin (2005).
23 Lorrain (2005) pp. 340–61.
24 Cohen (2005).

References

Anastossopoulos, J.- P., G. Blanc and P. Dussauge (1985) *Les multinationales publiques* (Paris: PUF).

Andrieu C. (1986) 'La France à gauche de l'Europe', *Le Mouvement Social*, 27 (January–March) 131–53.

Barrère, J., and Y. Bouvier (2003) 'L'Europe des électriciens', *Entreprises et Histoire*, 12 (October) 112–14.

Beltran, A. (2002) 'Internationaliser une société nationalisée: l'exemple de Gaz de France', in H. Bonin et al. (eds), *Transnational Companies 19th–20th centuries* (Paris: P.L.A.G.E.) pp. 389–97.

Bonin, H. (2005) 'Suez: from a French Flagship to a European Leader in Utilities (1982–2005)', unpublished paper presented at the international conference 'In Search of the European Enterprise', Bocconi University, Milan, 30 September–1 October.

Bussière, E. (2003) 'L'intégration économique de l'Europe au XXe siècle: processus et acteurs', *Entreprises et Histoire*, 12 (October), pp. 12–24.

Chick, M., and P. Lanthier (eds) (2004) 'Nationalisations et dénationalisations en France et en Grande-Bretagne: expériences comparées', *Entreprises et Histoire*, 13 (December) pp. 135–66.

Clifton J., F. Comín and D. Díaz-Fuentes (2003) *Privatisation in the European Union. Public Enterprises and Integration* (Dordrecht: Kluwer).

Cohen, E. (2005) *Le nouvel âge du capitalisme* (Paris: Fayard).

Delors, J. (2004) *Mémoires* (Paris: Plon).

Fridenson, P. (1993) 'Renault face au problème du franc et du risque devises (1957–1981)', in M. Lévy-Leboyer, A. Plessis, M. Aglietta and C. de Boissieu (eds), *Du franc Poincaré à l'écu* (Paris: Comité pour l'histoire économique et financière de la France) pp. 583–92.

Giandou, A. (1999) *La Compagnie Nationale du Rhône (1933–1998)* (Grenoble: Presses Universitaires de Grenoble).

Hamdouch, A. (1989) *L'Etat d'influence. Nationalisations et privatisations en France* (Paris: Presses du CNRS).

Kipping, M. (2002) *La France et les origines de l'Union européenne. Intégration économique et compétitivité internationale* (Paris: Comité d'histoire économique et financière de la France).

Lenglet, R., and J.-L. Touly (2006) *L'eau des multinationales. Les vérités inavouables* (Paris: Fayard).

Lorrain, D. (2005) 'La firme locale-globale: Lyonnaise des Eaux (1980–2004)', *Sociologie du Travail*, 47 (July) pp. 340–61.

Mucchielli, J.-L., and F. Puech (2003) 'Internationalisation et localisation des firmes multinationales: l'exemple des entreprises françaises en Europe', *Economie et Statistique*, 35 (November) pp. 129–44.

Quennouëlle-Corre, L. (2002) *La direction du Trésor 1947–1967. L'Etat-banquier et la croissance* (Paris: Comité pour l'histoire économique et financière de la France).

Sarre, C.-A. (2002) *Le dossier-vérité du Concorde 1959–2000* (Vallauris: Editions aéronautiques).

Tetreau, E. (2005) *Analyste: au cœur de la folie financière* (Paris: Grasset).

Thibault, P.-M. (2005) *Air Inter. La révolution intérieure* (Paris: Le Cherche-Midi).

Tixier, P.-E., and N. Mauchamp (eds) (2000) *EDF-GDF, une entreprise publique en mutation* (Paris: La Découverte).

Varaschin, D. (2002) 'EDF in the Global Market since the Beginning of the Nineties', in H. Bonin et al. (eds), *Transnational Companies 19th–20th Centuries* (Paris: P.L.A.G.E.) pp. 377–87.

6
When Ugly Ducklings Grow Up: Cases from German Utilities in Energy, Transport and Telecommunications

Harm G. Schröter

Introduction

This chapter focuses on four German utility companies – E.ON, REW, Deutsche Post World Net and Deutsche Telekom – and pays particular attention to their performance in recent years. These companies have several things in common: firstly, they all were state- or community-owned and secondly, they all experienced a phase of dramatic growth after privatisation. There are, on the other hand, many other utility companies that were also privatised, or continue to be state-owned, which have not grown like these four. The success story of these four companies is thus not representative of all the other firms. The railway company Deutsche Bahn provides a good counter-example. The questions posed in this chapter are related to the general ones in this volume. Since the expansion of these four firms was achieved to a large extent in Europe but outside Germany transnationalisation and integration are part and parcel of their process of expansion. But how have these firms achieved this growth to date? In what ways might they differ from other, less dynamic enterprises active in public utilities? What was the relationship between deregulation, privatisation and performance?

E.ON and RWE are among the largest private utilities in the world. Deutsche Telekom is one of the world's largest telecommunications providers. These three firms figure in the Stoxx 50 European stock exchange index. In 2004 Deutsche Post proudly announced a larger turnover than UPS (United Parcel Service), traditionally the world's largest logistics company.

Like most European states Germany had a state-owned PTT (Post, Telegraph and Telephone), Deutsche Post (previously Reichspost and then Bundespost). For decades a substantial profit was generated annually which went directly into the federal budget. In the interwar period, for several reasons, Germany was second to the USA in the rank of most developed countries for telecommunications and, in some fields, it even took the lead (for instance in the automatisation of switches). After 1945 Germany was no longer in this position, but was always near the top of the list of the most developed countries.

Energy supply used to be quite expensive but reliable: blackouts did occur in Germany, but they were extremely rare. All four firms can be understood as own entities not only in a juridical and economic sense, but also in a technical sense. All represent examples of what Thomas P. Hughes called Large Technical Systems with their special characteristics of behaviour.[1] One of these characteristics was a technical self-understanding of reliability, quality or even excellence. In the absence of competition (since all operated as monopoly organisations in their field), they provided a reliable (though not cheap) service. It was part of their self-understanding to provide quality, but not necessarily cheap services, a characteristic which was widespread in circles of German technicians and engineers: quality has its price!.[2]

I. Utilities Supplying Energy

While there was only one Post Office serving the whole country there were multiple suppliers of grid-bound energy. These were separated by type of energy (electricity, gas) as well as by territory. Some were relatively large, while others were extremely small. A number of utilities that supplied electricity and gas were organised as private enterprises, but most were owned by the state or by the municipality. Often municipalities did not keep the majority of shares but instead held voting rights by using multiple voting-shares. Nearly all firms represented the whole line of supply: generation, transfer, distribution and sales.

From the 1990s a new paradigm of utility companies emerged: they should compete with each other.[3] This new idea was part of a third wave of Americanisation of European economic life.[4] Though the new paradigm of competition had already started under the Thatcher government in the UK, it was the European Commission (EC) in Brussels that pressed for the introduction of competition into Europe. The EC stated in 1990 that the Single European Market required competition between utilities in order to force prices down. Though an evaluation in 1995 saw no connection between prices and ownership,[5] Brussels stood firm. Reform was to be initiated by deregulation and the establishment of guaranteed access to grid-bound transport capacity. It was not until December 1996 that the various governments agreed and the Council of Ministers issued their directive on electricity supply, which was to be transposed into national law within three years. This represented a change of paradigm because, from the emergence of electricity, supply prices had been calculated on costs after approval by state authorities. Now this system was to be abandoned and exchanged for market prices established by supply and demand. This new paradigm required a totally new way of thinking. In Germany governments thought that this could be best implemented by private owners and thus sold their shares.[6] At this time there was an urgent need for cash in public households as revenues did not meet public spending. Under the influence of Americanisation this meant politicians could do a good thing (get cash) and combine it with the right thing (privatisation). Large utilities such as RWE made tempting cash offers for a change of multiple-voting shares into ordinary ones, which then could be sold. Thus the owning municipalities could earn twice in such a deal: badly needed cash for their budget and praise for their up-to-date economic policy. However, the official aim of privatisation was not to balance so-called 'unforeseen' gaps in public households but to enhance competition. The respective shares were absorbed by the market; no decisive owners or groups of owners became established in the long term. In 2005, 30 per cent of RWE's shares were owned by local authorities, the rest were dispersed, with Allianz, a large insurance company, owning 4 per cent. E.ON's shares were owned in the following way: one half by German investors, funds, insurance companies and private persons; 17 per cent were registered by Americans; and the rest mainly by other Europeans.

The official reason for deregulating and privatising electricity utilities was to foster competition. The contrary was achieved, however. From 2004, after only five years of deregulation, only four companies dominated 90 per cent of the German market: E.ON, RWE, the Swedish state-owned firm Vattenfall and EnBW. EDF (Electricité de France) owns 45 per cent of EnBW, Germany's third largest supplier.

II. E.ON

E.ON is the official name of Europe's largest private public supplier of energy and, after EDF, represents the largest firm in this sector. E.ON's existence is the result of the merger of former state-owned enterprises Veba and Viag. Both were conglomerates, but their largest assets were electricity utilities PreussenElektra and Bayernwerk. This came into being on 1 January 2000, once the EU approved the merger. Initially the companies involved were active only in Germany, but not only in the sector of electricity supply. For instance, Viag Intercom, a telecommunications provider, had been set up by Viag. Another example was Viterra, a housing company which owned 150,000 flats, which had been part of Veba. A third was Degussa, the world's largest enterprise for fine chemicals, and a fourth was Gelsenwasser, the largest private-owned utility for water supplies in Germany. At the same time there were many more small firms; the reason for this eclectic portfolio was the tradition of state ownership under which various firms had been assembled under one umbrella. It was clear from the beginning that E.ON would sell these firms when the time was ripe. As predicted, Degussa, VAG Aluminium, Viterra and Viag Intercom were later sold for several billion euros each, providing cash for acquisitions fitting E.ON's core competences more closely. Since 2000 E.ON has regrouped and substantially reconstructed its organisation on an annual basis, reflecting not only the growth of the enterprise but also necessary swaps and sales connected to acquisitions partly ordered by state or EU authorities on competition. In 2005 E.ON's principal divisions were E.ON

Energy (mainland EU), E.ON UK, LG&E Energy, Sydkraft and E.ON Ruhrgas. From the very beginning E.ON understood the processes of privatisation and deregulation as an opportunity, not a threat. Like its main competitors E.ON systematically bought up smaller German electric utilities or drew them into its orbit by long-term contracts.

As regards foreign direct investment (FDI) PreussenElektra was already participating in enterprises in Sweden (such as Sydkraft), the Netherlands (EZH, Den Haag), Italy (Electra Italia) and Poland (Elektra Polska). The latter two were rather minor. In 2000, in its first annual report, E.ON presented at length its position in the Netherlands, Poland, Russia, Czech Republic, Latvia and Sweden. It suggested it saw itself as a ' "European" enterprise'. Moreover it was looking for nearby acquisitions which would open up possibilities of swapping electricity. These nearby regions could include Scandinavia, Germany's neighbours, as well as Italy and Hungary. One year later E.ON not only bought all of Sydkraft but also an entire Finnish company. More important was the acquisition of Powergen, one of Britain's principal suppliers. Powergen expanded further in the UK, taking over Enfield CCGT, a power station near London, in May 2005. Since Powergen owned LG&G Energy, a Kentucky-based American supplier of electric energy, E.ON from then on had an investment in the USA. E.ON Energy proudly stated in 2001 that one fourth of all customers, as well as one fourth of all employees, were situated outside Germany. Since E.ON Energy's second year this general expansion has been more focussed on Central and Eastern Europe. In its 2004 Annual Report E.ON Energy included a map indicating the countries where it was active. This map comprehended, besides Germany and Benelux, Poland, Czech Republic, Slovakia, Austria, Switzerland, Hungary and Bulgaria. In 2004 E.ON sold 1050 TWh of electric power. Together with its other companies this summed 1885 TWh (E.ON UK: 350, Sydkraft: 390, LG&E: 95).

In 2005 E.ON Energy entered the Romanian electricity market. The same behaviour was apparent: E.ON Energy first bought a minority stake, which was enlarged afterwards. This strategy was not entirely on E.ON Energy's own initiative, but related to the stepwise opening of energy markets in Central and Eastern Europe. E.ON cooperated and advised nearly all Central and South-East European states in their process of deregulation.

E.ON has major activities in the gas sector, carried out by Ruhrgas. In 2004 this represented Europe's third largest supplier, selling 4600 TWh. Ruhrgas is mainly active in transport and distribution with a concentration, besides its traditional home base of Germany, in Central and South-East Europe. It is, however, also engaged in the UK and in Norway in the production and prospecting of gas, owning a 6.5 per cent stake in the Russian GAZPROM. Its special relationship with GAZPROM suffered a setback in 2005 because of Russian political intervention. Ruhrgas wanted to raise its stake in one of GAZPROM's subsidiaries, but GAZPROM opted in favour of BASF-owned Wintershall, a competitor. Ruhrgas buys most of its gas from the Russian company. It prolonged its contract until 2036 buying 400 billion m³ in that period. Together with GAZPROM and BASF it is building a direct pipeline from Russia to Germany via the Baltic Sea for completion in 2011.

E.ON concentrated from the beginning on energy supply. It sold systematically not only non-utility assets, but also telecommunications and water supply activities. On the other hand, it expanded in Europe to nearly all countries, with the exception of France and Ireland. A significant move was the hostile bid for Spanish energy provider Endesa in 2006. In so doing, E.ON not only alienated the Spanish government, which preferred an indigenous solution, but also indirectly attacked EDF.

Through concentrated expansion E.ON made substantial progress within a short time. It still had some money left to please its shareholders, however: its most important initiative to influence share prices was a buy-back of 10 per cent of its own shares in 2001 when, after the breakdown of stock markets, share prices were low. This cost E.ON 4.5 billion euros. Since 2004 all major firms (except Sydkraft and LG&E) have been renamed in order to exploit the E.ON brand; for instance, Powergen became E.ON UK. During its five years in existence E.ON has established itself as one of the most aggressive enterprises in utilities in Europe.

III. RWE

Like E.ON, RWE (Rheinisch-Westfälische Elektrizitätswerke AG) was a holding company, governing a conglomerate of different activities. During the 1990s it was active in energy (electricity and gas), mining, mineral oils, chemicals, waste management, machine building, construction and telecommunications. All sectors were organised as separate stock companies. Many of them were majority-, but not entirely owned by RWE; there was, however, a strategy to acquire all stocks over the long run. Its 36.9 billion euro turnover in 1996/97 was derived mainly from Germany (81 per cent), plus 11 per cent from Europe and the rest mainly from North America. Broken down into branches of industry the energy sector was the largest, representing 33 per cent, together with mineral oil and chemicals (28), machine-building (14), construction (13), mining (7), waste management (3) and telecommunications (2). Mining was related to the generation of energy, thus where utility activities are concerned energy mining and waste management could be counted together, adding up to no more than 43 per cent. Despite the fact that in public RWE presented itself primarily as a utility company, in fact it was a holding company with a substantial interest in that sector. In 2005 RWE sold most of its non-utility firms.

In contrast to E.ON, RWE invested abroad early and substantially; by 1981 it had bought 50 per cent of Consolidated Coal Company, the third largest coal mine company in the USA, and invested in UEB, a uranium mine near Key Lake, Canada. FDI was carried out not by the holding company, RWE, but by the related subsidiary. Structurally RWE's portfolio was similar to

E.ON's: both divested non-core business, consolidated the market in Germany, invested abroad cautiously and tried to construct a network which in the future could be physically connected to their electricity and gas grids in Germany. The difference was that RWE applied the strategy first, and E.ON pursued it more vigorously later on. RWE used to be the largest utility in Germany until it was – to its surprise – overtaken by the merger which gave rise to E.ON. Since then, these firms have perceived each other as rivals. During the first half of the 1990s the new market in East Germany (up to 1990 the German Democratic Republic) was to be divided. Several new enterprises were established (such as VEAG and Laubag), all of which were finally consolidated in other firms. RWE and E.ON managed to keep EnBW (and thus EDF) outside. However, the German authorities made it clear that RWE and E.ON could not have everything and, since there were no other German players, some foreign investment had to be accepted. The real winner became Vattenfall which was able to acquire substantial investment in East and North Germany.

When it became legal to invest in utility companies in Central and Eastern Europe during the second half of the 1990s RWE started to do just that. At the same time, RWE invested in Portugal and bought a substantial part of Motor Columbus, an old Swiss holding company for electric utilities. In 1999 RWE announced a new strategy, the so-called 'multi-utility/multi-energy concept'. The idea was to combine as many utility aspects as possible in one given area: gas and electricity supply and, if possible, even waste management should all come from one enterprise. RWE claimed substantial savings by applying this concept. Later E.ON copied the idea, providing gas and electricity through E.ON Hanse. Telecommunications, though another utility service which would fit this concept, was not included. It turned out that competition in this sector became much stronger than expected, whilst it generated much lower profits than calculated.

The year 1999 brought several changes for RWE. It merged with VEW, another German utility active in RWE's home-region. But RWE's plan to merge with the French water-supplier Vivendi collapsed. CEO Dietmar Kuhnt was very angry when he heard that Vivendi had bought Seagram without informing him. This meant that Vivendi was no longer interested in a merger with RWE. However, Kuhnt at the same time had negotiated with Lyonnaise des Eaux, Vivendi's French arch-competitor. Despite this setback, RWE bid successfully for Thames Water, one of the world's largest suppliers of water, which was privatised in 1989. Together with Thames Water, the respective subsidiaries in the USA, Chile, Australia and Asia were incorporated. In the following two years RWE bought Transgas, an enterprise entirely dominating the Czech gas market, the US water giant American Water, as well as Innogy, the largest electricity supplier in the UK. In May 2005 RWE's relative position was as shown in Table 6.1.[7]

With all these acquisitions (except water) RWE positioned itself as a direct competitor of E.ON and its FDI activity. By selling non-core firms RWE

Table 6.1   RWE's Relative Position as of May 2005

Country/Region	Relative position in:			
	Electricity	Gas	Water	% of revenue in 2004
Germany	1	2	1	55
UK	2	3	1	21
Europe	3	6	–	9
USA	–	–	1	5
World	–	–	3	10

Source: Developed by the author based on RWE annual reports.

reduced its debts from 23 to 13 billion euros in 2005 and it was able to keep its A1 credit rating. In 2006 it announced the sale of Thames Water, thus further concentrating on energy. Of course not all its plans succeeded: especially when French connections were involved no result was achieved. Apart from the Vivendi and Lyonnaise des Eaux cases in 2001 EnBW successfully bid against RWE for the fourth largest Spanish supplier of electricity, HC/Hydrocantabrico. Both RWE and E.ON had announced that Italy would be their target market for the future, but it was EDF that bought Edison, the second largest supplier in May 2005. At the same time, EDF lined up with AEM, the distributor in Milan, as well as with Enel, Italy's number one in generation. It seems that EDF has successfully blocked the Germans not only in Italy but also in France. The German companies have not cooperated with each other abroad or at home but have competed in their main markets for electricity and gas, namely all Europe, except France. Further investment, especially in Eastern Europe, is predicted.

IV. Deutsche Post

Deutsche Post (DP) was privatised in 1995 and since 2000 shares have been sold stepwise. Though it had announced a total sell-out the German Federal State indirectly still owned a minority of 35.5 per cent in 2006.[8] DP's expansion was connected with Klaus Zumwinkel, who earlier served at McKinsey's and Quelle, a mail order house. Zumwinkel acted as CEO from 1990 and thus determined DP's fate to a large extent.[9] The old Deutsche Bundespost comprised postal, telecommunications and banking services. In the first 'Postreform' these services were separated and became state-owned stock companies. In 1997 the EU ruled that all postal services should be stepwise opened to competition. The last monopoly (on letters up to 20 g) was to fall in 2007. When Zumwinkel took over, DP was making losses of 7.6 per cent of its turnover in 1990. Signs of a turnaround were the closure of 17,000 out of 30,000 post offices, heavy investment in IT and a reconstruction of the remaining offices. Among other developments the old bullet-proof glass between customers and service personnel was removed as a sign of the new focus on customers.

Up to 1997 DP had no foreign investments, but since then the parcel service has been expanded. Its stated aim was to become in Europe what UPS and FedEX used to be in the USA. During its first year DP cooperated only with special services (not the respective post offices) in nearby countries Austria, Belgium, Poland and Switzerland. France, Italy and the UK followed the next year; and by 1999 DP claimed to be market leader for such logistic services in Europe. A strategic acquisition was the 25 per cent investment in DHL International Ltd in 1998, signalling a worldwide quest. A breakthrough was achieved in 1999. DP acquired Nedlloyd and ASG, with networks in Benelux and Scandinavia respectively. A key acquisition was Danzas, a Swiss firm with special competence in sea freight. The following year DP bought Air Express International with its seat in the USA. This step, together with the takeover of the remainder of DHL shares, made DP the world's largest logistics firm in air transport. It succeeded in integrating these different firms smoothly. Because of this well-known firms such as Amazon have used DHL as their first choice since 1999.

In parallel with the expansion in logistics a similar development was carried out for mail services. DP started via the acquisition of Global Mail in the USA in 1998 and two years later had established itself with its subsidiaries in 14 countries. DP bought the German Postbank in 1999. After privatisation Postbank and mail services never were physically separated. By owning Postbank DP not only could exploit this dual-use position without investment in new sales posts, but it acquired Germany's largest retail bank with 10 million customers. DP reorganised itself as a holding company called 'Deutsche Post World Net', of which DP is now referred to as the German branch.

In 2000 Zumwinkel stated he intended to make DP the world's largest logistics enterprise. Its IPO in 2000 was a great success: demand for shares was eight times larger than the offer. DP's Achilles heel remained the threat of opening the profit machine letter service up to competition. The EU suggested deregulation was slow. Some countries, such as France and Italy, hardly responded, while a few countries, such as UK, Germany, and the Netherlands, partly deregulated their market. Because of this Germany postponed its scheduled full opening until 2008. In doing so it gave DP some more time to exploit its monopoly position at home in order to plough the money back into DP World Net. In other words Germans and firms active in that country had to pay an extra levy in order to finance this service. However, this special move was taken also in the UK: in 2002 it was ruled that Royal Mail was to be protected in this sector until 2007. DP's strategic aim is to be generating at least 50 per cent of its turnover and its profits abroad when the letter monopoly expires.

DP decided to adopt the DHL logo worldwide (DHL Worldwide Express, DHL Global Mail), while the names DP and Postbank will be valid only in Germany. In contrast to DHL – logistics from mail to container – Postbank has no foreign subsidiaries. In 2005 DP had own subsidiaries in virtually every country in the world, except Japan. It employed 380,000 personnel, achieving a turnover of 43 billion euros in 2004. Its most important competitors in Europe were the former Dutch Post Office TPG and UPS in the USA. Relations with UPS were particularly competitive, with both CEOs openly expressing mutual hostility. UPS tried to keep DHL out of the US market, with not only economic but also political means. DP was surprised since the crude way UPS used its political connections was not widespread in Europe. For instance, UPS donated more to President Bush's election campaign than General Motors and Boeing combined.[10] UPS tried to block landing rights for DHL flights, and so on. Consequently DHL failed to capture more than 7 per cent of the US parcel market and amassed a deficit of 800 million euros for 2003–4. Break-even was not planned before 2007. In its home market DP – or more precisely DHL – enjoyed a 50 per cent market share in 2004. Next came DPD, a subsidiary of the French state-owned La Poste (19 per cent), GLS, Hermes and UPS, with about 10 per cent each. The market was totally deregulated except for light letters.

In April 2005 DP bid for Exel, as did UPS. British Exel was one of the world's largest logistics firms with a turnover of 10 billion euros, employing 111,000 personnel. DP was at that time without debt and could easily offer about 5 billion euros. Later in the same year Exel accepted DP's offer, making DP the world's largest logistics business.

V. Deutsche Telekom

Since Deutsche Telekom was part of the German Post Office it was privatised like Deutsche Bundespost in 1995. One year later the first tranche of shares was floated. Other tranches followed and in 2006 the German Federal State owned 31.25 per cent of shares.[11] Deregulation in 1998 turned Germany into one of the most liberal telecommunications services markets in the world. The traditional monopolist could not stop a steady decline of its share in all segments of the German market. In 2005 it provided 65 per cent of traditional telephone communication; its share in other services was lower. There are more than 200 competitors active in Germany. Like DP Deutsche Telekom viewed itself as a future global player. It raised its foreign turnover from 3 per cent in 1995 to nearly one half in 2006. In 1996 it founded a joint venture with France Télécom called Global One, to be used as a common platform for worldwide acquisitions. However, when three years later an opportunity arose to bid for Telecom Italia – the traditional Italian provider – Telekom did so only on its own account. Of course the strategic partnership went bust. At that time state intervention prohibited a foreign takeover in Italy (Olivetti won) and Telekom had to reassemble its shattered strategy.

Nevertheless Telekom underlined its aim of becoming market leader in Europe and, as a tool to achieve this, reorganised the concern into four divisions in 1999: T-Com for the traditional network of copper and fibre cables;

T-Online was the subsidiary for internet services; T-Mobile dealt with wireless communication; finally, T-Systems provided services for large customers. Expansion abroad was carried out by these subsidiaries.

Telekom introduced broadband technology (ISDN, DSL) early on and claimed to be the European market leader in this field from 2004. After a phase of financial stress in 2001/2002 the company broke even in 2003 and again made a substantial profit in 2004 (3 billion euros). In 2002 it had accumulated a loss of 24 billion euros (half of its turnover). The CEO had to go and some strategic investment, for instance in Russia, had to be sold.

In 1993, still state-owned, Telekom engaged itself in Hungary, taking over stepwise MATÁV, the traditional state enterprise. Other engagements of T-Com and T-Mobile in the Balkans followed later, but in traditional markets in Western Europe or overseas no large market-shares could be acquired. T-Mobile became more active with subsidiaries in the UK, Austria, Czech Republic, the Netherlands, the USA and Poland. In 2005 T-Online was active in France, Spain, Austria and Switzerland. Thus Telekom as a concern was among the most internationally diversified players in its field, with total employment of about 250,000. One of its last initiatives was to add its pink 'T' symbol to most of its subsidiaries in order to signal its integration into a single European enterprise.

Conclusions

European integration received a boost on various levels from these four companies. After privatisation and deregulation all four enterprises virtually 'exploded' over national borders and in their respective businesses. Their main thrust was in Europe. All four set up programmes to exchange personnel between national subsidiaries. Furthermore since all fall into the category of Large Technical Systems they integrate Europe technically as well as physically, via their wires, pipes, regular connections and so on.

In the background was a general wave of Americanisation, and in the foreground the official reason for deregulation and privatisation was not making money for the respective finance minister, but to inject competition. Competition, it was argued, would lead automatically to lower prices, better service and even more employment. Have these expectations been met? The answer depends on the sector: in 2005 telecommunications prices indeed had fallen, but this was not true of the other sectors. There is evidence of a comparative improvement of technical standards in all cases, but no qualitative leap. On the contrary, consumers have received warnings from energy suppliers that they can no longer uphold the same standards of security of supply under competition as before because they are too costly. The newspaper *Die Zeit* calculated that T-Com has invested less after privatisation than before privatisation, even when the investment of its main competitors is added to the whole of the telecom sector.[12] Employment has fallen in all four firms. Moreover there is much less competition in the German energy market than before. The precondition of deregulation and privatisation, that markets function better than regulation, can be questioned in the case of these firms. In the public utilities sector various companies have remained state-owned and have performed excellently, even in foreign markets, as Swedish Vattenfall has shown. Privatisation and deregulation have certainly benefitted big business. The four big firms have expanded to a large extent at the expense of their competitors; and they did this by external growth entailing economic concentration. General doubts that state or common ownership is inferior to private ownership in principle have been expressed several times before.[13] Our evidence only adds to such doubts; reality is more complicated than economic theory allows.

The metaphor of the ugly duckling transforming into a swan fits well these four companies. The exceptional expansion of all four mainly took place abroad, while they tried to maintain their position at home. In fact energy firms not only succeeded in maintaining but actually enlarged their market share at home, while the postal and telecom services managed to keep their position as market leader. All four became important world players. This success outside their home market is not easily explained. (1) Early privatisation and deregulation may have helped, but this happened to, for instance, British Telecom (BT) and Royal Mail even earlier. These British firms did not use this extra time to their advantage to overtake DP and Telekom in size. (2) All firms were already large in a European context when they were privatised, and their size may have helped. However, there already existed much larger enterprises to compete with, such as Vodafone or UPS. At the same time, there were also much smaller firms, such Vattenfall or the Spanish Telefónica, enterprises which grew even faster and today are a match for the four firms. Thus we have to exclude size as a reason. (3) Of course all firms were active in sectors of growth, but this applies to all competitors in this sector. (4) It may be that too much protection, as occurred in France and Italy, hindered French or Italian expansion. However, in these cases we have to wait and see what happens when enterprises such as France Télécom, Gaz de France or EDF are 'set free' from state intervention.[14] It is highly likely they will be formidable competitors. However, none of these reasons can explain the growth of the four German firms. There are, however, five other ways in which they differ from competitors: (1) All four firms engaged very early in the emerging markets of Central and Eastern Europe, though it was clear this would pay only in the long run. Geographical proximity and a traditional knowledge of these countries helped. For instance, in 2002, 30 per cent of the electricity sector in Hungary was German owned.[15] (2) All four firms had a self-understanding based on providing technically high-quality service; perhaps not cheap, perhaps not especially friendly but reliable. All firms are active in a sector where organisation really matters. In contrast to virtues such as flexibility or improvisation, organisational capability and reliability have been suggested to be traditional values upheld in Germany. Perhaps these cultural values gave the firms an additional boost. (3) All firms moved aggressively forward – but mainly in Europe. Most of their US subsidiaries had been acquired previously by British firms. There is therefore a special focus on Europe. Even Deutsche Bahn (German railways), rather a problem-laden enterprise, claimed 'our home-market is Europe. Germany would be too small for us'.[16] Perhaps such a pan-European understanding boosted activities abroad. (4) In contrast to the Anglo-Saxon model, the traditional Continental understanding of a 'good' firm is related to its size: successful firms grow. Consequently there is a focus on growth and less emphasis on profitability compared to British and US enterprises. Such values may have played a role. (5) Finally, all four firms are holding companies. Perhaps this traditional European concept is not as outdated as some Americans have suggested. Finally – and interestingly – all these factors explaining their exceptional growth are cultural, 'soft' ones.

Notes

1 Hughes (1983); Hughes (1987) pp. 51–82.
2 For how this actually worked see Schröter (1999) pp. 163–87.
3 See Clifton, Comín and Díaz-Fuentes (2003).
4 Schröter (2005), part 3, pp. 127–202. Clifton, Comín and Díaz-Fuentes (2003) p. 2.
5 'We cannot expect privatization to lower costs'. See Pollitt (1995) p. 189.
6 A summary of this history is in Mez (2003).
7 RWE (2005).
8 The state-owned bank Kreditanstalt für Wiederaufbau (KfW) owned 35.5 per cent and was bound to go on selling.
9 Zumwinkel (2003) pp. 47–65; Zumwinkel (1998) pp. 97–111.
10 *Manager-Magazin* (2003) p. 46.
11 14.62 per cent indirectly through KfW as in the case of DP (KfW homepage, 12 August 2005).
12 Lütge (2005).
13 See, for instance, Clifton, Comín and Díaz-Fuentes (2003), especially pp. 125–35 and Aharoni (2000) pp. 49–72.
14 EDF is the only enterprise with substantial investment in all large European markets (France, Germany, Italy, Spain and the UK).
15 Akbar (2003) p. 123.
16 Consequently Railion, the cargo subsidiary of Deutsche Bahn, bought its Danish and Dutch competitors and is, with Railion Italia, a major player in Italy.

References

Aharoni, Y. (2000) 'The Performance of State-Owned Enterprise', in P.A. Toninelli (ed.), *The Rise and Fall of State-Owned Enterprise in the Western World* (Cambridge University Press) pp. 49–72.
Akbar, Y. (2003) *The Multinational Enterprise, EU Enlargement and Central Europe: The Effects of Regulatory Convergence* (Basingstoke: Palgrave).
Clifton, J., F. Comín and D. Díaz-Fuentes (2003) *Privatization in the European Union. Public Enterprises and Integration* (Dordrecht: Kluwer).

Hughes, T.P. (1983) *Networks of Power: Electrification in Western Society, 1880–1930* (Baltimore: Johns Hopkins).

Hughes, T.P. (1987) 'The Evolution of Large Technical Systems', in W. Bijker, T.P. Hughes and T. Pinch (eds), *The Social Construction of Technological Systems* (Cambridge MA: MIT) pp. 51–82.

Lütge, G. (2005) 'Aufbruch oder Abbruch?', in *Die Zeit* (3 March).

Manager-Magazin (2003) 'Mit Pauken und Paketen. Deutsche Post/UPS: Sie sind Erzrivalen. Jetzt treffen sie zum Duell aufeinander nach amerikanischen Regeln. Können die Deutschen diesen Kampf gewinnen?', *Manager-Magazin*, No. 2, pp. 42–49.

Mez, L. (2003) 'New Corporate Strategies in the German Electricity Supply Industry', in J.-M. Glachant and D. Finon (eds), *Competition in European Electricity Markets. A Cross-Country Comparison* (Cheltenham: E. Elgar) pp. 193–216.

Pollitt, M.G. (1995) *Ownership and Performance in Electric Utilities: The International Evidence on Privatization and Efficiency* (Oxford University Press).

RWE Annual Report (2005).

Schröter, H.G. (1999) 'Innovationsverhalten, Mentalität und technologische Entwicklung: Vorreiterrolle und Servicedefizite der deutschen Reichspost 1920–1939,' in *Technikgeschichte*, 61 (1) (1994) pp. 11–34 (reprinted in C. Neutsch and H.-J. Teuteberg (eds), *Vom Flügeltelegraphen zum Internet*, VSWG-Beiheft, No. 145, Stuttgart, pp. 163–187).

Schröter, H.G. (2005) *The Americanization of the European Economy. A Compact Survey of American Economic Influence in Europe since the 1880s* (Dordrecht: Springer).

Zumwinkel, K. (1998) 'Der Transformationsprozeß einer öffentlichen Verwaltung zu einem marktwirtschaftlichen Unternehmen – dargestellt am Beispiel der Deutschen Post AG', in M. Becker (ed.), *Unternehmen im Wandel und Umbruch* (Stuttgart: Schäffer-Poeschel) pp. 97–111.

Zumwinkel, K. (2003) 'Deutsche Post World Net – von der nationalen Behörde zum globalen Konzern', in H. Hungenberg (ed.), *Handbuch Strategisches Management* (Wiesbaden: Gabler) pp. 47–65.

7
Transforming Network Services in Spain

Judith Clifton, Francisco Comín and Daniel Díaz-Fuentes

Introduction

Among the legacies of the Franco dictatorship was a bankrupt public enterprise sector. Most of these enterprises were in the manufacturing sector and had been placed under the control of the holding Instituto Nacional de Industria (INI), created in 1941 in the aftermath of the Civil War. Like the IRI in Mussolini's Italy, the INI originally had autarkic aims and its inward-looking policies continued until the 1970s.[1] During the democratic transition, between 1976 and 1986, the situation of and prospects for state-owned enterprises (SOEs) further deteriorated. The Spanish SOE sector was not as large as some scholars have claimed.[2] At the beginning of the 1980s Spain's SOE sector, compared to the European Economic Community (EEC) average, was relatively small overall, with an above-average industrial component. Many of Spain's service networks were either totally or partially privately owned. Spain thus was an exception to the rule within the EEC. Its pattern of industrial specialisation and above-average private participation in network services would have consequences during the privatisation and internationalisation of Spanish enterprises from the 1980s.

In the post-war period most Western democratic European countries adopted a model of economic regulation based on SOE network services with the aim of providing public services such as transport, communication, energy and water. Social regulation based on the welfare state aimed to provide social services such as education, health or social protection.[3] Admittedly there were important differences between democratic countries in terms of economic and social regulation. Differences, however, were much more dramatic between the democratic and non-democratic countries, where under-performing public and social services existed side by side with a weak welfare state.

During the democratic transition (1976–86) there were four key factors that helped bring about a change in politicians' attitudes towards public enterprises. Firstly, the industrial crisis, which began in 1975, affected both public and private enterprises. The government used SOEs as an anti-cyclical and anti-inflationary instrument (obliging them to invest, hire workers to avoid unemployment and restrict price increases). The INI also absorbed many bankrupt private enterprises during the years of crisis, further worsening the public sector situation. During the democratic transition new promises to build a welfare state were made. Loss-making SOEs were perceived as an unsustainable burden on the public budget. Secondly, in 1983 the Socialists came to power and embarked on a policy of industrial reconversion in which SOEs played a key role by becoming large enterprises through mergers with other national private enterprises and, in particular, with transnational corporations (TNCs). The Socialists' industrial policy aimed at sectoral concentration so as to forge competitive and efficient enterprises. So they sold off public enterprises to leading private groups from the same sectors. Simultaneously, the reorientation of industrial policy forced the government to reconsider the role of some public SOEs that had neither sectoral nor public service objectives. Thirdly, accession to the EEC in 1986 intensified the liberalising tendency of the government, forcing the opening up of the Spanish economy and the end of public monopolies and subsidies to public and private enterprises. Accession permitted the Socialists to implement certain industrial and fiscal policies since they could blame Brussels when imposing policy which had previously been impossible due to business and labour opposition. The fourth factor was the new ideological distrust of SOEs and the corresponding preference for privatisation around the world. The Socialists' manifesto, however, when they came to power at the end of 1982, did not contain plans to privatise; rather it stressed that some SOEs (including electricity) and financial services (such as banking) needed to be nationalised, as they had in other European countries in the post-war period. In Spain they had been left in private hands as a legacy of the dictatorship. Nevertheless the Socialists soon began to change their attitude towards public enterprises after the 1981 Mitterand-led French government failures and the 1985 Cavaço da Silva reversal from the 1976 Revolutionary Constitution which established that nationalisation was an irreversible achievement of the working class. This was compounded by the new pro-privatisation fashion coming from the UK, the USA and international organisations. Under these conditions the privatisation and internationalisation of Spanish enterprises occurred simultaneously.

The internationalisation of Spanish SOEs occurred in two main ways. Firstly, by significant inward foreign direct investment (FDI) which had begun in the 1970s but increased from 1985, triggered in part by the crisis from 1975. Part of this inward FDI consisted of the acquisition of SOEs sold by the government to foreign TNCs. Most SOEs bought by foreigners were industrial and would have been unable to survive without acquisition by TNCs with technological and strategic capabilities. Secondly, both private and public Spanish enterprises became internationalised via expansion abroad (outward FDI). This was not necessary in the past due to their inward-looking strategy and domestic protection. Some privatised SOEs providing public services opted to internationalise in order to be competitive in international markets as well as at home. This was possible because the privatisation policy in Spain opted to create 'national champions', whereby controlling shares were sold to Spanish institutional investors, sometimes allowing in a foreign technological partner or securing strategic or trade agreements abroad.

The rest of this chapter is organised into four sections. Section I examines the transformation of public and private enterprises in network services in comparison to other Western European countries. Section II analyses the policies of SOE privatisation and internationalisation with the aim of comparing the different approaches and objectives, in particular the promotion of national champions. Section III compares the dual policy of SOE transnationalisation whereby foreign TNCs were attracted to Spain whilst Spanish network service TNC activities were promoted abroad. Particular attention will be paid to Spain's two largest TNCs, Telefonica and Endesa. Conclusions follow.

I.   Spain in Europe: From Industrial State to Welfare State

The development of the public enterprise sector and the welfare state has been uneven and asymmetrical across the EU. In those countries which experienced long dictatorships, such as Greece, Portugal and Spain, there was a failure to develop either a strong welfare state or significant SOEs in public services. In contrast, other countries – including Sweden, Denmark, the Netherlands, Belgium and Luxemburg – developed a strong welfare state under a democratic government, but did not at the same time experience a corresponding growth in the SOE industrial sector.

In Spain, as in other Western European countries, specific industrial companies were created and/or controlled by the state for fiscal purposes.[4] The government managed various manufacturing activities or nationalised industrial companies, based on arguments such as market failures, natural monopoly, economies of scale, scope and networks, the need to promote strategic activities, defence and security and so on. These policies affected different sectors, including steel making, metallurgic industries, shipbuilding, automobiles and sugar.

As a result of the financial crisis and the bailout of bankrupt private firms during the 1970s, the proportion of employment in industrial SOEs increased significantly. Most of the large countries with a significant SOE sector also had large industrial sectors. Paradoxically Spain is included in this latter group of large industrial sectors, though it had a minimal number of SOEs in networks such as energy, transport, communication and water. Spain fell into the group of countries with a small overall SOE sector, along with the Benelux countries and Denmark. As shown in Table 7.1, at the beginning of the 1980s these countries had sectors half the size of those in the first group.

It was in the 1990s that the results of privatisation became apparent across the EU. The most extreme cases arose in the UK, Spain and the Netherlands

Table 7.1 Percentage of Salaried Employees in the Sectoral Activities of SOEs in Selected EEC/EU Countries

	1970–3	1974–7	1978–81	1982–5	1990	1995	2000
Manufacturing							
Belgium	0	0	0	0	2	2	2
France	4	5	11	17	13	6	3
Germany	5	5	4	4	1	1	2
Greece	1	1	3	6	1	3	2
Ireland	3	3	3	3	1	1	0
Italy	8	10	9	11	10	6	2
Spain	**7**	**7**	**10**	**6**	**4**	**4**	**1**
UK	14	15	16	14	1	0	0
Electricity, gas and water							
Belgium	16	17	19	19	24	24	22
France	74	81	85	85	79	75	75
Germany	29	34	27	21	60	43	51
Greece	16	17	39	56	62	66	53
Ireland	71	69	70	72	71	67	73
Italy	72	80	82	83	85	59	41
Spain	**28**	**29**	**31**	**35**	**41**	**17**	**6**
UK	97	99	98	99	67	13	9
Transport and communications							
Belgium	70	55	60	65	64	55	49
France	64	61	60	60	59	61	57
Germany	76	82	88	87	70	44	47
Greece	33	34	42	43	45	37	37
Ireland	89	85	87	84	80	93	59
Italy	60	63	67	73	81	88	63
Spain	**38**	**42**	**49**	**36**	**32**	**28**	**24**
UK	65	62	67	63	32	22	16

Source: Elaborated by authors based on in-house CEEP statistics on salaried employees in SOEs in Europe.

(and, to a lesser extent, Portugal), where percentages were reduced significantly. Indeed, they reached minimal levels during the processes of privatisation during the 1990s, though with different timescales. In Spain the process was intense during the second half of the 1990s, while in the UK the process had already stagnated. The differences between the indicators of countries and groups were maintained throughout the 1980s and these were significantly reduced in the 1990s when privatisation was implemented by most countries, as shown in Table 7.2.

When countries embarked on SOE reform during the 1980s by encouraging the pursuit of private criteria Spain followed suit. This was partly achieved through SOE reorganisation. Limited companies with majority state ownership were established, in various cases, under the control of one or more holdings

Table 7.2   Average Impact of Salaried Employees, Gross Added Value and Gross Capital Formation of Public Enterprises in the Non-Agricultural Merchantable Economy of the EEC–EU, 1982–2000

Country	1982	1985	1988	1991	1995	2000
UK	16.2	12.7	7.4	4.4	2.7	2.3
Spain	**12.0**	**12.0**	**10.0**	**9.0**	**8.0**	**4.1**
Netherlands	9.0	9.0	9.6	7.5	6.8	4.6
Luxemburg	7.5	7.1	7.2	6.4	6.4	5.7
Denmark	12.0	11.4	11.9	11.5	9.7	7.9
Belgium	12.1	11.1	12.0	11.0	11.6	10.9
Germany	14.0	12.4	11.6	11.1	10.7	10.9
Ireland	15.1	15.3	14.4	12.3	11.8	10.1
EEC-EU	**16.4**	**15.3**	**13.3**	**11.8**	**10.4**	**9.0**
Italy	20.0	20.3	19.0	18.9	14.2	9.6
Greece	22.3	23.2	20.8	20.2	15.4	14.2
France	22.8	24.0	18.3	17.6	14.7	11.8
Portugal	23.9	22.7	24.0	20.7	12.3	8.5
Austria	29.2	–	27.0	16.9	13.3	12.0
Sweden	18.9	–	–	–	12.9	13.1
Finland	23.5	–	–	–	17.6	10.9
StDv. EU-15	–	–	–	0.054	0.039	0.035
StDv EEC-12	0.051	0.056	0.053	0.055	0.038	0.036

Source: Elaborated by authors based on in-house CEEP statistics on salaried employees in SOEs in Europe.

of public participation (as in Austria, Belgium, Finland, Greece, Italy and Sweden). On the other hand, private management criteria and vertical and horizontal integration were promoted to increase international competitiveness through cleaning up and diversifying the portfolio of stake holding.

The programme to privatise and internationalise SOEs can be divided into two main stages, which correspond roughly to the governments of the Socialist Party (PSOE) from 1983 to 1996 and the Popular Party (PP) between 1996 and 2004. Although these two governments pursued different policies there were also elements of continuity in the sense that the PP's policy of 'total privatisation' could not have been implemented at such speed and with such dynamism if the PSOE had not cleaned up the public sector and implemented partial privatisation programmes.

II. SOE Privatisation and Transnationalisation

II.i The Socialist Experience: Third Way Politics?

Between 1983 and 1995 PSOE governments reorganised and cleaned up the public enterprise sector, improved its management and implemented some privatisation that was euphemistically referred to as 'de-investment'. This new policy was consolidated by Spanish accession to the EEC in 1986. Accession also forced SOEs to confront challenges which had been postponed until then in order to adapt to the requirements of deregulation and the Single Market Programme (SMP). For instance, some public monopolies (such as Tabacalera, Telefonica, Campsa, Iberia, Renfe or Correos) had to be opened up to competition. In addition, subsidies were cut to some sectors (Hunosa and the steel industry). Privatisation was implemented in an ad hoc way. As in other countries this process was not implemented directly by the government, but by the holdings or enterprises themselves, either with the support of, or by order of, the ministry to which the enterprise belonged. However, as elsewhere a lack of coordination between ministers and SOE holdings led to contradictory policies.[5]

The first objective of the PSOE privatisation programme was to promote industrial recovery by: (1) making the SOE sector profitable by eliminating loss-making businesses; (2) selling off enterprises that were not deemed to be of strategic interest, such as Textil Tarazona, Marsans (travel agency) and Entursa (tourism); (3) ensuring the sustainability of companies which could not be rendered competitive under public ownership because they lacked economies of scale, technology or commercial networks by selling the whole enterprise to TNCs (as occurred in the cases of Secoinsa, SKF, SEAT and ENASA) or merging them by cross shareholding in order to gain technological partners and business alliances with other companies; and (4) promoting reindustrialisation by favouring business concentration, as in the cases of INI's consolidation of smaller electricity enterprises into Endesa and the Instituto Nacional de Hidrocarburos (INH)'s consolidation of oil and gas companies into Repsol. Usually the whole company was sold. Between 1985 and 1994 the INI earned US$ 2.54 billion from SOE sales, but spent US$ 3.18 billion on cleaning the SOE sector up. In most of the larger cases of privatisation buyers were foreign TNCs since they were the only ones that had the technological, marketing and management know-how to ensure the survival of the privatised enterprises.

The second objective of privatisation during this period was of a financial nature and included: (1) reducing subsidies to loss-making enterprises; (2) forcing SOEs to become self-financing; and (3) finding additional revenues to eliminate the budgetary deficit. In order to achieve these objectives initial public offerings (IPO) took place of the most profitable SOEs. The idea was to introduce discipline and external financial control in business activities through stock market quotation and the introduction of private shareholders. However, in all these stock market sales public holdings remained the majority shareholder, as they were not prepared to lose control of the enterprises. Thus we could describe this as partial privatisation, good examples being the sale of shares on the stock market of INI enterprises such as Endesa, Gesa and Ence.

From 1994 privatisation started to be considered from a broader strategic perspective. The Ministry of Industry proposed that privatisation be used as an instrument of industrial policy, anticipating the participation of both national and international partners in SOEs so that they would constitute a 'hard core' of private shareholders that supported the established business policy of the company in question. In the same year the Ministry of Economy and Finance anticipated in the budget a privatisation plan aimed at reducing the public deficit and fulfilling the European Monetary Union (EMU) convergence criteria. The results were the partial privatisation of Argentaria (1994) and Repsol (1995). In March 1995 a law was approved that regulated 'a legal framework in the case of disposal of public participation in certain enterprises'. This allowed for the sale, dissolution, division or merger of public companies by decree whenever the sale was over 5 per cent and public participation in the enterprise was under 15 per cent. For the first time the use of 'golden shares' was introduced into privatisation law in Spain. In order to continue shrinking the SOE sector and to promote the privatisation of profitable enterprises, in June 1995 the plan of 'structural simplification' of industrial groups was passed. The State Industrial Holding Company (SEPI) was created as a shareholder of Teneo (profitable SOEs from the INI) and REPSOL (INH). SEPI assumed responsibility for INI's debt, estimated at around US$ 2.2 billion.[6] The State Industrial Agency (AIE) was also created to take over loss-making SOEs from INI, such as enterprises in the naval, steel-making (CSI), mining (particularly Hunosa) and defence sectors. As a consequence, the INI and the INH were formally wound up in June 1995.

II.ii 'Total Privatisation' and the Consolidation of National Champions in the Roaring 1990s

The PP's accession to power in 1996 brought about profound changes in the policy towards SOEs. The policy of 'total privatisation' changed not only the degree of privatisation but also its ideological approach. The PP believed there was no role for public enterprise in the global economy and the process of SMP, and so there was no need to maintain them. Placing SOEs in private hands would also render them more efficient, it was believed. In order to coordinate this process the SOE sector was reorganised and all the industrial SOEs were combined, including those belonging to the AIE and SEPI. Other important changes emanating from the policy of total privatisation were: (1) the government coordinated privatisation policy; (2) privatisation was managed by the holding agencies of enterprise shares, that is, SEPI and SEPPA (State Company for Property Participation that holds state shares in enterprises such as Telefónica, Tabacalera and Mediterránea); (3) privatisation would be implemented in accordance with principles of transparency, publicity and open competition, for which an independent body was created;[7] and (4) a timetable was set for the privatisation of all public enterprises to be undertaken by 2001, with the exceptions of RENFE (railways), RTVE (public broadcasting), Correos (postal services), Hunosa and Figaredo (mining). The official objectives of privatisation were to improve economic efficiency whilst maintaining jobs.

Proceeds from the 'total privatisation' policy were dominated by a small number of transactions in energy and telecommunications. Endesa, Telefónica and Respol accounted for 51 per cent and seven other companies for an additional

Table 7.3 Spain: Main Privatisation Operations, 1985–2003

Sector/Company	Transactions		Value (US$mill)		%
	1986–1996	1997–2003	1986–1996	1997–2003	
Energy	9	6	7 367	12 354	**38.4**
Endesa	2	2	1 708	10 794	24.3
Repsol	4	1	4 482	1 170	11.0
Gas Natural – Enagás	2	–	669	–	1.3
Telecoms	1	4	1 103	8 242	**18.2**
Telefónica	1	2	1 103	6 975	15.7
Retevisión	–	1	–	1 208	2.3
Transport	2	8	32	5 678	**11.1**
Iberia	–	3	–	1 507	2.9
EN Autopistas	–	1	–	3 277	6.4
Bank and finance	5	5	3 860	2 644	**12.7**
Argentaria	3	1	3 666	2 295	11.6
Manufacturing	22	14	3 237	5 582	**17.2**
CSI	1	1	1 777	832	5.1
Tabacalera	–	1	–	1 808	3.5
CASA-EADS	–	1	–	411	0.8
Other services	–	9	–	1 316	**2.6**
Total	39	46	15 601	35 815	85.1

Source: Elaborated by the authors based on Privatization Barometer database.

34 per cent (see Table 7.3). Public offerings (POs) formed the chosen route, making up about three quarters of privatisation income in both phases (1985–96 and 1997–2003). POs after 1996 differed from earlier ones and took advantage of the 'roaring nineties' financial boom. Additionally there was more participation of individual shareholders and institutional shareholders declined in importance.[8] Auctions were used, ranging from restricted to universal invitations to tender, direct sales and even POs.[9] Generally, objectives were reached: the state shed its participation in the privatised enterprises, companies survived and redundancies were insignificant. As a consequence of the PP's total privatisation the SOE sector practically disappeared in telecommunications, electricity, gas and oil.

The main problem with 'total privatisation' was that, despite intentions, the privatisation of public monopolies occurred before market liberalisation, as in other EU countries such as the UK.[10] The result was that public monopolies were replaced by private monopolies, as in the case of gas, or by oligopolies with enterprises which abused their position by avoiding effective competition. This occurred in such sectors as oil distribution, electricity, air transportation, telecommunications and tobacco. One of the main challenges that the government faced was the introduction of effective competition in these sectors through legislation, regulatory bodies and the defence of competition.[11]

Despite the fact that the government opened up the telecommunications market in 1998 following Council Directive 97/33/EC and European Directive 90/388/EEC, and went beyond the minimum requirements set by Electricity Directive 96/92/EC for an internal electricity market and Gas Directive 98/30/EC for gas market opening and competition, each of these sectors has remained dominated by incumbents at the national or local level.

Privatisation was a watershed for business power in Spain. Firstly, the initial structure of shareholding property of the privatised SOEs reflected the government's wish to favour the incorporation of individual shareholders, that is, to widen share ownership to promote popular capitalism. Secondly, the shareholding structure of privatised enterprises was affected by the significant proportion of shares bought by international institutional investors. Thirdly, it was the large national financial entities that benefited most from privatisation, not only by obtaining large shareholdings, but also because they were awarded control over companies through golden shares and administration boards. In addition, large banks and savings banks also established cross-shareholdings which allowed them to control the sectors that had until recently been managed by the public sector. The privatisation of strategic and network services was also a policy instrument to create national champions and increase the power of certain groups, and the government played an important role by appointing chairpersons close to the government. From 1999 the government prevented takeovers in strategic and network companies such as EDF's bid for Hidrocantábrico and KPN's bid for Telefonica.

Privatisation consolidated a shareholding structure that gravitated around two clusters of banks: Banco de Bilbao Vizcaya (which merged in 1999 with Argentaria) and La Caixa, on the one hand, and Banco Central Hispano and the Banco de Santander (which merged in 1999) on the other. Each of these groups of financial institutions had significant cross-ownership in the petroleum, gas, water, electricity and telecommunications sectors. Privatisation contributed to reinforcing the already stable links between banks and industry.

III. Public Enterprise Internationalisation

III.i Inward FDI: The Acquisition of Public Enterprises by Foreign TNCs

Some industrial public enterprises became internationalised because social and electoral pressures were opposed to their being closed down. Indeed one of the priorities of the privatisation process in Spain was to ensure the brand name of companies survived, as well as to guarantee jobs. For these reasons preference was awarded to companies presenting industrial investment plans rather than those offering the highest price. These industrial enterprises found themselves in a delicate financial situation when Spain opened up to international competition. Additionally, some had always depended on foreign technology, sometimes via the transfer of patents or technology, at other times with the participation of large TNCs in SOE capital, such as minority INI partners. In sum,

Spanish governments from 1985 perceived that the only way to ensure the survival of these SOEs was to sell them off to foreign TNCs. This is only an apparent paradox because the TNC bought the privatised enterprises for their worth: in other words, the state sold them for negative prices because it had already spent enormous amounts on cleaning them up, rescuing them from bankruptcy, subsidising them (before or after the sale) and financing redundancy packages. In reality this was the 'American' way to save companies in crisis, that is, via direct and indirect aid to a private enterprise or via privatisation.

The state's expenditure on dowries to encourage possible SOE suitors increased to such an extent that income for subsidies was greater than privatisation income. These privatisations were accomplished, generally, through direct sale: the processes of selection varied but their transparency left much to be desired (which is common in these commercial and business operations). Negotiations about the sales were generally long and complicated. Questions concerning the selection of the buyer were dominated by politics or guarantees of future state contracts or concessions. The main industrial sectors involved included: automobiles (SEAT and ENASA); equipment (La Maquinista Terrestre y Marítima); ball bearings (SKF and CSA); electronics (Secoinsa); aluminium (Inespal); steel (Aceralia and Sidenor); mining (Minas de Almagrera and Potasas); aeronautics (CASA); and aims (Santa Bárbara).

III.ii The Making of National Network Champions

The reason for privatising network services was not that they were loss-makers or unviable commercially. Rather these were large public service network enterprises that were usually profit-making, except for occasional losses due to the economic situation or to the policy of tariff fixing (to control inflation). These companies were known as the 'jewels in the crown'. During the first phase of privatisation the PSOE did not consider privatising them completely. The strategy rather was to offer small blocks of shares to obtain cash to balance the budget and finance capital investment in the public enterprises themselves or cover the losses of unprofitable enterprises. This was partial privatisation with strictly financial aims in which the SOE would remain publicly owned overall since the state would retain enough capital to control them.

The sale of these shares was accomplished via PO to list on the stock market. To increase the market value of these firms certain companies were subject to merger and acquisition. In addition, they were profoundly reorganised by introducing private management practices and profit-making criteria. The idea was to introduce some market capital discipline into the enterprises, as well as to improve their management. It was during this period that companies such as Telefónica, Endesa, Repsol, Gas Natural and Iberia started to invest abroad, particularly taking advantage of the opening of markets to FDI in Latin America.

Privatisation of these companies during this period was influenced by nationalism: privatisation without denationalisation. Large enterprises would remain under state control which would rear them as national champions. To this end some share tranches were reserved for selected Spanish institutional investors with whom special prices were agreed in exchange for the guarantee of remaining an investor over the long term. By acquiring shares these private groups gained positions on the administration boards of companies being privatised and gradually ended up in control.

This approach changed drastically from 1996 when the PP government implemented its policy of 'total privatisation' for all SOEs. No longer were large SOEs considered a necessary public policy instrument to provide public services and the role of the state was deemed to be only that of economic regulator. According to the liberalisation policy it was considered nonsensical that the state should continue to be involved as an entrepreneur or shareholder: simply, the enterprises should be privatised. What did not change, however, was the nationalist strategy since the aim was that privatised enterprises would remain in Spanish hands. To avoid allowing networks to fall into foreign hands the government reserved control of these enterprises via the golden share. The state could authorise or block operations, such as the sale of a percentage of capital or the closure of the enterprise, using its veto power. So 'total' privatisation of these companies meant that they remained in Spanish hands via golden shares and with members of the board and chairpersons nominated by the government. The new managers of these privatised enterprises – exploiting financial opportunities – decided to extend their operations and markets, increasing outward FDI, mostly in Latin America and Europe, and into activities with little or no connection to their main activity. The main Spanish TNC networks consolidated in this period included Telefónica, Endesa, REPSOL, Gas Natural, Retevisión-AUNA and Iberia. Their privatisation amounted to three quarters of all proceeds generated in Spain.

The origins of the three largest Spanish non-financial TNCs, Telefonica, Endesa and Repsol, are not in family or private small enterprises. Telefonica was a monopoly with mixed capital: the state owned, both directly and indirectly through the Bank of Spain, 51 per cent and nominated the CEO. However, it also had private shareholders including large institutional investors. In the electricity sector most companies were privately owned but INI participated in some companies that were consolidated as Endesa. Similarly, INH created Respol when the sector was liberalised in the 1980s. They were therefore the offspring of the inward-looking projects of state holdings. Private participation in public monopolies was common in many totalitarian regimes, such as the Nazi regime (Bell 2006). In the case of Franco's Spain a significant proportion of assets were transferred from public and foreign TNCs to national private owners close to the regime (Comín and Gálvez 2004).

Endesa

Endesa (Empresa Nacional de Electricidad S.A.) was founded in 1944 during the Franco dictatorship and belonged to the INI. In 1972 it was merged with

Hidrogalicia, but it was in 1983, during the first Socialist government, that the company started its expansion and consolidation via the acquisition of stakes in other regional electricity companies (Enher, Gesa, Unelco and Encasur, and ERZ). At the time Endesa was still a public enterprise whose shares were owned by INI. The privatisation of Endesa started gradually in 1988 during the second Socialist government and after EC accession. In this year, the state reduced its share slightly to 75.6 per cent, launching an IPO and the company was listed on the NYSE for the first time.

Between 1991 and 1993 Endesa underwent its second national expansion via horizontal acquisitions of 87.6 per cent of Electra, 40 per cent of FECSA, 24.9 per cent of NANSA, 61.9 per cent of CARBOEX and 55 per cent of Hidroeléctrica de Barcelona. Moreover in the same period its internationalisation commenced with takeovers of Electricidad de Argentina and Yacylec in 1992. This was followed by the takeover of Portuguese Tejo Energia and the Compañía Peruana de Electricidad and DistriLima in 1993.

In 1994 Endesa launched a second PO, but the state still held 66.9 per cent of capital and its capital diversification started with the purchase of 11.8 per cent of Sociedad General de Aguas de Barcelona and, one year later, 7.2 per cent of Airtel (Spain's second largest mobile phone company) as a result of an agreement with Banco Central Hispano. It also expanded into the electricity sector, buying Edenor (Argentina). Two years later Endesa led a consortium for the second largest fixed telecommunication operator, Retevision, and then continued its Latin American ventures, participating in Enersis of Chile.

In 1997 and 1998, under the PP, Endesa become a private company when it launched two significant POs for one quarter and one third of the capital, while the state had reduced its participation to 2.95 per cent by the time of writing (2006). Thus, from 1988 Endesa has been transformed from a local public enterprise into a global TNC in the world's top four electrical companies. In 2004 it participated in the generation, transportation and distribution systems of twelve countries. Nevertheless Endesa kept its core activities in Spain and was still the largest domestic power supplier in 2006 (45 per cent of power generation, 40 per cent of distribution and 50 per cent of turnover). Endesa has diversified its activities and is exploiting network competitive advantages in water treatment, gas distribution and telecommunications. It has been the leading investor (30 per cent of the capital) in AUNA, the second global telecom operator in Spain, with Banco Santander Central Hispano (23 per cent), Unión Fenosa (19 per cent) and ING Bank (10 per cent).

Telefónica

Telefónica has its origins in the concession awarded by the military nationalistic dictatorship of Primo de Rivera to ITT in 1924 with the aim of integrating and interconnecting the three main national private operators. In the aftermath of the Civil War ITT supported Franco and in 1939 tried to sell Telefónica to German private business (against opposition from the USA). Despite ITT's strong support for Franco in 1945 the regime nationalised – or 'Spainised'[12] – Telefónica, taking 41 per cent of its capital (12 per cent went under the control of the central bank, Banco de España, and the rest to Spanish private share-holders). Thus the Franco regime opted for a different model from the, PTT that dominated in the rest of Europe. Spanish state ownership of Telefónica never exceeded 47 per cent and was managed by Spanish private banks, though the government chose its presidents.

Telefónica's internationalisation started earlier than that of most other European telecommunications operators, partly because of its private participation and management. Its internationalisation of capital commenced in 1987 when it was listed on the NYSE and other international markets. Telefónica, along with smaller European PTOs (KPN, Telia and Swiss Telekom), established a strategic alliance with Unisource, that was tightly linked to ATT. In 1985 Telefónica Internacional (TISA) was created and soon embarked on a significant internationalisation drive, acquiring 43.6 per cent of CTC (Chile) in 1990, followed by more acquisitions across telecom markets in Argentina, Brazil, Colombia, Ecuador, El Salvador, Morocco, Mexico, Peru, Puerto Rico and Venezuela. In October 1995 the PSOE privatised another 12 per cent stake through a PO raising US$ 1.1 billion. In 1997 the PP used Telefónica as a key example of its total privatisation policy by selling the remaining 20.9 per cent of capital for US$ 4.2 billion. A golden share of 0.11 per cent was maintained to dissuade hostile takeovers and to block mergers or acquisitions by SOEs. At the same time the PP president chose a new company president, Juan Villalonga, a close school friend, supported by a *nucleo duro* of financial investors including BBV, Argentaria and la Caixa. After an ambitious expansion strategy the stock market crash led to Villalonga's replacement by Cesar Alierta who adopted a strategy of asset consolidation centred in Europe, bidding for third generation licences in Austria, Germany, Italy and Switzerland (even though they did not have a network). In June 2005 it acquired 69.4 per cent of Cesky Telecom and in December 2005 it took 100 per cent of the UK's O$_2$ Plc for 1.2 billion euros. Telefónica is Spain's largest TNC and since 2000 has been listed among the top 70 companies in the FT Global 500 list and, since 1998, among the world's 50 largest TNCs by UNCTAD. Telefónica has diversified its markets and operations beyond the EU more than any other EU PTO: in 2005 only one third of its 173,500 employees were based in Spain, only one quarter of its customers were based in Spain and most of its activities are in Latin America where Telefónica was the first-mover telecom operator.

Conclusions

An examination of Spanish SOE transformation reveals a twofold process of privatisation and internationalisation. On the one hand, inward FDI flows sustained the transformation of SOEs in the manufacturing sector. These accounted for over half of privatisation transactions but less than one fifth of all privatisation revenues. In contrast, the consolidation of SOEs in financial and network services was clinched by the outward transnationalisation of Spanish enterprises into the EU and beyond. Four network services in particular dominated the process: Endesa, Telefónica, Repsol and Argentaria, whose privatisation made up two thirds of total proceeds. These firms, along with participating companies such as Gas Natural (Repsol) and AUNA, are Spain's leading network TNCs. The privatisation process can be summarised in terms of the number of significant financial operations (which were similar in both periods 1985–96 and 1997–2003). However, the proceeds of the first period represented only 30 per cent of the overall total. Privatisation of some of the larger enterprises started before 1997, when the PSOE was in power, but accelerated in the second phase, when Argentaria, Repsol, Gas Natural, CSI, SEAT, ENASA, EFERSA and INESPAL were sold. The bulk of privatisation proceeds was due to a small number of operations involving large companies from 1997, when the PP was in government and stock markets were booming. During this period Endesa, Telefónica, Retevisión, Iberia, Tabacalera and CASA were privatised. So a pro-privatisation ideology fused with favourable financial conditions during this period.

In terms of the internationalisation of Spanish firms Guillén noted that a few years ago a book on Spanish TNCs 'would have been regarded by many as a work of fiction. Nowadays, however, Spanish TNCs are making a dent in international competition just like firms from other EU countries'.[13] In fact, there are only three Spanish TNCs quoted in UNCTAD's list of the world's top 100 non-financial TNCs. These are: Telefónica (from 1998, ranked 52, 30, 9, 14, 28); Repsol-YPF (from 1999); and Endesa (42 from 2003). As has been shown, the rise of these three TNCs can be attributed to three factors: (1) the firms' internationalisation strategies; (2) the promotion of 'national champions'; and (3) the new international environment boosting FDI (M&A and privatisation proceeds) and increased regional competition in network services favoured by technological development.

But were global or regional forces most important? Aharoni observed that the recent FDI boom is more of an 'intraregional' (European) than a global trend.[14] The emergence of TNCs from public services is a generalised trend, particularly in the larger EU countries. Europe played an important role in the processes of privatisation and internationalisation.[15] As a result of the SMP implemented since the 1980s most privatisation transactions were in sectors that had been opened up to competition. For instance, the opening up of manufacturing and financial services from 1992 led to the privatisation of Argentaria, Tabacalera, CASA-EADS, SEAT-ENASA and CSI. In fact, before sectoral liberalisation of telecoms or electricity, Spain anticipated reforms by restructuring Endesa, Telefónica, Gas Natural and Respol. Schröter questions whether, after decades of European integration, the 'European firm' is finally emerging.[16] In the case of Telefónica, Repsol, Endesa and the two largest banks, BSCH and BBVA, transnationalisation went beyond the EU, indeed, they ventured into

Latin America before the rest of Europe. Finally, although these examples could be taken as Spanish 'success stories', all could be subject to takeovers or M&A in the future.

Notes

1   Comín and Martín Aceña (2003).
2   Arocena (2004) states 'The nationalisation of a large number of loss making companies led to the creation of a huge unprofitable PES (public enterprise sector) suffering from overcapacity, overstaffing and chronic financial needs'.
3   Flora and Alber (1981); Esping-Andersen (1990); Guillén and Alvarez (2001); Comín and Díaz-Fuentes (2005).
4   See Comín and Díaz-Fuentes (2004).
5   See Comín (1999); Comín, Martín Aceña and Jiménez (1992); and de la Dehesa (1992).
6   It was thought that SEPI could be listed on the stock exchange in 1996, but this did not occur due to changes in the direction of privatisation policies by the PP.
7   Consejo Consultivo de Privatizaciónes (Consulting Council for Privatisation).
8   Individual shareholding was overlooked in the sales of Gas Natural (1996) and Aldeasa (1997). See Cuervo (1998); Gámir (1998); and Mañas (1998).
9   According to the Consulting Council for Privatisation (1998).
10 Newbery (2004) and Parker (2004).
11 Lasheras (1999).
12 Comín and Gálvez (2004).
13 Guillén (2005) p. vii.
14 Aharoni (2004).
15 Clifton, Comín and Díaz-Fuentes (2003, 2004 and 2006).
16 Schröter (forthcoming 2007).

References

Aharoni, Y. (2004) 'World Investment Report. The Shift to Services', *Transnational Corporations*, 14 (1), pp. 157–67.
Arocena, P. (2004) 'Privatisation Policy in Spain: Stuck between Liberalisation and the Protection of National Interests', CESIFO Working Paper No. 1187.
Bell, G. (2006) 'Against the Mainstream: Nazi Privatization in 1930s Germany', Working Paper, Universitat de Barcelona.
Clifton, J., F. Comín and D. Díaz-Fuentes (2003) *Privatisation in the European Union: Public Enterprises and Integration* (Dordrecht: Kluwer Academic Publishers).
Clifton, J., F. Comín and D. Díaz-Fuentes (2004) 'Nationalisation, Denationalisation and European Integration: Changing Contexts, Unfinished Debates', *Enterprises et Histoire*, no. 37, pp. 24–52.
Clifton, J., F. Comín and D. Díaz-Fuentes (2005) 'Empowering Europe's Citizens? Towards a Charter for Services of General Interest', *Public Management Review*, 7 (3), pp. 417–43.
Clifton, J., F. Comín and D. Díaz-Fuentes (2006) 'Privatisation in the European Union: Ideological, Pragmatic, Inevitable?', *Journal of European Public Policy*, no. 5.
Comín, F. (1999) 'Luces y sombras en la historia de la empresa pública en España', *Economía Industrial*, no. 329 (Madrid: Ministerio de Ciencia y Tecnología).
Comín, F., and D. Díaz-Fuentes (2004) *La empresa publica en Europa* (Madrid: Síntesis).

Comín, F., and D. Díaz-Fuentes (2005) 'Sector público administrativo y estado del bienestar', in A. Carreras and X. Tafunell, (eds) *Estadísticas históricas de España SXIX y XX* (Madrid: FBBVA).

Comín, F., and L. Gálvez (2004) 'Enterprises publiques et multinationals sous l'autarcie franquiste', *Enterprises et Histoire*, no. 37.

Comín, F., and P. Martín Aceña (2003) 'La política autárquica y el INI', in L. J. Tascón Fernández and G. Sánchez Recio (eds), *Los empresarios de Franco: política y economía en España, 1936–1957* (Barcelona: Crítica) pp. 23–46.

Comín, F., P. Martín Aceña and J. Jiménez (1992) 'Problemas actuales de la empresa pública en España', *Papeles de Economía Española*, nos 52–3.

Cuervo, A. (1998) 'La privatización de las empresas públicas. Cambio de propiedad, libertad de entrada y eficiencia', *ICE*, no. 772 (Madrid: ICE).

De la Dehesa, G. (1992) 'Privatización europea, el caso de España', *ICE*, no. 707.

Esping-Andersen, G. (1990) *The Three Worlds of Welfare Capitalism* (Cambridge: Polity Press).

Flora, P., and J. Alber (1981) 'Modernization, Democratization and the Development of Welfare States in Western Europe', in P. Flora and A. J. Heidenheimer (eds), *The Development of Welfare States in Europe and America* (New Brunswick and London: Transaction Publishers) pp. 37–81.

Gámir, L. (1998) 'Privatizaciones, eficiencia y transparencia', *ICE*, no. 772, pp. 27–44 (Madrid: ICE).

Guillén, M. (2005) *The Rise of Spanish Multinationals: European Business in the Global Economy* (Cambridge University Press).

Guillén, A.M., and S. Álvarez (2001) 'Globalization and the Southern Welfare States', in R. Sykes, P. Prior and B. Palier (eds), *Globalization and European Welfare States* (London: Macmillan).

Lasheras, M.A. (1999) *La regulación económica de los servicios públicos* (Barcelona: Ariel).

Mañas, L. (1998) 'La experiencia de una década de privatizaciones', *ICE*, no. 77 (Madrid: ICE).

Newbery, D. (2004) 'Privatising Network Industries', CESIFO Working Paper 1132.

Parker, D. (2004) 'The UK's Privatisation Experiment: The Passage of Time Permits a Sober Assessment', CESIFO Working Paper 1126.

Schröter, H. (forthcoming 2007) *In Search of the European Enterprise* (Springer).

Further Reading

Clifton, J., F. Comín and D. Díaz-Fuentes (2005) 'Las transformaciones de las empresas públicas en red en la época de las privatizaciones globales', in Julio Tascón (ed.), *Redes de empresas en España. Una perspectiva teórica, histórica y global* (Madrid: Editorial LID) pp. 155–76.

Comín, F. (2004) 'El gasto y la industria de defensa en la España contemporáneá, *Cuadernos Aragoneses de Economía*, 2, pp. 297–320.

Gálvez Muñoz, L., and F. Comín (2003) 'Multinacionales. Atraso tecnológico y marco institucional. Las racionalizaciones de empresas extranjeras durante la autarquía franquistá, *Cuadernos de Economía y Dirección de la Empresa*, 17, pp. 139–79.

8

Privatisation and Transnationalisation of Network Services in Portugal, 1980–2005

Ana Bela Nunes, Carlos Bastien and Nuno Valério

Introduction

This chapter assesses the relationship between privatisation and transnationalisation processes in Portugal from the 1980s to the present, with particular attention to network services. We argue that the privatisation process transformed the Portuguese economic system from one of strong state capitalism to one of weakly regulated capitalism, whilst simultaneously promoting both passive transnationalisation (the penetration of foreign economic groups into the Portuguese economy) and the formation, restoration or reinforcement of Portuguese economic groups, some of which started an active transnationalisation process. All of these processes unfolded according to what could be expected in a European and world context, although Portuguese investments abroad revealed some specificities, mainly related to the importance of the Portuguese-speaking countries, the network services and strategic alliances with Spanish enterprises. The rest of the chapter is organised into five sections. Firstly, the public enterprise sector in Portugal and privatisation are briefly presented. Secondly, we provide a general view of the main trends of privatisation and transnationalisation. An analysis of inward and outward foreign investment in Portuguese network services follows in parts three and four. Finally, in the conclusions we enquire to what extent Portugal is a typical case with regard to the transnationalisation of network services.

I. The Portuguese Public Enterprise Sector in 1980 and Privatisation

The extensive nationalisation process which took place between 1974 and 1976 – during the transition from the authoritarian regime that ruled the country until the revolution of 25 April 1974 to the democratic regime that prevailed after the enactment of the Constitution of 1976 two years later – created the largest public enterprise sector that has ever existed in the Portuguese economy.[1] Article 83 of the new Constitution established the irreversibility of the direct nationalisations carried out between 1974 and 1976 and included provisions limiting the possibility of privatisation of the indirectly nationalised enterprises. Law 46/77 of 8 July 1977 sought to settle the limits of the public and private sectors, guaranteeing the freedom of private enterprise (in particular within the context of specific legislation about foreign investment), but at the same time banning it from several sectors. These were: banking (except for savings banks, agricultural credit cooperatives and parabanking companies), insurance (except for mutual insurance societies), electricity and gas production and distribution, the distribution of water for public consumption, sanitation, postal services, telegraph services, telephones, air transport, rail transport, urban public transport (except in taxis), ports, airports and arms industries, oil refining, basic petrochemical industries, iron and steel, fertilisers and cements (and also allowing the government to ban private enterprise from the tobacco and match industries, if it so wished). In the mining sector public ownership of mines was established together with the possibility of the temporary concession of the right to their exploitation. Thus by 1980 a significant part of the Portuguese economy (roughly 23 per cent of gross added value, 19 per cent of employment and 43 per cent of the gross fixed capital formation) was under state control in the form of public enterprises.[2]

At the beginning of the 1980s, however, the political climate surrounding the public enterprise sector began to change in the world in general and in Portugal in particular. This resulted in new laws establishing the limits of the public and private sectors, successively more open to private enterprise.[3] From the end of the 1980s the agenda ceased to be simply a question of reducing the number of sectors reserved exclusively for public enterprise and began to be a question of reprivatising nationalised enterprises. Portugal's accession to the European Communities in 1986 was certainly not unrelated to this turnaround, although there was a transitional period for the adoption of the so-called *acquis communautaire* (Community patrimony) originally envisaged to last until 1995 (the end of this period was later brought forward to 1993).

The constitutional revision brought about by the Constitutional Law 1/89 of 8 July 1989 introduced profound changes to the former Article 83 (now Article 85) of the Constitution, providing for 'The reprivatisation of the ownership or the right to exploit means of production and other assets nationalised after 25 April 1974', 'under the terms of a framework law approved by an absolute majority of the members of parliament'. This framework law was Law 11/90 of 5 April 1990. According to this law public enterprises could be transformed into joint-stock companies after a prior independent valuation had been carried out and could be privatised through the sale of shares or capital increases effected by means of a public call for tenders, a public offer for sale, a public subscription, a restricted call for tenders or a direct sale. Whatever the case, it was established that part of the capital to be privatised would be reserved for emigrants, small subscribers and workers of the company itself. The possibility was also established that restrictions could be placed on the purchase of shares by foreigners. A framework was therefore established whereby enterprises could be handed to Portuguese or foreign economic groups, in combination with a scheme of popular capitalism.

Over the next 15 years nearly 200 operations were undertaken to sell off nearly 150 firms. This process did not follow any general plan. Rather it attempted to benefit from market opportunities, as was also the case in other European countries. Most of the firms were sold without much concern for the future of their activity, which was clearly not considered as involving any public interest. In some cases schemes such as residual public participations or golden shares were established so that the Portuguese government retained some control of their destiny. In many cases privatisation was not undertaken, either because of strategic reasons or because of the difficult financial situation of the firms (which were nevertheless maintained because they were considered of public interest). As a consequence the public enterprises in the beer, tobacco, iron and steel, maritime and road transport, and telecommunications sectors were completely privatised. The public enterprises in banking, insurance, the production, transport and distribution of electricity and gas, cellulose and paper pulp, cement, oil refining, the chemical industry, shipbuilding and repairing, arms industries and the media were partially privatised. Public enterprises in sectors such as water distribution for public consumption, sanitation, air transport, rail transport, urban public transport, ports, airports and postal services remained under public ownership.[4]

II. Privatisation and Transnationalisation: A General View

Privatisation promoted transnationalisation in two ways:

(a) Passive transnationalisation, that is, the penetration of foreign economic groups into the Portuguese economy. This happened either by direct purchase of privatised firms or by secondhand purchase from Portuguese entrepreneurs seeking to cash the surplus value of the firms they had bought from the government. In some cases the Portuguese government promoted the formation of groups of core owners involving alliances of Portuguese capitalists and foreign strategic partners.

(b) Active transnationalisation, that is, the penetration of Portuguese economic groups into foreign economies. This happened by means of the formation, restoration or reinforcement of Portuguese economic groups strong enough to start a transnationalisation process. In some cases active transnationalisation was made by enterprises that remained in the hands of the government.

Parts three and four will review the main aspects and cases of passive and active transnationalisation in the Portuguese economy, with special attention to network services. The cases of privatisation that did not give rise to significant transnationalisation (that is to say, where Portuguese groups bought the firms and did not engage in active transnationalisation) will not be dealt with. Of course passive and active transnationalisation often mingled in the same sector and even the same firm. Cases will be considered in part three or four according to the relative importance of passive and active transnationalisation elements in each sector or firm.

III. Foreign Capital in the Portuguese Network Services

Foreign investment in the Portuguese economy dates back many centuries. Italian and Flemish traders, among others, participated in various ways in the financing of Portuguese discoveries and the exploitation of overseas trade from the fifteenth century onwards. Foreign capital, mainly British and French, was very important in the introduction of economic innovations to Portugal, such as railroads, telephones and modern urban transportation, during the nineteenth century. The Portuguese colonial empire and specific sectors in which Portugal had traditional comparative advantages (such as wine, cork and canned fish) also attracted significant foreign investment during the first half of the twentieth century. These flows increased in size and diversified by sector during the third quarter of the twentieth century, both because this was the golden age of Portuguese modern economic growth and because of Portuguese participation in the process of European economic integration (at the time in the framework of the European Free Trade Association).

Foreign capital invested in Portugal was not directly disturbed by nationalisations. Thus foreign firms operating in Portugal in the early 1970s kept their business more or less successfully during the following years. Others began to operate in Portugal after sectors previously restricted to public enterprises began to open to private initiative during the 1980s. Privatisation opened new opportunities and several foreign firms profited. The cases of passive transnationalisation linked to privatisation may be divided into three groups according to their final result:

(a) Successful endeavours leading to the stable presence of foreign firms in the Portuguese economy. These may be found mainly in the banking and insurance, beer, tobacco, mining and chemical industry sectors.
(b) Unsuccessful endeavours leading to the closing down of the Portuguese firms involved. These may be found mainly in the shipbuilding and repairing and iron and steel sectors.
(c) Dubious situations of (often uneasy) partnership between foreign firms, Portuguese entrepreneurs and the Portuguese government. These may be found mainly in the energy and air transport sectors. As important network services these will be analysed in more detail (see Table 8.1).

Table 8.1   The Largest Portuguese TNCs

Name	Sector	% of cash-flow abroad	% of work force abroad	Privatised	Spanish partners	Countries*
PT	Telecommunications	29	38	Y	Y	12 (7)
EDP	Energy	25	32	Y	Y	5 (4)
GALP	Energy	–	–	Y	Y	5 (4)

Notes: Firms ranked by cash-flow abroad.
* Number of countries of activity abroad (number of Portuguese-speaking countries of activity abroad).

Source: Elaborated by authors using *Público* (7 November 2005).

III.i   Energy

The main firms in the energy sector were directly nationalised in 1975. Reorganisation of the energy sector of the Portuguese economy during the nationalisation period left in place two main public enterprises: Electricidade de Portugal (EDP), a producer and distributor of electricity formed in 1976 by the merger of the previous Portuguese electricity producers and distributors, and Petrogal, a refiner and distributor of oil derivatives formed also in 1976 by the merger of the previous Portuguese oil enterprises, together with a few branches of important foreign oil companies.

The strategy of the Portuguese government was to privatise EDP and Petrogal, choosing as the core of the new owner groups Portuguese entrepreneurs linked with important international energy firms. Meanwhile the Portuguese government was to maintain golden shares to ensure adequate consideration of the Portuguese public interest. None of these processes went smoothly. Sluggish capital markets and formal problems with European Union competition law have prevented a definitive solution until the time of writing (2006).

The French firm Total was the first strategic partner chosen for Petrogal in the early 1990s, but it quit after suffering heavy losses during the crisis of the mid-1990s. New strategic partners were sought in oil-producing countries, but both Saudi Ameco and Angolan Sonangol failed to fulfill hopes. As a consequence a new scheme was devised involving the transformation of Petrogal into a new firm, GALP, potentially interested in all the energy sector, but especially in gas, and an alliance with the Italian firm ENI. This scheme was at a critical point at the end of 2005 with ENI trying to acquire strategic control of GALP and the Portuguese government trying first to keep the *status quo ante* and later to interest a Portuguese enterprise group – Amorim – to compete with ENI for control.[5]

Attempts to privatise EDP came much later, around the turn of the century. As a preliminary to privatisation EDP was broken up into three firms: CPPE, an electricity producer, fully controlled by EDP;[6] REN, the controller of the high voltage distribution network;[7] and EDP proper, an electricity distributor. The capital of EDP became widely spread, with the Spanish firms Iberdrola (5.7 per cent) and CajAstur (5.53 per cent) leading, together with the two main Portuguese financial groups, CGD (4.80 per cent)[8] and BCP (5.98 per cent).[9]

Meanwhile both EDP and Petrogal engaged in some active transnationalisation. In the case of EDP the main target was Brazil. EDP came to control the Empresa Bandeirantes de Energia, one of the main producers and distributors of electricity in the state of São Paulo, and Escelsa, one of the main producers and distributors of electricity of the state of Espírito Santo. It also became partner of Petrobrás in building and exploiting the hydroelectric plant of Lajeado in the state of Bahia, one of the biggest projects in the country. A second target of EDP was Spain, where it acquired Hidrocantábrico, a firm that ranks fourth in the Spanish energy market. Cape Verde, Guatemala and the Chinese Special Administrative Region of Macao played minor roles as targets.

Petrogal directed its attention mainly to African Portuguese-speaking countries, namely Cape Verde (Enacol), Guinea-Bissau (Petromar and Petrogás), Angola (Petrogal Angola and Agran) and Mozambique (Petrogal Moçambique and Moçacor), and to Spain, always in the sector of oil refining and distribution. It is also trying to improve its position in crude exploration and extraction in Brazil.[10]

III.ii Air Transport

Air transport also deserves brief mention here. This is another example of privatisation failure, not only because the firm directly nationalised in the mid-1970s, TAP (Transportes Aéreos Portugueses), later renamed Air Portugal, became unprofitable, as most air companies did after the oil shocks, but also because of an unfortunate choice of strategic partners for its first international alliance. Swissair and the Qualiflyer Group, to which TAP was linked, proved even less successful than TAP itself, as the collapse of its two main companies – Swissair and Sabena – proved. TAP is now a member of the Star Alliance led by Lufthansa and engaged in a significant effort of active transnationalisation, trying to participate in a rescue operation of the Brazilian air company Varig.

IV. Portuguese Investments in Network Services Abroad

As a rule, capital exports flow mainly from highly developed economies to other highly developed economies and to emerging economies. Portugal became a highly developed country only in the last quarter of the twentieth century. Thus until then it was not a significant source of investment abroad. The only exception that is worth mentioning is Portuguese investment in the Portuguese colonial empire between the late nineteenth century and the early 1970s, which was greatly harmed in the decolonisation process of the mid-1970s.

The situation changed in the late twentieth century. As Portugal became a highly developed country it started to be a significant capital exporter, and often a net capital exporter since 1995. The privatisation process favoured such movements in two ways: it allowed the formation of Portuguese groups, more or less linked to the government, capable of investing abroad; and it allowed Portuguese private groups to rebuild or consolidate and thus to become better able to perform as active transnational actors. The main cases of active transnationalisation occurred in the banking and insurance, telecommunications, highway management, cement and pulp and paper sectors. The main cases of network services transnationalisation are highlighted next.

IV.i Telecommunications

Privatisation of the telecommunications sector was also the basis for the formation of a significant Portuguese group, Portugal Telecom (PT), which became engaged in active transnationalisation.[11] In Brazil PT became the main national mobile operator in the state of São Paulo – Telesp Celular – and the main pager operator, Mobile. It also acquired control of the mobile operator Global Telecom in the states of Paraná and Santa Catarina, and significant holdings in other telecommunications firms, such as Companhia Riograndense de Telecomunicações (in Rio Grande do Sul). In spite of the support of three important banking institutions – CGD, Espírito Santo[12] and BPI[13] – there were some financial difficulties in developing all these endeavours. This pushed PT to accept an alliance with a Spanish firm in the same sector, Telefonica, to handle its Brazilian investments. They are now joint (50/50) owners of Vivo, the main South American mobile operator, which operates in 19 Brazilian states (including Acre, Amapá, Amazônia, Bahia, Espírito Santo, Goiás, Maranhão, Mato Grosso, Mato Grosso do Sul, Pará, Rio de Janeiro, Rondônia and Sergipe) and the Federal District of Brasília.[14]

In Africa PT established operators in all Portuguese-speaking countries – Angola, Cape Verde, Guiné-Bissau, Mozambique and São Tomé and Príncipe – and also in Morocco and Kenya. In the Far East it established operators in China and Timor.

IV.ii. Highway Management

Brisa – a firm with mixed public and private participation formed in 1972 to build and manage Portuguese highways and later nationalised – became after privatisation the main endeavour of an important Portuguese enterprise group, the Mello group.[15] Its most successful initiative was linked to the electronic payment system devised for Portuguese highways, which proved a very competitive patent in international terms, allowing Brisa to become a partner of other highway managers in several countries: Italy – Autostrade (1999), Brazil – CCR (2001) and Spain – Acesa (2002).

Conclusions

Is Portugal a typical case of the privatisation and transnationalisation of network services? Privatisation and transnationalisation have certainly been very important processes in shaping the main characteristics of the Portuguese economy during the last two decades of the twentieth century and the early twenty-first century. The privatisation process in Portugal developed in line with European trends, both in its timing and in its characteristics.[16] It transformed the Portuguese economic system from strong state capitalism to weakly regulated capitalism. This is mainly a consequence of the fact that the existence of an effective competition authority and independent regulatory bodies in sectors with natural monopolies was not designed from the beginning of the process and had to be added as it unfolded, with the inevitable result that these institutions are still building their credibility. Judged by the standards of the usual goals presented in privatisation processes – increasing economic efficiency by means of increased competition, both among privatised firms, and between private firms and those possibly remaining in public hands; fostering the activity of capital markets; raising public revenue, while reducing the government's weight in the economy; and contributing to wider share ownership – it can be assessed as quite successful, although to different extents depending on which goals are being discussed.[17]

The main characteristics of transnationalisation movements related to the Portuguese economy corresponded to what might be expected given the general characteristics of the Portuguese economy. Being an emergent economy with not particularly fast growth for nearly a century (from the middle of the nineteenth to the middle of the twentieth century), it was not a significant source of direct investment abroad and it attracted a significant, although not particularly important amount of foreign direct investment. The definitive take-off of modern economic growth and participation in the process of European integration accelerated the inflow of foreign capital during the third quarter of the twentieth century and the nationalisation process put a brake on it between the mid-1970s and the mid-1980s. Then, as Portuguese modern economic growth matured and the Portuguese economy liberalised, both capital inflows and outflows increased. As might be expected, capital inflows came mainly from big multinational companies and more or less neighbouring European, and especially Spanish, firms. Again as might be expected, capital outflows came mainly from the largest Portuguese economic groups and went mainly to neighbouring European, and especially Spanish, endeavours.

There are, however, some specificities that deserve mention. Concerning the privatisation and passive transnationalisation aspects it is worth noting that the Portuguese public enterprise sector was rather large and diversified when the privatisation process started, mainly because of the recent and highly ideological nationalisation process of the mid-1970s. This meant that a significant number of profitable firms, especially in the industrial sector, were brought to the market and afforded good revenue for the government and good business to the buyers.

With regard to active transnationalisation three items must be emphasised:

(a) There are very important capital outflows to Portuguese-speaking countries, first of all towards Brazil, but also towards ex-Portuguese colonies in Africa. This is easily explained by the reduced communication costs of establishment in these countries, which of course rank in attractiveness by size and degree of development.[18]

(b) Investment in the service sector is roughly of the same importance as investment in the industrial sector. This can be explained not only by the tertiarisation of both the Portuguese economy and the world economy in the last decades of the twentieth century, but especially by the fact that the main Portuguese economic groups more often than not have their core business in the service sector and stick to it in the transnationalisation process. In other words, horizontal integration has prevailed over vertical integration. As a consequence, network services became a key sector in Portuguese active transnationalisation.

(c) Strategic alliances with Spanish enterprises are quite common.[19] As a matter of fact the three largest Portuguese multinational firms originated in the privatisation process, have their core business in network services, concentrate abroad in Portuguese-speaking countries and have engaged in some kind of alliance with Spanish partners.

Notes

1   On the long-term evolution of the public enterprise sector see Nunes, Bastien and Valério (2005).

2   On the public enterprise sector around 1980 see Martins and Rosa (1979).

3   Law 88-A/97 of 25 July 1997 restricts sectors from which private enterprise is banned to the distribution of water for public consumption, sanitation, postal services, railway transport and ports, although it opens up the possibility of the concession of such activities to private enterprise under public regulation. Moreover it establishes a special restrictive regime for the arms industry.

4   On the privatisation process, see GAFEEP (1995); Vilar et al. (1998); and DGEP (1999).

5   As a result, by end 2005 ENI and Amorim were almost on level pegging, holding, respectively, 33.34 per cent and 32.25 per cent of outstanding shares, while the third shareholder, the Spanish firm Iberdrola, owned only 4 per cent. However, few, if any, believe this is a stable situation.

6   CPPE supplies around 75 per cent of the electricity produced in Portugal. The second largest producer is Tejo Energia (fomerly controlled by the French EDF, now controlled by the British National Power) with a share of 10 per cent.

7   Owned by the state (70 per cent) and EDP (30 per cent).

8   CGD was created as a state-owned savings bank in 1876 and remained state-owned throughout its existence, although it underwent several transformations. In the period under consideration it clearly aimed at being the head of a universal financial

group. During the privatisation process this group was enlarged with the acquisition of other important banking – Banco Nacional Ultramarino (the former issuing bank for the Portuguese colonial empire) – and insurance (Fidelidade, Mundial-Confiança, part of Império-Bonança) firms. At the same time, CGD engaged in an active transnationalisation process in Spain, African Portuguese-speaking countries, countries with a high concentration of Portuguese emigrants and the Chinese Special Administrative Region of Macao.

9 BCP is an important Portuguese financial group formed during the 1980s which was consolidated by the acquisition of banking – Banco Português do Atlântico, Banco Mello – and insurance (Império, Bonança) institutions during the privatisation process (later, BCP gave up the insurance business). BCP has been very active in transnationalisation, acquiring banking institutions in Poland (Millennium), Greece (Nova Bank) and Turkey (Bank Europa and Site Bank), and has cooperated with Spanish banking institutions, firstly, Banco Central Hispano, later Banco Sabadell.

10 On the transnationalisation of Petrogal, see Cruz, Rodrigues, Hofschulsz and Valadas (1999).

11 The telecommunications sector was also a field for passive transnationalisation, although unrelated to privatisation. The main examples were the acquisition of the mobile phone network Telecel by Vodafone and the participation of France Telecom in another mobile network, Optimus.

12 Espírito Santo was one of the main Portuguese financial groups of the pre-nationalisation epoch. During the privatisation process the banking – Espírito Santo – and insurance (Tranquilidade) firms it had held before the nationalisation process of the mid-1970s were restituted. It also engaged in an active transnationalisation process as a financial institution in Spain and Brazil.

13 BPI is an important Portuguese financial group formed during the 1980s which was consolidated by the acquisition of several banking institutions – Banco de Fomento e Exterior, Banco Borges & Irmão and Banco Fonsecas & Burnay – during the privatisation process. It is now simultaneously a case of active transnationalisation, mainly in Angola – Banco de Fomento Angola – and passive transnationalisation by means of capital holdings on the part of La Caixa (Spain), Itaú (Brazil) and Allianz (Germany).

14 Because of the cross holdings between PT and (the much bigger) Telefonica, PT may also be considered a case of passive transnationalisation. Telefonica holds 9.58 per cent of the outstanding capital of PT, almost the maximum allowed by the statutes for a single owner (10 per cent).

15 Before the nationalisation process of the mid-1970s the Mello group was mainly an industrial group, owner of the most important (chemical) Portuguese firm, Companhia União Fabril. The Mello group obtained control of a number of firms in several sectors – banking, insurance, tobacco, shipbuilding and repairing – during the privatisation process, but later concentrated mainly in the highway management and health care businesses. Mello holds 30.92 per cent of the outstanding capital of Brisa, followed by the Spanish highway manager Acesa (10.08 per cent) and the Portuguese financial group BCP (9.59 per cent).

16 Even concerning unfavourable conditions brought about by the rigidities of the labour market and the scarcity of liquidity in the capital market in some periods.

17 A systematic assessment of the impact of privatisation on public accounts is presented in Valério (2004). It is widely believed that most of the shares acquired by emigrants, small subscribers and company workers on special terms were sold for cash as soon as possible and convenient, thus frustrating any programme of popular capitalism.

18   Some analyses explain the relatively low level of investment in highly developed economies as a consequence of the lack of financial leverage of the rather weak and fragmented Portuguese banking system and the immature stage of Portuguese economic development.

19   On these specific characteristics of Portuguese investment abroad see A. Mendonça et al. (2001) and Silva et al. (2002).

References

Cadernos de Economia, various issues.

Cruz, C., R. Rodrigues, S. Hofschulsz and T. Valadas (1999) 'A estratégia de internacionalização da Petrogal', Centro de Estudos de Gestão, Instituto Superior de Economia e Gestão, Working Paper no. 41.

DGEP (1999) *Privatizações e regulação – A experiência portuguesa* (Lisbon: Ministério das Finanças).

DN Empresas (Lisbon: various issues).

Economia Pura (Lisbon: various issues).

GAFEEP (1995) *Privatizações em Portugal – Uma reforma estrutural* (Lisbon: Ministério das Finanças).

Martins, M.B., and J.C. Rosa (1979) *O grupo Estado* (Lisbon: Expresso).

Mendonça, A., M. Farto, E. Ribeiro, J. Dias and M. Fonseca (2001) 'O investimento directo das empresas portuguesas no Brasil: sectores, tipos de operação e principais determinantes, 1996–1999', Ministério da Economia, Working Paper no. 32.

Nunes, A.B., C. Bastien and C. Valério (2004) 'Nationalisations et dénationalisations au Portugal (19ème et 20ème siècles): une évaluation historique', special issue of *Entreprises et Histoire*, no. 37.

Nunes, A.B., C. Bastien and N. Valério (2005) 'Nationalizations and De-nationalizations in Portugal (19th and 20th Centuries): A Historical Assessment', Gabinete de História Económica e Social, Instituto Superior de Economia e Gestão, Working Paper no. 22.

Público (Lisbon: various issues).

Silva, J.R, F.C. Fernandes and C.G. Costa (2002) 'A internacionalização das empresas portuguesas no Brasil – territorialidade, dimensão e sectores de origem em Portugal', CEDIN, Instituto Superior de Economia e Gestão, Working Paper no. 8.

Valério, N. (2004) 'Nationalisations and Privatisations in Portugal during the Last Quarter of the 20th Century: Were They Profitable to the State?', *Revista de História Económica e Social*, 2nd series, no. 7.

Vilar, E.R. et al. (1998) *Livro Branco do Sector Empresarial do Estado* (Lisbon: Ministério das Finanças).

9
Transforming Air Transport in Ireland

Sean D. Barrett

Introduction

The case of air transport in Ireland represents one of the most radical experiences of deregulation worldwide in terms of market entry, price reductions and increases in passenger volumes. The change in public policy from national airlines to a competitive single European market in aviation has stimulated a change in corporate culture throughout the industry. The market entry of new airlines and airports, the 'disintermediation' of retailing of air tickets, as Internet sales replace travel agents, and the unbundling of the airline product have all changed the air transport network. Air transport integrated networks are being replaced by point-to-point travel. Moreover the creation of a single integrated European market in aviation has extended the scope for new point-to-point services between third countries. These markets were not available when airlines were restricted to routes according to the nationality of the airline. Airlines have been transferred from the public utility sector to the commercial sector and have been privatised. Following free trade in aviation in Europe is the prospect of liberalised aviation agreements between Europe and the USA, as well as other aviation partners. Aviation is thus moving towards the general pattern of international trade, in contrast to its traditional special treatment in trade negotiations. This chapter examines the case of Aer Lingus, the national airline of Ireland, and its evolution from the protectionist economic policies of the 1930s to the deregulated single European market of the last decade. Table 9.4 below shows the transformation of the Irish airline sector from an Aer Lingus monopoly with 2.3 million passengers in 1985/6 to four airlines with 38.6 million passengers in 2004/5. The new entrants since deregulation were Ryanair, founded in 1985 and Europe's leading lowcost airline, Cityjet, founded as a full service airline in 1993 and now owned by Air France, and Aer Arann, founded in 1970 to serve three islands off the west coast of Ireland.

I. Ownership, Power, Governance and the National Airline

The establishment of Aer Lingus as Ireland's national airline in 1936 was part of a policy of state enterprise and protectionism espoused by Irish nationalists for one and a half centuries. Independence in 1922 had allowed these policies to be implemented. The interventionist tradition was based on a nostalgic, romanticised view of the independent interventionist Irish parliament between 1782 and the Act of Union in 1800, as well as a belief that infant industries should be protected, based on the German economist Friedrich List.[1] In addition, a British government policy of 'killing Home Rule with kindness' involved placing Irish nationalists on public boards in the hope of diluting their separatist aspirations. Irish politicians after 1800 became successful rent-seekers at the Westminster parliament and used their position when holding the balance of power to leverage concessions in the form of state boards. Sir Robert Peel, Chief Secretary for Ireland (1812–18) stated that 'everyone in Ireland, instead of setting about improvement as people elsewhere do; pester government about boards and public aid. Why cannot people in Ireland fish without a board [for fishing] if fishing be so profitable?'. By 1914, there were 40 government departments in Ireland. Although 11 were branches of British departments, 29 had no British equivalents.[2]

The first Irish tariffs on industrial imported goods were introduced in 1924. By 1929 the government claimed that 60 per cent of non-agricultural jobs were subject to tariffs creating an extra 15,000 jobs.[3] The first state companies were established in 1927. These included the Electricity Supply Board to acquire 160 electricity undertakings in the state, the Agricultural Credit Company to provide credit for this sector and the Dairy Disposal Company to acquire creameries. During the 1930s new state enterprises were established in areas such as aviation, shipping, steel, industrial credit, sugar manufacture, chemicals and insurance. The telephone service was operated by the Department of Posts and Telegraphs. Water services were provided by the local authorities and small local gas companies in cities and towns were privately owned.

Nationalism rather than socialism was the motivation. According to Chubb the growth of public enterprises in Ireland owed little to socialist theory: 'After the eclipse of the left wing of the labour movement during the latter part of the First World War, there were few socialists in Ireland, no socialist movement worth the name and no developing body of socialist doctrine'.[4]

In the parliamentary debates on the foundation of the Dairy Disposal Board concern was expressed that the creameries would be taken over by Lovell and Christmas, 'the biggest grocers in the world'. The foundation of the Sugar Company in 1933 was motivated, in the words of its official historian, by 'a national wish to be independent of foreign supplies of basic needs'.[5] The Minister proposing the State Insurance Company in 1936 stated that 'we are taking steps to promote the extension of native insurance by prohibiting the entry of any further insurance companies into the Saorstat' (Irish Free State).[6]

As late as 1965 when the state acquired the B. and I. Line, a shipping company operating on the Irish Sea, the Minister stated in parliament that 'a greater measure of Irish participation in the cross channel trade for a long time has been an important objective of government policy'.[7] The acquisition was warmly supported by the opposition parties. 'It is a good thing that the B. and I. Line is now in Irish hands ... there are far too many foreigners buying land and public firms in this country'.[8]

The formation of state companies in the 1920s and 1930s was also promoted by a number of other factors at the time. Ireland did not have its own currency and thus lacked the capability to use an independent monetary policy. In the 1930s a dispute with Britain over land annuities payable in respect of land transfer from colonial landlords to peasant proprietors led to an 'economic war' with the country with which Ireland conducted 95 per cent of its foreign trade. There was a general indifference to the loss of foreign export markets such as the Ford company transfer of some operations from Cork to Dagenham, the Guinness transfer of some operations from Dublin to London, the Jacob company transfer of some operations to Liverpool and the decline of the Irish whiskey sector because of lack of imported inputs. The new state identified state companies with economic progress and an advance from a pre-independence state of economic backwardness.

Recent economic and historical research disputes the nationalist belief that Ireland needed state enterprises to rescue it from a pre-independence stagnation. Geary and Stark estimate that Ireland's economic performance was good enough to locate it among the richest in the world in the 1870s and on the eve of the Great War.[9] Cullen states that at the end of the nineteenth century 'its large foreign trade, its export oriented industries, its highly developed infrastructure of banking, commerce and railways, and its foreign investment yielding a sizeable income made Ireland comparable in some respects to a handful of highly developed nations'.[10] The progress of Ireland to a country with GDP per head above the OECD average from 1990 in the Celtic Tiger era may be merely a return to the country's relative position between 1870 and 1914. Ireland thus could be seen to prosper in eras of free trade and decline in periods of protectionism and interventionism.

II. Protecting the National Airline

It was in this context of protectionism and nationalism that Aer Lingus was established as Ireland's national airline in 1936. These themes are captured in the official history of Aer Lingus by Share (1988). Public policy protected Aer Lingus even before it commenced operations. The Air Navigation (International Lines) Order of 1935 gave the Minister for Industry and Commerce control over air services 'with a view to the limitation or regulation of competition as may be considered necessary in the public interest'.[11] In 1935 Crilly Airways sought to operate air services between Ireland and Britain and was informed that 'the Minister was unable to entertain his proposals. The reason given was the government's intention to set up a national airline at the earliest possible date'.[12] In 1949 a proposal for a service from Cork to Britain by Cambrian was refused 'on the grounds that air transport policy did not contemplate that airlines other than Aer Lingus would operate a scheduled service between the two countries'.[13] In 1950 a proposal from Silver City, a British airline, for a car carrying service from Liverpool to Dublin was refused because Aer Lingus 'was considering the opening of a similar service on the route'.[14] Share also records that 'other airlines were in this period equally unsuccessful in their intentions to serve Ireland' and that proposed Rome–Paris–Dublin and Milan–Paris–Dublin services were successfully opposed by the Aer Lingus board.[15]

Share also records that the thinking behind the bill establishing Aer Lingus 'which enshrined the position of the State as sole international carrier, had been influenced by European developments. KLM had been set up in 1919, Lufthansa in April 1926 and Air France in 1933: these were all state entities benefiting from official restriction of competition.[16] Such was the strength of protectionist opinion in the governing party that the Minister explained that 'though he wished to minimize competition on economic grounds, he recognized that no one country could hope to reserve to its own nationals the whole of air transport between its own territory and that of another country'.[17] Today the idea of minimising competition 'on economic grounds' may sound bizarre, particularly in the case of a small country such as Ireland which was to prosper under free trade in the 1990s and lagged behind the OECD countries in the decades of protectionism. It is also ironic that a country so staunchly opposed to competition in aviation proved to be the major beneficiary of the single European market some 60 years later when Ryanair, an Irish company, became the first major airline to exploit the deregulated European aviation market in competition with national airlines in third-country markets.

At the Chicago international aviation conference in 1944 US proposals for an open skies regime for postwar aviation were defeated because of European fears that the larger US fleet would dominate aviation. The defeat of multilateralism brought about a bilateral aviation system in which aviation between countries was controlled by agreements between the governments and their national airlines. The typical international air transport agreement provided for one airline per country to agree the capacity on a route in advance, to share the market, to pool the revenues and to charge the same fares. The airlines typically agreed to act as each other's sales and airport agents, to accept tickets issued by the partner airline and to broadly standardise the airline product between the partner airlines. This way of organising the aviation market was believed to avoid wasteful competition between airlines, to stabilise the market and to avoid excess capacity and predatory pricing. The passenger gained from a worldwide integrated network of interline services of connecting flights, mutual acceptance of tickets and a common standard of service.

There were, however, inherent dangers in the economics of the Chicago-based bilateral model. Bodies that collude and are exempted by government from the threat of new market entrants become complacent about costs. Managements and employees in the protected organisations become rent-seekers rather then efficient producers. Where the protected bodies are in public ownership regulatory capture of the supervising government department by producers at the expense of consumers is likely and the Aer Lingus record in lobbying against new market entry is not surprising.

In 1962 Dr Garret FitzGerald, a future prime minister (Taoiseach), published the first major volume on Irish state companies. He attributed the dearth of analysis of state companies to their relative novelty as an instrument of government.[18] FitzGerald gave two main reasons for the establishment of state commercial enterprises: 'a desire to maintain in existence a bankrupt, or virtually bankrupt, undertaking, whose preservation is believed to be in the national interest' and 'a desire to initiate an economic activity deemed necessary in the national interest – but one which for one reason or another private enterprise has failed to inaugurate or to operate on a sufficiently extensive scale'.[19] He included Aer Lingus in the second category, that is, filling a role where the private sector did not exist. We have seen that far from filling a void left by the private sector Aer Lingus successfully lobbied governments to keep other airlines out of the market.

FitzGerald noted two important characteristics of Irish state enterprises: capital intensity and high wages. State companies accounted for 30 per cent of gross national fixed investment in 1960 and 'earnings per head in this sector appear to be about 40 per cent above the national average for employees'.[20] These factors became matters for concern in the 1980s when the low efficiency of Irish public sector investment and the low productivity of labour in Irish state companies became causes for concern.

III. Disillusionment with State Enterprises and National Airlines in the 1980s

The consequences of protectionism and state commercial enterprises in Ireland are seen in retrospect to have had several detrimental impacts on the economy. Daly states that 'one major legacy of the thirties was the institutionalization of an Irish dependence on the State, and on politicians, for economic benefits'.[21] Political patronage was also a feature of the policies. Keogh noted that there were in 1992 some 2200 appointees to state boards compared to 1500 locally elected public representatives.[22] Lee noted the 'gradual growth of an insidious, if initially discreet spoils system in the army, the judiciary, and the state sponsored bodies'.[23] With political loyalty rather than commercial ability influencing board appointments the system of political patronage undermined the quality of state company boards, reduced the independence of the state commercial companies and diminished their public standing.

Lee notes that the Labour Party proposal for a National Development Corporation in the early 1980s failed to generate enthusiasm because

> the public had so lost confidence in the capacity of any state organization to serve any purpose except its own self-interest that the proposal generated more skepticism than enthusiasm. A series of poor returns on several enterprises and the apparent casualness with which public sector trade unions resorted to the tactic of inflicting suffering on the public, the same public they claimed to serve in their more esoteric flights of fancy, in order to intimidate the government into concessions left public opinion increasingly dubious about the likely results of direct state intervention.

The evidence of the problems of public enterprises in Ireland accumulated steadily over the 1970s and 1980s. In 1979 the Dargan Report (Daigan 1979) found that the telephone operations of the Department of Posts and Telegraphs were overstaffed by a factor of three compared to Britain, four compared to the USA and almost eight compared to Switzerland. The Report of the Enquiry into Electricity Prices in 1984, chaired by E.G. Jakobsen, managing director of ELSAM Denmark, found manning levels double those in Scotland, three times those in Denmark and six times those in Vermont.[24]

The general disillusionment with state enterprises in Ireland extended to Aer Lingus mainly because of popular dissatisfaction with the level of airfares on its European routes. Research by the Civil Aviation Authority on 11 short haul routes from London showed that between 1980 and 1985 fares between London and Dublin rose by 75.2 per cent, compared to an average price rise on the routes of 43.7 per cent and a retail price index increase of 41.5 per cent. Passenger number growth on London–Dublin between 1980 and 1985, at 2.8 per cent, was the lowest of the 11 routes, which had an average growth of 29.9 per cent in passenger numbers. The lower fares to London available from Belfast, a domestic UK route, compared to Dublin, Cork and Shannon, caused public resentment in Ireland. Reports of low fares following deregulation in the USA in 1978 also called into question the costs to an outer offshore island of the bilateral cartels which controlled aviation in Europe. A government emergency bill to fine, imprison and remove the licences of travel agents charging less than government approved fares was stalled by parliamentary opposition in 1984 and deregulation of the Dublin–London route followed in May 1986. Fares fell by 57 per cent on deregulation day, from £208 to £94.99. Passenger numbers in August 1987, the first full year of deregulation, were 92 per cent higher than in August 1985 and the route became the busiest international route in Europe and one of the busiest in the world. The OECD Report on Regulatory Reform in Ireland (2001) found that this deregulation 'provided a clear demonstration of the potential benefits of competition to all consumers in Ireland, having a significant effect on public opinion'.[25] The Ireland/United Kingdom airline deregulation of 1986 was also influential in providing a case study some 11 years before the full deregulation of European aviation in 1997.

IV. Privatising and Adjusting Europe's National Airlines

Ownership of national airlines moved from the public to the private sector. Goldman Sachs found that of 18 European national airlines only five were wholly in state ownership.[26] These were Air Malta, Czech Airlines, Malév, Olympic and TAP. The ownership structure of European national airlines is shown in Table 9.1.

The move away from full state ownership of European national airlines shown in Table 9.1 was influenced by factors such as the perceived high fares charged by national airlines in Europe compared to fares charged by charter airlines and new low-cost carriers in Europe since deregulation and perceived high fares in Europe compared to airlines based in North America and the Asia/Pacific regions. The difficulties of reforming state airlines in Europe were described as 'distressed state airline syndrome' by Rigas Doganis who has experience both as an academic specialising in air transport and as chief executive of Olympic Airways. Table 9.2 contrasts distressed state airline syndrome with the performance of Ryanair. Established in 1985 Ryanair was the first low-cost airline in Europe and in 2005 only the merged Air France–KLM group carried more international passengers in Europe.

Table 9.1 Ownership Structure of European National Airlines, 2004 (%)

	State	*Employees*	*Private*
Adria	–	6	94
Aer Lingus	85	15	–
Air Baltic	53	–	47
Air France*	44	11	45
Alitalia	62	12	27
Austrian	40	–	60
British Airways	–	10	90
Czech Airlines	100	–	–
Finnair	65	–	35
Iberia	–	9	91
KLM*	25	–	75
Lufthansa	–	1	99
Luxair	21	–	79
Malév	100	–	–
Olympic	100	–	–
SAS	54	–	46
TAP	100	–	–

Note: *The government of France announced in December 2004 its planned reduction of its holding in Air France–KLM from 44% to 18%.
Source: Elaborated by author based on Goldman Sachs International (2004), Appendix E.

Table 9.2   Distressed State Airline Syndrome and Ryanair Contrasted

'Distressed State Airline Syndrome'	*Ryanair*
Substantial losses	High profit margin
Overpoliticisation	Independent
Strong unions	Minimum unionisation
Overstaffing	High productivity, outsourcing
No clear development strategy	Cost reduction strategy
Bureaucratic management	Low management costs
Poor service quality	Eliminating expensive services

Source: Elaborated by author based on Doganis (2001) (column one) and author's analysis (column two).

Table 9.3   The Ryanair Deregulated Airline Product

1. Customer service items deleted:
   Sweets, newspapers, free food and beverage service, seat allocation, business class. More seats per aircraft and a higher load factor.

2. Airport service items:
   Secondary airports are typically used. No interlining or connection journey tickets are issued. Passengers and baggage must be checked in at each airport on a multi-sector journey. No airport lounge service.

3. Ticket restrictions:
   Tickets are not sold through travel agents. There are no airline sales offices. No frequent flyer programme. Stricter penalties for 'no show' passengers.

The seven problems identified by Doganis are illustrated by government interference in national airlines through the political appointment of directors and airline reliance on government financing. Union power, built up from the decades in which Europe's airlines colluded rather than competed, places legacy airlines at a serious productivity disadvantage compared to new entrant airlines. For example, Ryanair raised its number of passengers per staff member from 4890 in 1998 to over 11,200 in 2004/5. This contrasts with 1000 in Alitalia which has 20 million passengers and 20,000 staff.

The lack of a clear development strategy is illustrated by the failure of national airlines to exploit the opportunities of the single European market. The final problem included in the Doganis list of difficulties facing legacy airlines in Europe is poor service quality which is somewhat surprising considering the high fares and high costs involved. The Ryanair approach has been to redefine the traditional airline product in Europe and to unbundle services from the traditional package offered by the traditional airlines. The new airline product is illustrated in Table 9.3.

Table 9.3 shows some 17 aspects in which the Ryanair product is possibly inferior to the traditional European airline product. The tradeoff in choosing this product is major price savings and, perhaps surprisingly, some product improvements.

The 2004 average Ryanair fare was €40 one-way. This contrasts with the €264 fare on Dublin–London when Ryanair entered the route in 1986, or €448 at 2004 prices. The fare reduction is therefore 82 per cent. Larger reductions have been achieved on routes between Ireland and mainland Europe where in the early 1990s fares were as high as €825 between Dublin and Paris and Brussels. Product improvements by Ryanair include better punctuality, based on the use of secondary airports with less congestion and fewer bags lost because of the simple point-to-point product. Since the burden of no-show passengers is not borne by those who turn up at the airport the risk of being bumped from overbooked flights by traditional airlines does not arise for Ryanair passengers.

The service items dropped from the Ryanair product in Table 9.3 were acceptable to the 30 million passengers carried in 2004/5. From their fare savings passengers can buy newspapers and meals at points of departure or arrival. Secondary airports have proved a surprising success. On the longest deregulated route, Dublin–London, more than half the passengers now use Gatwick, Luton, Stansted and London City rather than the previously dominant Heathrow. Prestwick has a 64 per cent share of Dublin–Glasgow traffic and Charleroi has 66 per cent of Ireland–Brussels traffic. Skavsta and Vasteras have 37 per cent of London–Stockholm traffic and Torp has 26 per cent of London–Oslo traffic. Shorter walking times within terminals and between car and bus parks and terminals added to less confusion at small airports and less waiting around for bags on arrival have made small airports a, perhaps surprising, passenger benefit from deregulation.

Ticketing, sales and promotion staff were a major part of the excess costs of Europe's legacy airlines. The Internet removes this part of the cost base, including the expensive downtown sales offices of the airlines, and makes prices far more transparent than when travel agents had an incentive to sell the highest price fare in order to maximise commission or to route passengers through airlines offering larger 'over-ride' commissions.

As the country with the longest experience in Europe with the deregulation of scheduled airline services and the first with a new entrant airline to grow several multiples of its national airline, Ireland has the most experience with the implications for established national airlines and networks of airline deregulation.

V. The New Aviation Market and the Future of National Airlines – the Aer Lingus Response

Airline deregulation in Ireland is seen unequivocally to have been a huge benefit to the national economy. Tourist visits to Ireland, stubbornly stuck at 2 million for 20 years, have grown to over 7 million since access deregulation.

This sector employs more people than either Irish or foreign-owned industry. These national benefits so outweighed the costs of transforming Aer Lingus from a traditional national airline to a new competitive one that there was little doubt about the policy direction which the airline management would take. Losses of €52.1 million in 2001 became operating profits of €63.8 million in 2002, €83.0 million in 2003 and €107.0 million in 2004 through a strong survival plan. In 2004, however, €104 million was allocated to the cost of fundamental restructuring as an exceptional item in the Aer Lingus accounts. The year end staff numbers fell from 4281 in 2003 to 3906 in 2004.

Aer Lingus pursued a 'diversification programme' from 1966 because it was felt that aviation was inherently uneconomic and would require to be subsidised from a wide range of aviation-related, catering, hotel, engineering, travel agency and leisure activities. The official history of the airline lists 40 companies owned by Aer Lingus under its diversification programme (Share, Appendix 7). The current plan is to focus on the core airline business and the subsidiaries have been sold.

The steady reduction of the average Ryanair fare has left Aer Lingus with little option but to follow. The average Aer Lingus European fare fell from €103.10 in 2001 to €79.70 in 2004, a fall of 23 per cent, while average journey length increased by 36 per cent, from 597 km to 813 km. The Aer Lingus product now resembles the Ryanair one as shown in Table 9.3 with the exception that seat reservation has been retained for all passengers. In-flight service is provided on a pay basis. The airline found that unbundling service in business class from restricted access tickets has resulted in rarely more than ten passengers traveling business class and 50 per cent of flights had less than 5 business class passengers. A 24-hour help desk phone service for premium customers was closed at nights and evenings when there were typically only five callers. Business class passengers have declined by 50 per cent since October 2002 and will be retained only on routes such as London and Brussels. The frequent flyer club will be confined to business class passengers, with a target membership of 7000 high-yield customers. Travel agent commission has been reduced and the Aer Lingus.com website now accounts for 75 per cent of business.

Outsourcing is being sought in catering and handling with in-house catering being virtually eliminated. Airline staff numbers have been reduced by a series of survival plans from a peak of over 7000 to 4000, with a target in 2005 of 3000 and a recognition that further reductions towards 2000 will be required in a falling yields market. The carriage of 6.6 million passengers by 3000 staff will mean an annual 2200 passengers per staff member compared to 10500 at Ryanair and 6293 at Easyjet in 2003. Aer Lingus has just over 30 per cent of the market between Dublin and London compared to 46 per cent for Ryanair. Its Heathrow competitor on the route, British Midland, has also relaunched as a low-cost carrier.

Aer Lingus launched 36 new routes between 2002 and 2004. Its total route network increased from 42 to 65 routes in that period and the airline left the main internal Irish route, Dublin–Cork, and several UK provincial routes serving Ireland. The new routes are direct from Dublin and Cork to low-cost local airports in mainland Europe. The choice of low-cost airports allows the airline to achieve the economies of 25-minute turnaround while yields are better than feeding traffic through hubs. The airline sees some seven interline deals as likely in the future and will pursue its present low-cost policies while a member of the One World Alliance. Only 7 per cent of Aer Lingus passengers to New York are interline passengers booked through to the US airline networks. Many passengers instead make Internet bookings on point-to-point airlines such as Jet Blue. Some 30 per cent of Aer Lingus passengers at Heathrow are on interline journeys. This share is likely to decline with the development of more direct services from Ireland and increased use of Internet bookings.

The Aer Lingus 'virtual Ryanair' strategy is working in financial terms. The airline in 2004 had an operating margin of 11.8 per cent, the highest of Europe's legacy airlines. The annual reports for other legacy airlines in Europe show operating margins per airline as follows; British Airways 7.2 per cent, Air France 6.9 per cent, Lufthansa 5.6 per cent and SAS 2.9 per cent. The Aer Lingus load factor was 82 per cent. The Insead Report notes that 'low cost carriers such as Ryanair and easyJet had costs per ASK (available seat kilometer) as low as half that of full-service airlines' in 2002.[27] INSEAD also notes that the breakeven load factor, that is, the percentage of seats required to be sold in order to cover costs, is as low as 53 per cent for Ryanair, compared to 76 per cent for KLM and 68 per cent for Lufthansa.

VI. Transnationalisation, Irish Airlines and the Commercialisation of Aer Lingus

Table 9.4 contrasts the Irish aviation sector before deregulation, when Aer Lingus was a monopoly national airline in coordination with other European national airlines, and the free market situation since 1997.

As an outer offshore island in high fare coordination with other European airlines the development of Irish aviation was limited before deregulation, as shown in Table 9.4. By contrast, under deregulation only 44 of Ryanair's 220

Table 9.4   Passengers and Staff Employed, Irish Airlines, 1985/6 and 2004/5

		Passengers (m)	*Staff*
1985/6	Aer Lingus	2.3	6,500
2004/5	Ryanair	30.0	2,500
	Aer Lingus	7.0	4,200
	Cityjet	1.0	500
	Aer Arann	0.6	300
2004/5	Total	38.6	7,500

Source: Elaborated by author based on company annual reports.

routes in 2004/5 served Ireland. Only 2 of its 12 bases were in Ireland. Ryanair thus contrasts with the traditional national airline in availing itself of the market opportunities afforded by the single European market. It is the leading transnational airline in Europe. Most of its routes are between other EU countries and it also operates internal UK and Italian routes. Its bases outside Ireland included: Stansted (75 routes), Luton (12), Liverpool (13), Prestwick (17), Skavsta (12), Charleroi (11), Hahn (22), Bergamo (17), Ciampino (16) and Girona (22). Aer Lingus in the years since the opening up of the single market in 1997 and its 2001 reform package emphasised efficiency and the profitability of its network rather than exploitation of the single market. Its most likely expansion of transnational services is likely to be charter services from other EU countries to the US after liberalisation of this market in late 2006. The long-haul markets served by Aer Lingus from Dublin are New York, Boston, Chicago and Los Angeles, with a Dubai service starting in 2006. US routes accounted for 39 per cent of Aer Lingus passenger revenues in 2004. Long-haul markets served by feeder routes to a Dublin hub are likely to grow with liberalisation. A cautionary note is that other attempts by national airlines to serve routes outside their traditional bilateral agreements were unsuccessful, such as Lufthansa on Rome–Bari and Alitalia on Porto–Lisbon.

The Civil Aviation Authority analysis of the impact of liberalisation on aviation employment found that overall airline employment increased from 380,199 to 402,775 between 1992 and 2001, an increase of 6 per cent in 18 European countries examined.[28] The largest increase was in the UK where there were 27,811 extra employees, a 39 per cent increase. France had an increase of 8652 (14 per cent) and Spain 3898 (13 per cent). The countries which lost employment in aviation were Switzerland (–36 per cent), Portugal (–18 per cent), Greece (–48 per cent) and Belgium (–86 per cent). The CAA attributes the decline in aviation employment in these countries to 'downsizing or the collapse of the national carrier'.[29] Aviation employment in Ireland increased by 16 per cent.

Goldman Sachs states that 'we note that the European Commission actively promotes the idea of a consolidated European airline sector, based around British Airways, Lufthansa, and Air France. In our view this vision may be unrealistic and is based on the political aspiration of creating European "champions" as global leaders in the sector.'[30]

Taking the US precedent of the southwest case of a large 'home' liberalised market in Texas before the federal government deregulated interstate aviation, British Airways and Ryanair enjoy a similar advantage in Europe. Air France and Lufthansa have large home markets and their hubs at Paris and Frankfurt have strong intercontinental services. With London as the lead hub, Paris and Frankfurt are likely to increase their market shares at the expense of smaller hubs such as Brussels and Zurich.

Aer Lingus is an interesting case study of the evolution of a national airline from protectionism through regulatory capture to market adjustment and successful commercialisation. It has achieved the highest operating margin of Europe's legacy carriers while facing competition from Ryanair in many of its markets. In 2004 its profit after the allocation of €104 million for restructuring was a mere €1.2 million on a turnover of €907 million. The final steps from national airline and legacy carrier to commercialisation require the completion of restructuring without recurrence of the 2004 costs. The privatisation of Aer Lingus was announced in May 2005 and took place in September 2006.

Aer Lingus has made considerable progress in its reforms since 2001 and has successfully reinvented itself as a virtual low cost airline in competition with Ryanair on Ireland–UK routes while serving mostly different mainland European markets at falling fares. Aer Lingus management sees opportunities for the airline in a liberalised North Atlantic market, with the airline serving many more cities outside its present markets confined to New York, Boston, Chicago and Los Angeles. Success for Aer Lingus looked unlikely throughout the period from 1986, when it first faced new entrant competition from Ryanair on its major route, through to 2001 when it faced bankruptcy. The legacy of the extraordinary regulatory capture of the Department of Transport by Aer Lingus is a difficult one for management seeking to change the corporate culture of the airline. There have been frequent management changes since the mid-1990s. The government as owner of Aer Lingus has been heavily influenced by trade union opposition to change at the airline. Completing the successful commercialisation of Aer Lingus is on balance likely to succeed but there is no guarantee that the new owners will not face the same problems after privatisation.

Notes

1   Daly (1992) p. 5.
2   Guiomard (1995) p. 207.
3   Daly (1992) p. 41
4   Chubb (1970) p. 274.
5   Foy (1976) p. 23.
6   PDDE, Vol 63, Col. 2650 (1936).
7   PDDE, Vol. 214, Col. 974 (1965).
8   PDDE, Vol. 214, Col. 974 (1965).
9   Geary and Stark (2002) p. 927.
10 Cullen (1972) p. 206.
11 Share (1988) p. 3.
12 Ibid. p. 3.
13 Ibid. p. 69.
14 Ibid. p. 71.
15 Ibid. p. 70.
16 Ibid. p. 22.
17 Ibid. p. 22
18 FitzGerald (1962) p. 3.
19 Ibid. p. 15.
20 Ibid. p. 2.
21 Daly (1992) p. 178.

22   Keogh (1994) p. 331.
23   Lee (1989) p. 322.
24   Jakobsen (1984) p. 83.
25   OECD (2001) p. 29.
26   Goldman Sachs International (2004).
27   INSEAD (2003) p. 15.
28   Civil Aviation Authority (2004).
29   Civil Aviation Authority (2004).
30   Goldman Sachs International (2004) p. 14.

References

Barrett, S.D. (1987) *Flying High, Airline Price and European Regulation* (London: Adam Smith Institute).

Barrett, S.D. (2004a) *Privatisation in Ireland*, CESIFO Working Paper 1170.

Barrett, S.D. (2004b) 'The Sustainability of the Ryanair Model', *International Journal of Transport Management*, 2, pp. 89–98.

Chubb, B. (1970) *The Government and Politics of Ireland* (London: Longman).

Civil Aviation Authority (1987) *Competition on the Main Domestic Trunk Routes*, CAA Paper 87005.

Civil Aviation Authority (2004) *The Effect of Liberalisation on Aviation Employment*, CAA Paper 749.

Cullen, L.M. (1972) *An Economic History of Ireland since 1660* (Dublin: Gill and Macmillan).

Daly, M. (1992) *Industrial Development and Irish National Identity, 1922–39* (Dublin: Gill and Macmillan).

Dargan, M. (Chairman) (1979) *Report of the Posts and Telegraphs Review Group* (Dublin: Government Publications) ('The Dargan Report').

Doganis, R. (2001) *The Airline Business in the 21st Century* (Routledge).

FitzGerald, G. (1962) *State Sponsored Bodies* (Dublin: Institute of Public Administration).

Foy, M. (1976) *The Sugar Industry in Ireland* (Dublin: The Sugar Company).

Geary, F., and T. Stark (2002) 'Ireland's Post-Famine Economic Growth', *Economic Journal* (October) pp. 919–35.

Goldman Sachs International (2004) *Evaluation of Ownership Options Regarding Aer Lingus Group* (Dublin: Department of Transport).

Guiomard, C. (1995) *The Irish Disease* (Dublin: Oaktree).

ICAO (annual) *Surveys of International Fares and Rates* (Montreal: ICAO, various years).

INSEAD (2003) *Note on the European Airline Industry* (Fontainebleau: INSEAD).

Jakobsen, E. (Chairman) (1984) *Report of the Inquiry into Electricity Prices* (Dublin: Government Publications) ('The Jakobsen Report').

Keogh, D. (1994) *Twentieth-Century Ireland: Nation and State* (Dublin: Gill and Macmillan).

Lee, J.J. (1989) *Ireland 1912–1985* (Cambridge University Press).

OECD (2001) *Regulatory Reform in Ireland* (Paris: OECD).

Parliamentary Debates Dail Eireann (PDDE) (various years) *Parliamentary Debates*, especially Vol. 63, Col. 2650 (1936); Vol. 214, Col. 974 (1965) (Dublin: Dail Eireann).

Share, B. (1988) *The Flight of the Iolar: The Aer Lingus Experience 1936–1986* (Dublin: Gill and Macmillan).

10

Scandinavian Experiences of Network Industries: Public Enterprises and Changing Welfare Policies, 1950–2005

Lena Andersson-Skog and Thomas Pettersson

Introduction

Large welfare systems, small public enterprise sectors, a large degree of local autonomy and a long tradition of social democratic governments are a common description of the Scandinavian countries.[1] However, Scandinavian experiences of network industries do not easily fit into the general picture of the 'Scandinavian model'. In most European countries, and perhaps especially in Scandinavia, welfare policies have been integrated into transport policy and regulation, so that explicit concerns for regional development were considered. But the generalisation to a Scandinavian model sometimes colours the understanding of publicly regulated sectors, such as the network industries. It is clear that, at different times, various paths have been chosen by Denmark, Sweden and Norway in regulating their respective network industries.[2] However, most of these similarities and differences have not been examined over time, but rather regarded as rigid general frameworks.[3] The aim of this chapter is to examine the development of public enterprises in two Scandinavian network industries, international civil aviation and railways, with an emphasis on regulatory development paths and performance in national and international markets. Transnationalisation and integration, as well as ownership and governance, are considered as major driving forces in these processes. The shift from a Keynesian to a Schumpeterian welfare model and its impact on these network industries will also be examined with regard to the organisation and transformation of public enterprises. We will among other things argue that the overall changes in welfare policy also shifted the government's focus from subsidising operations to investments in infrastructure in the network industries.

I. Public Enterprises in the Network Industries – The Best or Worst of Both Worlds?

State intervention in the economy was once again put on the agenda in the 1950s. In the aftermath of the Second World War most countries had to adapt to the new economic, social and political circumstances. Public enterprises in a number of industries were established in many countries, sometimes as a result of nationalisation, and sometimes they were founded as a state company or public utility. In the transport industry generally the postwar era witnessed a strong tendency towards political regulation and nationalisation. This can be explained largely by the changing competition that existed in the transport market, primarily between rail and road, but also between land and water transport. Railways, for instance, had faced stiffening competition during the interwar period, but had survived intact throughout the war. In the face of changing demands in the late 1940s, however, railways required investment and increased levels of organisational efficiency. Nationalisation was an answer to these problems in many countries. A public enterprise solution in this case seemed to ensure both long-run safety capital provision as well as public accountability.

Naturally, questions of ownership and political power affected the way the transport industries were regulated. The general discourse on welfare, rights and obligations at the societal level resulted in political demands in terms of tax spending, investment in infrastructure and an expansion of the health care sector. A striking example from Swedish transport policy during the 1940s was the urge in all official reports to 'connect Sweden'. This meant that the state was responsible for increasing accessibility in and between all regions across all transport industries. To a large extent, this can be understood as traditional political interest groups disguising their attempts to allocate resources to a specific region.[4]

Transport Policy as Welfare Policy?

Today there is a lively international scholarly debate concerning the shift from a Keynesian to a Schumpeterian welfare state model.[5] In the Keynesian model the government uses the welfare state to balance changes in the business cycle. In the Schumpterian model, on the other hand, the government must not interfere in the functioning of markets, for example by trying to reduce unemployment. Moreover the Schumpterian welfare model recommends an independent central bank. In Scandinavia national governments have used the transport sector as an instrument of welfare policy, emphasising regional equality such as equal transport conditions, access to communication services, and so on.[6] This has been achieved via public investments in infrastructure, such as roads, railways and airports, or through subsidies to passenger traffic and goods transportation. Thus it is infrastructure rather than individual enterprises or their operations which has been at the centre of transport policy. Examples of this Keynesian strategy include the investment in new regional railways and the construction of regional airports in Sweden from the late 1980s. At the same time, however, the emergence of a more Schumpetarian-oriented policy is apparent, for example, in post-1993 Swedish telecommunications policy when deregulation created a formal market that was in practice still controlled by the public enterprise Telia. In 1998 Parliament had to reinforce deregulation by actually privatising Telia and at the same time strengthening the role of the government agency in control of regulation.[7] The different strategies deployed across Scandinavian countries to regulate investments in, and ownership of, the 3G networks are other examples of the emphasis upon services rather than enterprises. The Swedish government awarded concessions to those companies that promised to invest in 3G infrastructures in sparsely populated areas.

These patterns seem to be connected to the scale and scope of public enterprises in different sectors. Tightly coupled national networks, such as railways and electrical systems, were protected over the long term from deregulation and privatisation. The idea of public enterprise as the optimal organisation of the industry remained very strong. Loosely coupled national networks, however, such as aviation, were easier to deregulate and to incorporate into national and international private enterprises.[8] The scope of public enterprises can be categorised in accordance with various forms of governance. A major dividing line in terms of the political ambitions concerning public enterprises is whether they are to be subsidised or expected to deliver revenue. Another important issue is whether the public enterprise is expected to be reactive to demand, or active ahead of demand. A third difference is between backward and forward linkages. It is, for example, easier for regional interests to argue for government support of a visible infrastructure with strong regional backward linkages. The outcome of forward linkages is to be found in the future and, as such, is more difficult to justify as a political resource. It is important to bear in mind that this governance structure is the result of institutionalised ownership and political legacies. It also, however, highlights a potential tension between political regulation and market development in regulating scale and scope for a specific public enterprise. On the other hand, economic performance and technological development may be hampered by political control or lack of expertise if operated by the state.

In Scandinavia we can also see a dual development from the 1950s. On the one hand, there is increasing political influence in the transport sector through a more extended and detailed regulatory process. On the other hand, from the 1980s transport policy has become increasingly influenced by market principles and, most recently, by consumer demand.

II. Public Enterprises in Scandinavian Network Industries – The Case of Railways and Civil Aviation

In the nineteenth century, when national transport infrastructures were constructed, Foreign Direct Investment (FDI) in infrastructure was scarce in the Scandinavian countries. Instead, the respective state and private interests cooperated in raising capital or in regulating performance and operation. In both Norway and Sweden private and state interests commenced railway construction in the 1850s. In Norway Norske Statsbaner (NSB) was established in 1854, and Statens Järnvägar (SJ) was set up in Sweden in 1856. In Denmark the state railway administration Danske Statsbaner (DSB) was established as late as 1885 as a result of the bankruptcy of a number of private railway companies that the state took over. A rare but striking example of transnational cooperation is the Great Nordic Telegraph Company, established in 1869, which was a private company which ran the concession granted by national governments to take care of international telegraph communication to and from Scandinavia.[9] In most other cases each country created their own infrastructures which were owned in different proportions by state and private interests. Private interests and the state cooperated and competed in building railways and telephone networks. From the 1920s the state got the upper hand and a long reign of strong national political regulation and state-run national transport administration dominated most sectors from road management to telephones. This was the case in the railway sector where nationalisations took place between the 1920s and the 1950s. This was also true for the telephone sector which became state-owned during the same period.[10] The era of dual ownership was thus transformed into the national governance of public enterprises. A specific feature, especially in Sweden, was the formation of sector-specific administrative agencies under political regulatory bodies, governed by a staff of experts and technical specialists who acted at their own discretion on a day-to-day basis. This created strong, independent national public enterprises, each the ruler at home and subject to varying degrees of independence from government. One important exception, however, was the formation of Scandinavian international civil aviation after 1945. The founding of Scandinavian Airlines Systems (SAS) in 1946 continued a tradition of trans-Scandinavian cooperation in the network industries after the Second World War.[11]

II.i Civil Aviation in Scandinavia

Politics and economics in national and international aviation have, since the First World War, continuously been in conflict. Airlines, like any other network industry, are dependent on network externalities, which result in high barriers to market entry and high fixed costs: the textbook definition of a natural monopoly.[12] In practice the airline industry has been regarded as a natural monopoly and this has, together with national concerns about being excluded from international airline networks, shaped national and international policies governing the industry. Therefore the so-called national 'flag-carriers' have not traditionally been operated as commercial enterprises geared towards markets and consumer demand, nor have they been managed entirely in the public interest like the state-owned railways. This has been particularly true of European airline carriers which have been subsidised by national governments for a long time under conditions that minimised competition and cost savings and, as a consequence, allowed carriers to charge relatively high fares compared to the American experience. A history of strong European national concern for the industry resulted in a generally low level of trans-nationalisation and integration, together with strong direct government influence until the 1980s, especially if compared with the American case.[13] From the late 1980s national airline industries were deregulated. The new market-liberal regulations forced SAS, for example, to negotiate mergers with Dutch KLM, Austrian Airlines and Swissair, though none of these mergers were finally realised. SAS is now, instead, part of the Star Alliance together with Lufthansa, Air Canada, United Airlines and others. However, as a consequence of historical developments European airlines and governments faced a unique situation during the liberalisation policies of the 1980s and 1990s compared to other countries. It is interesting to enquire how the Scandinavian countries as early as the 1940s managed to blend private and public interests in the formation of a Scandinavian transnational airline industry in contrast to the European context. Analysis of this Scandinavian 'joint venture' offers a fruitful analysis of multinational collaboration within an international network industry that otherwise favoured national political concerns and public monopolies.

II.ii   Civil Aviation and Regulations in Scandinavia – Forward Linkages and Transnational Markets

Comprehensive economic regulation of the international airline industry began in the aftermath of the Second World War when more than 50 countries, including the Scandinavian ones, attended a convention in Chicago and agreed on the basic regulations for international aviation.[14] An international division of regulation was also established. National governments concluded bilateral agreements to regulate airport entry and capacity, while the authority for setting fares and terms of service in international markets was delegated to the airlines through the International Air Transport Association (IATA). Combined, the bilateral agreements and IATA supported national airline monopolies connected to the strictly regulated international market. In Europe the national 'flag carrier' became the dominant model.[15] However, in Scandinavia civil aviation was organised differently. The first step towards Scandinavian collaboration in the international civil aviation industry was taken in 1946 when the Scandinavian governments agreed to merge the existing national airlines into SAS.[16] During the first five years the SAS consortium only handled transatlantic traffic. On other international routes and in domestic markets, national airlines still competed until the 1950s, when SAS became the only international Scandinavian carrier. Technological break-throughs during the Second World War laid the foundations for transatlantic traffic and the creation of transcontinental routes and markets, which was the driving force for Scandinavian countries to pool their resources. The shares were divided between Scandinavian governments and private shareholders. In 2005 the Swedish state owned 21.4 per cent of the shares, the Danish and Norwegian states each owned 14.3 per cent, while private investors owned the remaining 50 per cent. With 21 million passengers a year SAS is one of the largest airlines in Europe and the 15th largest in the world. It has had a mix of public and private ownership from its beginnings. Small domestic markets, together with influences from private business interests, explain why the Scandinavian countries pooled their resources as early as the 1940s. Representatives from the three Scandinavian countries had little to offer other countries' airline companies in terms of traffic flows due to their relatively small populations. This was a crucial point since the Chicago Convention stated that international airline routes were derived from bilateral agreements on traffic flows and the pooling of revenues. Although the governments were eager to protect the national interest and played an active role in the negotiations, industrialists such as Marcus Wallenberg (Sweden), Thomas S. Falck (Norway) and Per Kampmann (Denmark) also played key roles in hammering out the final agreement. SAS's mix of public and private management and ownership is unique in the international context and was an important factor in facilitating international integration at later stages, which will be shown below. The SAS joint venture also increased the levels of integration and transnationalisation in other areas. There were, for example, consequences for labour market policy in Scandinavian countries when the world's first international collective labour market agreement was struck in 1951. SAS and the trade unions from each country negotiated the same salaries and benefits for all SAS employees in the three countries.

By the late 1950s the arrival of jet aircraft quickly raised the total supply of tonne kilometres above demand and hit the airlines' balance sheets hard. SAS as a transnational company was questioned in the late 1950s when it, like all other flag carriers, showed a large deficit. The reorganisation of SAS changed the relationship between the company and national governments. The regional (national) heads, who had previously been expected to represent their country in SAS, would now have the reverse function: to represent SAS in their respective countries. The ability to quickly reorganise and adapt to the new circumstances resulted in a relatively quick return to profitability. In 1963 SAS was the first airline to return to profitability among airlines that had to deal with the introduction of jet aircraft. The oil crisis in the 1970s was the next major challenge to the aviation industry. The airlines within IATA lost a combined total of US $400 million in 1971 and US $1400 million in 1974 in current prices. SAS, however, managed remarkably well. With the exception of 1972 the company showed net profits every year during the oil crisis. This was mainly due to the flexible composition of the fleet of aircrafts. Thus SAS managed to balance the overall stagnation of the economy with a more efficient use of the fleet compared to its competition.

The next major challenge to national airlines came in the 1980s when new, more liberal rules were introduced in the aviation markets. In Europe this process started in 1986 when the European Court of Justice ruled that the competition rules in the Treaty of Rome also applied to air transport. In 1986 the Commission formally charged ten airlines with infringement of competition rules. Among other things British Airways was forced to give up certain routes.[17] In 1989 the Court decided to extend competition rules to international flights between EC members and other states. Furthermore these new rules aimed at creating a single air market within the EEC. All traffic within and between member states was now considered as domestic traffic, which gave states and their flag carriers little room for defining the national interest.[18]

In 2004 SAS established three independent national companies under the SAS consortium with separate economic responsibilities. The SAS board also decided to establish wholly owned subsidiaries of the SAS consortium in Norway, Denmark and Sweden to conduct the airline operations that the consortium undertook through its regional business units. These organisational changes were motivated by economic difficulties following the terrorist attacks on September 11, as well as growing competition from so-called 'low-cost carriers' from the 1990s.

Over the years SAS has managed to adapt to changing competitive circumstances. In 1952 it was the first airline in the world to introduce 'Tourist Class', a discounted ticket with certain conditions. The entire airline industry followed suit. In the 1960s SAS became the first airline in the world to fly over the North Pole. At the beginning of the 1980s it launched a new service concept for business travel, 'SAS Euro Class', and as a consequence of this innovation received the 'Airline of the Year Award' in 1984.

To summarise the historical development one can argue that both private and public actors and ownership were critical components during the formation and further development of SAS. This background can help explain how SAS managed to respond to rapid changes in aircraft technology such as in the early 1960s when other airliners were less profitable. This special mix of both private and public interests makes civil aviation in Scandinavia extraordinary in comparison with other public enterprises in the network industries. A combination of public and private transnational ownership is therefore a unique and historically important characteristic of SAS in an international perspective.[19]

II.iii Railways in Scandinavia

Even though competition from cars affected both performance and profitability in the railway sector, the Scandinavian railway administrations faced somewhat different challenges from the 1950s. In Denmark the short distances between the major cities had always made road transport a harsh competitor. Investments in railways were delayed and, along with only a few other European countries, the Danish main railways were not electrified in the late 1970s.[20] However, in the 1980s a plan to modernise the Danish railway system was agreed upon which entailed the electrification of main lines and investment in new track and railway bridges. Moreover in 2001 a bridge connection to Sweden, the so-called Öresundsbron, was opened. During the 1990s competitive national and international passenger traffic was proclaimed the key objective for DSB. In 1997 DSB was converted into a private limited company with responsibility for operations, whereas the rail administration remained a public utility.

In Norway restrictions on car imports until 1960 postponed the most obvious signs of competition in the transport market but by the 1960s it became clear that the heyday of railways was over.[21] In 1964 parliament decided on a plan to stimulate and invest in roads and road traffic and, a few years later, questions about dividing the railway system into profitable and unprofitable lines were discussed. In 1996 NSB was divided into a rail administration and a state company, NSB BA, with responsibility for traffic operations. In 2002 the latter was converted into a private limited company owned by the Norwegian Ministry of Transport and Communications. In the 1990s NSB and SJ cooperated both in the passenger market, on the lines Oslo–Stockholm and Oslo–Copenhagen, and in transnational freight transport.

In Sweden the nationalisation of the vast private railway network was completed in 1952. From this time onwards 25 per cent of the railway network was closed down until 1972.[22] Despite this attempt to improve performance from 1958 subsidies were paid to keep operations running. In the 1980s these subsidies amounted to SEK 1 billion annually, but losses continued to grow. In an attempt to create a competitive state railway in 1988 SJ was divided into a national rail administration, Banverket, and a public enterprise, SJ, in charge of traffic on the main lines.

This brief overview shows that there are several similarities in the steps taken by the respective Scandinavian countries. In the 1990s, due to investments in infrastructure linking Denmark, Sweden and Norway, integration and cooperation as well as competition grew – but without transnational ownership. Instead national governments met market demand with national solutions. However, the Swedish trajectory stands out for its radical institutional changes. Great Britain and Sweden are the first European countries to have abolished the railway monopoly. The shift in Swedish railway policy from that of a public enterprise with far-reaching social responsibilities in the 1950s to a situation in 2005 with a national rail administration, a public transport administration with socioeconomic responsibilities and a handful of national companies, where SJ handles passenger traffic as a competitive national limited company, requires further analysis.

II.iv   Railways and Regulations in Scandinavia – From Backward Linkages to Emerging Transnational Markets

In 1963 a decision was taken by the Swedish parliament aimed at full cost coverage in each traffic sector. Even though the principle was never implemented, and in fact was changed to marginal pricing in 1979, it raised the questions of how and which social cost responsibilities and equal transport preconditions should be upheld. The traffic policy decision entailed the division of the railway network into profitable commercial railway networks and unprofitable low-traffic networks where the state covered the losses. The goal was for SJ to attain a predefined return requirement on the commercial part and to minimise losses on the low-traffic network.[23] From this time onwards the state wanted to obtain greater insight into SJ's operations. As a consequence, former sector-specific experts and railway managers were replaced by politically appointed civil servants, amongst other things. Pricing was also altered: first, freight transport was deregulated and later, passenger traffic in order to make competition with civil air and bus transport possible.[24]

In 1988 more radical changes were introduced. SJ was divided into a public enterprise responsible for rail traffic and a rail administration in charge of infrastructure. The state took over responsibility for tracks through the rail administration and SJ had to pay a fee in order to gain access to the tracks. Planning for new investments from now on officially would have to have a socioeconomic focus and was to be carried out by the Rail Administration and its decentralised regional departments. This accelerated the need for new railway lines and, from the beginning of the 1990s, regional interest groups siding with regional Rail Administration departments succeeded in obtaining the capital for new regional railways for fast speed trains.[25] In 1994 the government also appointed a private consortium, partly foreign, which won the contract to build and operate the new railway line between Arlanda International Airport and Stockholm city.

The first steps towards competition on the railway network were also taken in the decision of 1988. The state bought selected unprofitable inter-regional traffic through the County Public Transport Administration (CPTA), which was granted trafficking rights in passenger traffic on regional branch lines. CPTA could procure this traffic in competition, but it was not until 2000 that a handful of private operators gained the contract in competition with SJ.[26] From 1995 a parliamentary decision opened up the railway network to free competition for freight and passengers. From then on, also CPTA could operate traffic on the trunk lines in the respective counties. As a result of this possibility SJ lost commuter traffic in Stockholm in 2000 to a company owned partly by the French state and partly by Swedish private interests. So far, changes have resulted in the reconstruction of the existing traffic in the hands of new operators and not in new traffic flows, which was one of the main objectives behind the change.

In 1998 parliament took yet another decision on transport policy to enhance deregulation and competition. In 1999 a new authority, the National Public Transport Agency, Rikstrafiken, was set up to manage the procurement of socioeconomically justified inter-regional public transport, including railways. The government authorised transport procurement to the amount of SEK 3.7 billion over a five-year period. In 2003 rail transport accounted for roughly SEK 443 million.[27]

In 2001 SJ was converted into six independent companies in order to be able to compete under the same conditions as other actors on the market and to be free to cooperate and form international alliances. The limited company form also highlights the focus on profitable business. Travel and transport consumer satisfaction is currently the clearly defined goal for SJ AB, the company running passenger traffic. SJ Green Cargo AB manages freight traffic.

Market deregulation and the exposure of national companies to competition is a necessary stage in the railways encompassed by the common market and increases their possibilities of competing with transnational truck transport in Europe. Still, a lot remains to be accomplished regarding transnational integration in the European railway network. The Swedish example, however, shows that a radical change towards the liberalisation of institutional frameworks and organisation is possible in combination with a social welfare policy that remains in state hands.

Conclusions

From the 1980s the state-dominated regulatory order in the Scandinavian network industries started to erode. One major driving force was the consolidation of what later became the European Union (EU). From the early 1970s Denmark was a full member of the European cooperation, whereas Norway and Sweden were associated through special agreements, that is, the European Economic Area agreements. Economic regulation enforced competition on equal terms, which affected the economic environment for public enterprises. Technological development became increasingly international, which also put pressure on the infrastructure industries. Political and economic cooperation within the EU created a general move towards integration in different respects. This gave national governments fewer opportunities to argue for public economy considerations, such as subsidies or welfare effects from investments.

Welfare policies generally started to change in many areas in Scandinavian countries from the 1990s. Direct government support to public enterprises eroded, giving way to market-oriented principles regarding financial solutions and earning capacity. Another definite change was the movement from nationally decided levels of social support or other benefits to more individually oriented solutions decided on a local level. An important ideological change concerned what constituted a natural monopoly. Traditionally, network industries were often regarded as natural monopolies and, as such, could be suitably organised as public enterprises. In the more recent period market principles were considered as the most effective way of organising network industries. Together these changes had a major impact on the way the public enterprises in the network industries were organised and governed. They also represented indications of a shift from a Keynesian to a Schumpeterian welfare regime and, at the same time, a move from national to European markets, accompanied by a shift from public economy to market values.

Is it possible for national governments to use public enterprises to obtain Keynesian welfare goals? Or have market integration and the transnationalisation of organisations rendered national autonomy outdated? It is argued that there still exist dominant Keynesian features in the investment policies in infrastructure in the Scandinavian countries that give governments a platform for political initiatives. Backward linkages in the network industries are still important arguments for publicly financed infrastructure investments, whereas forward linkages, which are dependent on the flow in the networks, have been connected to private business. Moreover the decision-making process is no longer inevitably national, but perhaps more often regional or European in its origin. At the same time, a general Schumpeterian pattern in the changes to public network enterprises for the last 25 years is that, whereas investments in infrastructure still reflect Keynesian principles, the welfare principles guiding the public enterprises nowadays are Schumpeterian. This divide between infrastructure and societal responsibility on the one hand and the profitability of operations on the other constitutes a definitive change in the Scandinavian welfare policy's consequences for network industries as it has been understood over the last 50 years. To sum up, it has been shown that there has been a strong connection between changes in overall national welfare ideologies and organisations on one hand and changes in public enterprises in the network industries on the other, although this policy shift has not changed all aspects of public enterprise. Public enterprise may be the best or worst of all worlds – as private enterprise may be. The important thing to keep in mind is that performance and outcome depend on the institutions that govern the sectors in question.

Notes

1   Esping-Andersen (1990).
2   Andersson-Skog (2000).
3   Thue (1995); Kaijser (1999).
4   Andersson-Skog (2001) and Andersson (2004).
5   For a general discussion, see Torfing (1999); Cox (2001); and Blyth (2001).
6   Regional interests have always been of importance, see for instance Hodne (1988).
7   Murhem (2003).
8   There are exceptions. For example an attempted merger in the late 1990s between the Swedish and Norwegian telecommunications enterprises failed. A similar attempt succeeded between the Swedish and Finnish companies.
9   Jacobsen (1997).
10   Andersson-Skog (2000).
11   Buraas (1979).
12   Button (1991).
13   Sochor (1991) pp. 187.
14   Sochor (1991) pp. 16–21.
15   Lyth (1997) p. 175.
16   The paragraph on SAS is based mainly upon Buraas (1979).

142   *Transforming Public Enterprise in Europe and North America*

17 Sochor (1991) p. 184.
18 Sochor (1991) p. 189.
19 Ottosson (2003) p. 95.
20 The paragraph on Denmark is based mainly upon Ousager (1988), Johansen (1997) and Nørgaard Olesen (2000).
21 The paragraph on Norway is based on Børrehaug Hansen, Gundersen and Sundin (1980) and Gulowsen et al. (2004).
22 Andersson-Skog (1993).
23 Andersson-Skog (1993) pp. 162–9.
24 Ibid.
25 Carlsson (2001) and Andersson (2004).
26 Alexandersson, Hultén, Nordenlöw and Ehrling (2000).
27 Rikstrafiken (2003).

References

Alexandersson, G., S. Hultén, L. Nordenlöw and G. Ehrling (2000) 'Spåren efter avregleringen', KFB-rapport 2000:25 (Stockholm: KFB/Banverket).
Andersson, F. (2004) 'Mot framtiden på gamla spår? Regionala intressegrupper och beslutsprocesser kring kustjärnvägarna i Norrland under 1900-talet', *Umeå Studies in Economic History*, no. 28.
Andersson-Skog, L. (1993) 'Såsom allmäna inrättningar till gagnet, men affärsföretag till namnet. SJ, järnvägspolitiken och den ekonomiska omvandlingen sedan 1920', *Umeå Studies in Economic History*, no. 17.
Andersson-Skog, L. (2000) 'National Patterns and the Regulation of Railways and Telephony in the Nordic Countries up to 1950', in *Scandinavian Economic History Review*, no. 2.
Andersson-Skog, L. (2001) 'Compensating the Periphery – Railways and Interest Groups in Northern Sweden', in L. Magnusson and J. Ottosson, (eds), *New Perspectives on Interest Groups and the State* (Cheltenham: Edward Elgar).
Blyth, M. (2001) 'The Transformation of the Swedish Model. Economic Ideas, Distributional Conflict, and Institutional Change', *World Politics*, 54 (October) pp. 1–26.
Buraas, A. (1979) *The SAS Saga. A History of Scandinavian Airlines Systems* (Oslo: SAS).
Button, K. (1990) *Airline Deregulation: International Experiences* (New York University Press).
Børrehaug Hansen, T., H. Gundersen and S. Sundin (1980) *Jernbanen i Norge* (Oslo).
Carlsson, M. (2001) 'Det regionala särintresset och staten. En studie av beslutsprocesserna kring Mälarbanan och Svealandsbanan 1983–1992', *Uppsala Studies in Economic History*, no. 53.
Clifton, J., F. Comín and D. Díaz Fuentes (2003) *Privatisation in the European Union. Public Enterprises and Integration* (Kluwer Academic Press: Dordrecht).
Cox, R.H. (2001) 'The Social Construction of an Imperative. Why Social Reform Happened in Denmark and the Netherlands But Not in Germany', *World Politics*, 53 (April) pp. 463–98.
Esping-Andersen, G. (1990) *The Three Worlds of Welfare Capitalism* (Cambridge: Polity Press).
Gulowsen, J., H. Ryggvik and T. Bergh (2004) *Jernbanen i Norge 1854–2004* (Bergen: Vigmostad and Bjørke).
Hodne, F. (1988) *Statens grunnlagsinvesteringer. Stortingssalen som markedsplass 1849–1914* (Oslo: Universitetsforlaget).

Jacobsen, K. (1997) 'The Great Northern Telegraph Company. A Danish Company in the Service of Globalisation since 1869', in S. Tønnesson, J. Koponen, N. Steensgaard and T. Svensson (eds), *Between National Histories and Global History* (Helsinki: Finska Historiska Sanfundet) pp. 179–197.

Johansen, H.C. (1997) *Jernbanerne i bilismens skygge 1950–1997*, part III (Copenhagen).

Kaijser, A. (1999) 'The Helping Hand. In Search of a Swedish Institutional Regime for Infrastructural Systems', in L. Andersson-Skog and O. Krantz (eds), *Institutions in the Transport and Communications Industries. State and Private Actors in the Making of Institutional Patterns, 1850–1990* (Canton MA: Science History Publications).

Lyth, P. (1997) 'Institutional Change and European Air Transport 1910–1985', in L. Magnusson and J. Ottosson (eds), *Evolutionary Economics and Path Dependence* (Cheltenham: Edward Elgar).

Murhem, S. (2003) 'Turning to Europe. A New Swedish Industrial Relations Regime in the 1990s', in *Uppsala Studies in Economic History*, no. 68.

Nørgaard Olesen, M. (2000) *Danske jernbaner gennem tiderne* (Lamberth).

Ottosson, J. (2003) 'Staten och kapitalet – SAS', in Y. Hasselberg and P. Hedberg (eds), *I samma båt. Uppsatser i finans- och företagshistoria tillägnade Mats Larsson* (Stockholm).

Ousager, S. (1988) *Politikk på skinner. Lokalbanesporsmålet og Nordfyns privatbaner i dansk trafikpolitik ca 1920–1970* (Odense).

Rikstrafiken (2003) *Annual Report* (Stockholm).

Sochor, E. (1991) *The Politics of International Aviation* (Basingstoke).

Thue, L. (1995) 'Electricity Rules – The Formation and the Development of Nordic Electricity Regimes', in A. Kaijser and M. Hedin (eds), *Nordic Energy Systems. Historical Perspectives and Current Issues* (Canton MA: Science History Publications).

Torfing, J. (1999) 'Towards a Schumpeterian Workfare Postnational Regime: Path-Shaping and Path-Dependency in Danish Welfare State Reform', *Economy and Society*, 28 (3) pp. 369–402.

11

Ownership and Transnationalisation in the Benelux: The Case of Belgian Railways, 1834–2004

Frans Buelens, Julien van den Broeck and Hans Willems

Introduction

At the beginning of the twenty-first century debates on the transformation of state-owned enterprises focus on rapid changes in ownership, as well as processes of the transnationalisation of previously nationally based enterprises into European or global networks. In the Benelux area this process is evident in many sectors, including communications and public utilities. It is, however, perhaps best reflected in the transportation sector, in which railways play a key role. The aim of this chapter therefore is to shed new light on key developments by examining this network in historical perspective. The case of the Belgian railway system was selected because the railways have played a central role for Belgian state companies for nearly two centuries.[1] The Belgian national railroads are not only the oldest state-owned company but they are also the most important public enterprise. Moreover historical analysis is highly valuable when discussing contemporary debates on the railways. In recent years the Belgian National Railway Company (Nationale Maatschappij der Belgische Spoorwegen – NMBS) has also been affected by the European debate on privatisation and transnationalisation of public companies; in that respect some important steps have already been taken. Railways constitute an important actor among network services such as transport, electricity, gas, water or telecommunications, as seen in Table 11.1. In 2003 NMBS was the biggest company measured by staff, followed by Belgacom (telecoms) and Electrabel (electricity). NMBS was the third company as far as sales are concerned. In recent years tremendous changes have occurred in all these sectors. In the telecom sector it was state-owned Belgacom (former RTT, which changed its name to Belgacom in 1992) that had a strong position; as a state company it was already highly profitable at the time and it adapted quite well to new business conditions and new competitors such as Mobistar. Belgacom became one of the strongest European telecom companies at the beginning of the twenty-first century. In electricity a private monopoly exercised by Electrabel – which was acquired by the French holding company Suez – continued for years, Distrigaz, the Belgian state-owned gas company, was

Table 11.1   Largest Home-Based Belgian TNCs in Network Services, 2003

Company	Industry	Sales*	Employees
NMBS	Railways	5,009	56,557
Belgacom	Telecommunications	5,377	17,541
Electrabel	Electricity, gas and water	10,845	17,360
Mobistar	Telecommunications	1,160	1,676
Distrigaz	Electricity, gas and water	3,882	88

Note: * Millions of euros.
Source: UNCTAD, World Investment Report, 2005.

privatised too, split into Distrigaz and Fluxys. Again, Suez acquired a major stake in both. In the course of a decade all these companies have witnessed tremendous changes as they have adapted to new European conditions.[2]

Belgium was the first country on the European continent to follow Britain in constructing a national railway network in the 1830s and was also among the first to embrace industrialisation.[3] Other countries would follow. Only one decade later the country was equipped with a national railway system that served at the same time as an international transit system.[4] The network was essentially state-owned but after a while Belgium became an interesting laboratory where private railway companies coexisted alongside the state railway system.[5] This situation continued until the end of the nineteenth century, after which the state gradually embarked on a programme to take over the private railway companies. In the first half of the twentieth century this situation changed dramatically, as new, competitive means of transport were introduced. Railways had existed for almost a century enjoying a near-monopoly environment; they were then faced with operating in a competitive environment where other modes of transport offered superior alternatives for customers. A secular decline set in: investments and market shares diminished. It was only during the last two decades of the twentieth century that renewed attention was paid to railways as a necessary transport system to overcome the disadvantages of road and air transport.

In the meantime the institutional environment had completely changed. Indeed in the nineteenth century nation states took the lead, often using national railway companies as agents for reaping monopolistic profits, making them part of policies of national defence and exploiting their military potential. By the end of the twentieth century the European integration process took hold, placing unification policies on the agenda whilst, increasingly, nation states withdrew. The geopolitical situation changed too. Whilst in the nineteenth century a few European states dominated the international scene now Europe was in the process of creating one large-scale European economy capable of competing with the American and Japanese economies on a world level. It is unavoidable that regional and national particularities should disappear in such an environment and subsequently national railroad policies were adapted rapidly to fit these new institutional settings.

Over the last two centuries railways have operated within three different sets of structural conditions. During the first period, which started in 1835 and lasted until the 1920s, they operated as a natural monopoly. From the 1920s the natural monopoly on transportation was gradually eroded by increasing competition from firms operating in other means of transport, such as road and air. Railways in many countries were nationalised, as they were no longer viable. From the 1980s onwards a new impetus was generated with European-driven restructuring and investment programmes for the railway sector.

This chapter is organised as follows. Firstly, the historical background to Belgian railways is presented, since this was a veritable laboratory for all kinds of experiments and some of the experiences are of value for contemporary debates. Secondly, the ongoing transformation process of the railways is examined until the present day. The historical experience of Belgium can be highly valuable for current European transport policy: first because current European policy (like Belgian policy in the nineteenth century) is aimed at developing a railroad system that can respond to the urgent transport needs of the economy; second because the same problems are still visible. Indeed the Belgian railroad system from 1835 onwards had a lot of private railroad operators alongside the state: this was known as the 'Belgian model'. In a short time the country witnessed the transformation of many of these private companies into a few big private ones, competing strongly with state railroads but offering fewer services, having a poorer safety record and asking higher prices compared to the state-owned railroads. Starting around 1870 this caused the government, urged by passengers and private companies, to take the plunge and nationalise the private railroads, a process that was nearly complete by the end of the nineteenth century. The European Union (EU) should be well aware that it could be confronted with many problems, such as interoperability between different lines, keen competition, safety questions and the rapid concentration policies of big firms; indeed, the same old problems that have characterised Belgian railroads for decades.

I. Belgian Railways in the Age of National Environment and Natural Monopoly

This period can be divided into two lengthy stages.[6] In the first stage railways enjoyed an environment of near-natural monopoly. Alternative solutions to the transportation problem hardly existed. This made railroads a comfortable sector as an investment and operations platform. In the second stage alternative modes of transportation appeared on the scene and increased in popularity. Their arrival heralded heavy losses in profits and market share, consequently requiring massive governmental support for the sector.

Belgium became independent in 1830 and its newly established government commenced railway construction in 1835. The government undertook a series of crucial decisions about the – at the time – new transport system.[7] Firstly, the government unequivocally opted to fully support the railway network, secondly, the system was to be state-owned and state-run; thirdly, it was to be constructed as part of a European network system by taking, from the very beginning, neighbouring countries as crucial connections for railroads. Indeed as Belgium was a rather small country it was at the same time highly dependent upon imports and exports. During the nineteenth century the coal mines of the southern part of the country were so enormous that they had to look for customers in neighbouring countries, especially in northern France and Paris, the Rhineland and the Netherlands. The highly developed steel industry (with the Cockerill steel works at Liège) were delivering steel products all over Europe. Besides, the country was able to reap significant profits from the transit function it fulfilled for British goods exported to France and the Rhineland. For a decade the state continued to invest in the sector, allowing private investors to enter only from 1843 onwards,[8] when concessions were granted for 90 years (with a few exceptions prior to that date); also, British and French capital was allowed in.[9] Between 1845 and 1847, following the British railway mania, British capital exports to Belgium went into 10 railroad projects to the tune of BEF 50 million. Later on French capital also became interested as the French Compagnie des Chemins de Fer du Nord (controlled by the French banker Rothschild) succeeded in gaining control over many private railroads in the southern part of the country.

Notwithstanding private railway investments the Belgian conceptual framework for this sector was heavily based on the state being the representative of the whole nation, reaping the benefits of this natural monopoly and distributing them among companies and consumers by way of extremely low prices.

As a state company, the Belgian railways were soon depicted as a wholly different alternative to the British railway system, which was essentially a private one. Moreover it proved to be a highly successful alternative.[10] Indeed during the period 1845–47, when private companies were allowed to enter, virtually none was successful except for the Chemins de Fer de Tournay à Jurbise. Out of ten concessions granted, nine were nearly a complete disaster by the end of 1850. Private firms abdicated and resigned, capital needs proved too large so private capital was rapidly withdrawn since it seemed profits were not to be expected very soon. The state thus had to intervene by guaranteeing a fixed minimum level of 4 per cent return on investment. Due to the state guarantee system many companies joined in but by the end of 1868 the sector was dominated by a few giant private railway companies in competition with the state railroads. These few companies by exploiting their position of economic power precipitated the rise of several monopolistic practices.

There was a massive outcry in favour of government intervention and the takeover of the private railroads as private companies commanded high prices on their lines while rendering low quality services in return. Companies from all sectors, as well as passengers demanded low and equal prices for all customers wherever they lived in the country. Gradually the government gave in, beginning with those railroad companies that risked use in the political and military battles of the time between European powers such as France and Germany. Indeed as railroad companies could be used to transport military forces, French and German capital tried to acquire Belgian-based railroad companies. This prompted the Belgian government to take over these railroads.[11] Indeed as part of his military strategy Napoleon III (1808–1873) had encouraged big French railroad companies such as Compagnie de l'Est to gain control of the Belgian eastern railroads such as the Grand Luxembourg (connecting Luxembourg with Brussels) and others. As this could be taken as a hostile act towards Germany the Belgian government heavily opposed the takeover, as it did German efforts to acquire interests in other Belgian railroads. This rather particular situation was followed by the Belgian government's takeover of those companies that went bankrupt,[12] and finally by the takeover of the biggest private railroad company, the Grand Central Belge of the Belgian holding company Société Générale in 1897.[13] A few minor companies continued to exist; when their concession period expired after 90 years these railroads too were taken over by the state. Often they were even taken over before expiration date on condition they were prepared to negotiate a takeover price. This process would continue until 1957 when the last private railroad company was taken over. The final balance of the whole privatisation process was rather negative. After all, it had cost the state an enormous amount of money to take over these railroads in order to save the Belgian railroad network from destruction, while complaints about the service and the security of these private companies were copious.

However, this was a highly successful period in terms of railway construction and organisation. The service provided was a good one and prices were very low, at least in the case of the state railways.[14] Transport of goods by rail appeared to be faster and more reliable than by any other means of transportation. Bottlenecks in transportation could be avoided as capacity could be enhanced whenever necessary. The opening of Belgium to the continent was a key factor in its economic development, as mining, industrial and agricultural products could be exported easily. Moreover state ownership was preferred over private ownership: private intervention in this sector met with heavy resistance and it became quite common to consider the railways a sector key to the national interest to be operated solely under the aegis of the state. Moreover as the state put no limits on investments in new technology at the time (in contrast to the private companies) this too was welcomed warmly: nearly all state railroads, for instance, had double tracks, whereas many private companies primarily used single track systems. Private companies employed different tariffs for different connections, whereas the state used a single unified (and low) tariff throughout the country. The temporary character of the concession system for private companies did not encourage them to make significant investments in their networks since they were scheduled to revert to the state at the expiration of the concession period. The state railroad system could boast high performance levels; no losses were incurred and profits were not very high owing to the low pricing system.

By the first half of the twentieth century it had become clear that the natural monopoly argument was nearing its end. Increased competition from road (and air) transport threatened the future of the railroad system.[15] A secondary railroad system was even completely dismantled. In several countries where private railroad systems existed the state took over operations that were increasingly suffering losses. The expansion of the railroad sector came to a halt and the network was partially dismantled; new investments and modernisation programmes were scarce. In 1926 the Belgian National Railroad Company, NMBS, was created, amalgamating all state railways into one. This did not solve all of the problems as the institutional environment was now completely different. Admitting top men from private industry, such as Alexandre Galopin (future governor of the Société Générale) or Jules Jadot (brother of the governor of the Société Générale) to the board of directors did not solve the problems either. During this period state railways met with increasing criticism: their profit-making days were a thing of the past and state subsidies had to be used to support the companies. Moreover prices rose, making alternative transport systems even more attractive.

II. Railways in the Age of European Integration and Competition

From the 1980s onwards,[16] as European integration advanced, old questions raised their heads. The first was whether railways had a future at all, operating as they were side by side with other modes of transportation. The second was whether, if indeed they had a future, how this future was to be organised?[17] The European Commission decided to stimulate railroads as an important means of solving the transportation problem. Indeed the natural limitations of the road transport system, together with the polluting effects of road traffic, called for a new transport policy. This policy required the modernisation of the existing railroad system, as railroads were faster (high-speed trains) and thus able to offer an attractive alternative to other means of transportation. Finally, the policy could propose railroads to connect the whole of Europe and thus physically unify the new European integrated economy. The European decision to favour railroad transport was accompanied by an institutional setting such that this should be done in an environment of competition, interoperability and private companies. For the Belgian situation this meant a revolution in the traditional approach.

From 1926 the NMBS had been considered a state company with nearly complete autonomy. The government had a decisive voice in all important questions, such as prices or investments. Low prices were considered an important means of supporting the industrial and mining sectors, as well as a weapon against foreign competition. Together with shrinking market shares as a consequence of increasing competition from road and air traffic, increasing losses were the result. As financing investments for the NMBS was never the government's highest priority the railroad company's competitive position diminished further; even more so as orders had to be placed with other Belgian companies, such as ACEC and BN. Indeed the government was more inclined to finance road transport and the bulk of investments, especially after the Second World War, were made in road construction and maintenance. Within half a century this policy proved to be disastrous as the efficiency of road transport had become severely compromised through heavy congestion by the rapidly expanding volume of traffic. During the 1980s a decision was taken to participate in the high-speed train project but, once again, the government refused to finance it, thus directly undermining the financial situation of the NMBS. However, as the NMBS loans were guaranteed by the state incurring losses was never an obstacle to acquiring and keeping AA+ ratings on the capital market. Moreover the company could concentrate for years on other important aspects of railroad traffic, such as high safety and high punctuality, in both of which it achieved a leading position worldwide. It is understandable that such a sheltered position would not be easy to abandon.

It took several years before any serious response was given to the 1991 European directive (91/440). Although the NMBS was transformed into a public limited company in 1992, following the Belgian law of 21 March 1991 on the autonomy of state companies, this had no real consequences. As the EU urged the separation of operations and infrastructure the only action taken in consequence was the Royal Decree of 5 February 1997 by which this required separation was restricted to maintaining separate accounts for operations and infrastructure.

In the meantime NMBS made significant efforts to transform itself into a real European multinational company by making several important acquisitions throughout Europe. Its strategy consisted in realising rapid growth at the EU level in many activities, more or less related to railroad traffic. The aim was to control the forward and backward linkages of the cornerstone activity of the railroad company and thus bring additional traffic and assure its survival. Besides, certain profit opportunities were exploited such as its telecom activities (B-Telecom). As a result at the end of 2004 it had 171 foreign affiliate companies, ranking NMBS in first place among Belgian multinational enterprises as far as the number of foreign subsidiaries is concerned.[18] For example, one of the basic activities of the NMBS had always been the national distribution of packages. In 1993 ABX Logistics was established as a separate domestic transport company; in 1998 it started its international expansion with the acquisition of some major transport companies abroad, extending the scope of NMBS operations in the logistics sector beyond Belgian borders. Thyssen Haniel Logistics and Bahntrans (Germany), Saima Avandero (Italy), the Dubois Group, Testud and Delagnes (France) were acquired. Within three years (1998–2001) the company underwent a major transformation from a Belgian company into an international concern established in over 30 countries. It became not only a leading

European distribution centre but an international one (USA, South Korea, the Philippines).[19] The same occurred in the harbour terminals sector with IFB (Interferry Boats), another NMBS affiliate. This traffic is essential for NMBS as it brings a lot of additional traffic for railroads, especially for NMBS's goods division, B-Cargo. Indeed much traffic was connected to goods imported and exported through West European harbours (Antwerp, Dunkirk, Zeebrugge). Controlling these terminals seems to be a logical strategy. IFB was founded in 1998 as a merger between Ferry Boats, Interferry and Edmond Depaire BV. Its core business is intermodal rail haulage. It has made acquisitions in France (steel terminal Acimar), thus extending its already extensive experience in Belgium in linking railroad transport to ports. Furthermore NMBS has participated in two European networks: the Eurostar project, the high-speed train connection with London, and the Thalys project, a high-speed train connection with Paris, Amsterdam and Cologne. In fact NMBS's policy has not differed much from that of Deutsche Bahn, which acquired Stinnes. Big railroad companies were indeed intensively preparing for survival. Indeed, this is considered one of the most probable outcomes of the ongoing privatisation process due to the well-known economies of scale effect.

This European expansion strategy was extremely ambitious and centred around the concept of growth, without giving enough attention to profitability. Expansion and growth became the primary motive, not sound economics. Managers were assured that what was successful at the national level would be successful at the European level too, although they lacked capital and managerial capacity for this strategy. This expansive and ambitious diversification strategy was not always successful in the case of the NMBS. It brought about heavy losses for some affiliate companies, such as ABX Logistics and IFB. In the case of ABX Logistics this was due to many factors, including insufficient use of synergies between different ABX Logistics companies and managerial mistakes in the invoice department. One of the most important was the rapid and massive takeover of too many companies worldwide, which were often loss-making.[20] In the case of IFB overcapacity in their harbour terminals and bad contracts with private firms (such as with Arcelor for handling its steel transport) were responsible for this. In the case of Eurostar keen competition from airlines puts heavy pressure on profit margins, causing heavy losses. There have been many other general problems such as lack of attention to bookkeeping methods due to a long tradition of government subsidies; Belgium's relatively small market; insufficient working capital and too high debt servicing; insufficient investment and heavy political influence on strategic decision-taking.

This forced the NMBS into selling or downscaling some of these activities. The strategy switch entails developing specialised niches instead of doing everything everywhere. Besides the regional transportation function, the NMBS wants to continue its strategy to manage international corridors of goods, if possible in collaboration with SNCF (France) or Deutsche Bahn (Germany). Another key strategic element is to allow the private sector to come in, even in profit-generating activities. This is the case for B-Telecom (the telecom activities of the NMBS) that ensures all internal telecommunication activities. The history of B-Telecom goes back to the major fibreglass network of 3800 km for NMBS's own use. This network makes the company number two on the Belgian market, after Belgacom, giving it high potential for future growth. In 1998 NMBS received permission to commercialise its internal network and offer capacity on the professional user market. This permission enabled B-Telecom to provide all kinds of telecom services (speech, data, bandwidth, LAN, WAN, internet transport) to private companies such as BT and Mobistar.[21] Private investors were then sought to join B-Telecom.

Although neither the NMBS board nor the government was convinced of the new European strategy to split operations and infrastructure with the objective of increasing competition they had no choice. By the end of 2000 they still had not managed to realise any of the three main objectives of European Directive 91/440. They had even failed to take over the historical railroad debt which was a vital pre-condition to guarantee the future of these companies. Due to the huge public debt/GDP ratio (over 100 per cent), the government delayed taking action. However, the new directive 2001/14 required them to join the European reform process by 15 March 2003. Indeed from then on the separation of accounting was no longer sufficient. Separate companies had to be founded. The final solution adopted by the Belgian government was to split up activities into several companies. First of all, the record debt (7.4 billion euros) as well as railroad assets (not the operation of these assets), were collected in FIF (Fonds de l'infrastructure ferroviaire),[22] meaning that the financial burden of these debts would no longer be carried by the railroad company but by the state. This does not mean that all the debts have been taken over, however, as commercial debts are not included in this operation. Secondly, three separate companies with three different boards of directors have been established: Infrabel, responsible for the management of infrastructure and distribution of licenses to run trains among several competing operators; operating company NMBS Transport that has to pay to use the infrastructure and will have to meet competition from other operators; a holding company owning the majority of shares of the other two companies (NMBS Holding). All the former NMBS staff were transferred to the NMBS Holding Company. Infrabel and NMBS Transport can transfer staff to one of these companies. High safety standards have to be implemented without further delay, this being an aspect of government control. Moreover the Belgian railroad sector (as well as other international railroad companies) is working on a European Train Control System (ETCS) for high-speed traffic. It offers automatic warning and control to train drivers as regards speed, signal indicators and target distances.[23] This system thus can be used throughout Europe to make interoperability technically feasible. Thus it may be that companies do not need to change their locomotives whenever borders are passed. The state will hold the majority of votes and/or capital in these different companies.[24]

Competition has already been introduced into the Belgian railroad system. As of 15 March 2003 on the Trans Europe Network international transportation of goods throughout Europe was opened up to other operators. Dillen and Lejeune Cargo managed to acquire transport contracts for several routes connecting the port of Antwerp with the hinterland. As liberalisation of European railroads will be complete by 2007 for goods and by 2010 for passengers, little time remains for adaptation.

The ongoing process is a witness to the confidence of the European Union in the future of railroad transport. This appears to be the right decision for Europe, as high concentration levels of industries and people practically leave no other choice. Huge investment and modernisation programmes for existing national railroads can contribute strongly to this. The European Union intervention has highlighted some of the long-known failures of the national railroad company such as inadequate attention to commercial activities, financial control and analytical bookkeeping systems. Finally, within a few years a real European railroad transport system will be possible. However, unifying an array of rules and procedures (safety standards, licence to drive for operators) as intended can only offer favourable results if the highest standards are set and maintained.

However, by engaging all of Europe in a privatisation and competition process the EU is playing a risky game and providing only one option for organising rail transport amongst many. The EU promises an improvement in transport conditions, but there are dangers as illustrated in section one on the historical background. Furthermore the British experience of privatisation does not offer an ideal case either. Some of the pitfalls can already be discerned. As competition is opened up the practice of cherry picking will be ever present, meaning that the private railroad companies will concentrate on the most lucrative transport routes, leaving the others to the national railroad companies. Passengers will be crucially dependent on one of the competing companies: they will not be able to use whatever train passes by. Although safety measures are crucial it cannot be taken for granted that in a competitive environment they will be considered as carefully as in a non-competitive one. Moreover private firms seeking high profits will certainly try to save money on quality, training programmes and staff remuneration, and as workload increases this will exacerbate the coordination problems that are already very high and bound to become even higher in the future. Indeed as the former NMBS is now divided into three different companies conflicts will arise: for example, it will be in Infrabel's interest to make sure that whenever some work has to be done on infrastructure no trains pass, whereas it will be in the interest of operators that as many trains as possible can continue their normal schedules. Nor will the question of responsibility in case of accident be settled easily when Infrabel and the operator come into close contact. Last but not least, due to increasing returns to scale it is possible that within a few years only a few major European railroad companies will survive, with the dangers of monopolistic practices and neglect of national interests never far away. As the national network infrastructure manager already occupies a monopoly position, high prices can be charged for making use of these national networks, implying higher end prices and loss of traffic.

Conclusions

Free market reform of state-controlled NMBS in Belgium signals a major change in how the railroad sector has operated for the last 200 years. The old NMBS was split up into three separate companies in 2003, with NMBS Holding and two affiliate companies: Infrabel, responsible for infrastructure, and NMBS Transport, an operating company. In future NMBS Transport will meet increasing competition from other national and international operators. As increasing competition is but one part of a well defined European-wide transport policy to favour intra-European railroad transport the whole picture has to be taken into account. The European Commission considers diminishing transport prices and better services in the future as natural outcomes of increasing competition but the Belgian experience over 200 years shows that this cannot be taken for granted. Indeed during the nineteenth century Belgium was a laboratory where private companies existed alongside state-owned railways with the private sector underperforming in such important areas as prices, services and safety systems. This problem became so important that finally the overwhelming majority of private consumers as well as private companies from all sectors called for the nationalisation of the railroads.

Lessons from Belgium also provide an ex ante evaluation of this new European policy. Indeed contrary to the past when lucrative activities on some Belgian railroads cross-subsidised others, from now on this will no longer be the case. Competing operators will undoubtedly cherry-pick. Moreover huge attention will have to be given to safety questions as it cannot be expected to be a priority for free market companies, in contrast to state-owned ones; the British experience of increasing accident rates due to privatisation is likely to be repeated. Finally it can be envisaged that due to increasing returns to scale a few big multinational European companies will dominate the railroad-operating sector within the next few decades, bringing familiar monopolistic problems with regard to prices and poor services.

Quite apart from issues of privatisation or nationalisation it is quite clear that the EU is undertaking a revolutionary transformation of its communication and transportation systems. From the many different national transport systems within a few years a new Europe-wide transport system will arise. This transport system will heavily emphasise railroads as a basic transportation means. This is intended to solve increasing traffic problems and to merge all of Europe into one well connected transport system that will serve as a vast infrastructural base for a highly competitive European economy.

Notes

1 Laffut (1998).
2 Laffut (1998).
3 Lebrun et al. (1981).
4 Avakian (1936) pp. 449–82.
5 Veenendaal (1995) pp. 186–93.
6 This section is based on Buelens and van den Broeck (2004).
7 De Brulle (1967) pp. 25–93.
8 Van der Herten (1994) pp. 861–912.
9 Caron (1973).
10 De Laveleye (1862).
11 Kurgan-van Hentenryk (1972) pp. 395–446.
12 Kurgan-van Hentenryk (1982).
13 Jamar (1972).
14 Nicolaï (1885).
15 Van der Herten (2004).
16 This section is based on Fremdling (2002).
17 Fremdling (2002).
18 Graydon Belgium (2004).
19 ABX Logistics, http://www.abxlogistics.com/corp/History.aspx.
20 Meeussen (2003) p. 11.
21 NMBS, various years.
22 FIF is responsible for railroad infrastructure.
23 Alcatel, http://www.alcatel.com/tas/etcs/etcs.htm
24 NMBS (2003).

References

ABX Logistics, http://www.abxlogistics.com/corp/History.aspx
Alcatel, http://www.alcatel.com/tas/etcs/etcs.htm
Avakian, L. (1936) 'Le rythme de développement des voies ferrées en Belgique de 1835 à 1935', in *Bulletin de l'Institut de Recherches Economiques*, vol. 7 (August) pp. 449–82.
Buelens, F., and J. van den Broeck (2004) *Financieel institutionele analyse van de Belgische beursgenoteerde spoorwegsector 1836–1957* (Antwerp: Garant).
Caron, F. (1973) *Histoire de l'exploitation d'un grand réseau, la Compagnie du Chemin de Fer du Nord 1846–1937* (Paris: Mouton).
De Brulle, D. (1967) 'Les chemins de fer belges, Charles Rogier et l'Etat', in *Annales de l'Economie Collective*, 55 (1) (January–March) pp. 25–93.
De Laveleye, A. (1862) *Histoire des vingt-cinq premières années des chemins de fer belges* (Brussels–Paris).
Fremdling, R. (2002) *European Railways 1825–2001. An Overview*, Groningen, Growth and Development Centre, Research Memorandum GD-54 (August).
Graydon Belgium (2004) *Graydon Database*.
Jamar, A.M. (1972) 'Contribution à l'étude des chemins de fer belges. Le rachat du Grand Central Belge par l'Etat Belge', MA dissertation, Free University of Brussels.
Kurgan-Van Hentenryk, G. (1972) 'Une étape mouvementée de la réorganisation des chemins de fer belges: le rachat du Grand-Luxembourg par l'Etat (1872–1873)', in *Revue Belge de Philologie et d'histoire*, L(2) pp. 395–446.

Kurgan-Van Hentenryk, G. (1982) *Rail, finance et politique: les entreprises Philippart 1865–1890* (Brussels: Editions de l'Université Libre de Bruxelles).

Laffut, M. (1998) *Les Chemins de Fer Belges 1830–1913. Genèse du réseau et présentation critique des données statistiques,* (Brussels: Académie Royale de Belgique, Série: Histoire Quantitative et Développement de la Belgique et de ses régions aux XIXe et XXe siècles, 1ère série (XIXe siècle), vol. VIII 1a en 1b, *Les moyens de Communication en Belgique* Brussels: Palais des Académies) vol. 2.

Lebrun, P., M. Bruwier, J. Dhont and G. Hansotte (1981) *Essai sur la révolution industrielle en Belgique 1770–1847,* Série: Histoire Quantitative et Développement de la Belgique et de ses régions aux XIXe et XXe siècles, 1ère série (XIXe siècle), vol. II, *La révolution industrielle* (Brussels: Palais des Académies).

Meeussen, G. (2003) 'Laurent Levaux: 'ABX Logistics is als een onontgonnen schat', in *De Financieel Economische Tijd* (20 June) p. 11.

Nicolaï, E. (1885) *Les chemins de fer de l'etat en Belgique, 1834–1884. Etude historique, economique et statistique* (Brussels: Félix Callewaert Père).

NMBS *Annual Reports,* various years.

NMBS (2003) Het organigram: nieuwe structuur van de NMBS (http://www.b-rail.be/php/news).

Van der Herten, B. (1994) 'De spoorlijn Antwerpen-Gent, 1841–1897. De wisselwerking tussen privé initiatief en overheidsinterventie in de Belgische Spoorwegen', in *Belgisch Tijdschrift voor Filologie en Geschiedenis,* 72, pp. 861–912.

Van der Herten, B. (2004) *België onder stoom* (Leuven: Universitaire Pers Leuven).

Veenendaal, A.J. (1995) 'State versus Private Enterprise in Railways. Building in the Netherlands 1838–1938', in *Business and Economic History,* 24 (1) pp. 186–93.

12
The Transformation of State Enterprises in Russian Networks, 1990–2005

Marina V. Klinova

Introduction

Huge corporations emerged in Russia as a consequence of the privatisation programme which started in the early 1990s with the transition to a market economy.[1] The state, however, often retained a significant share in a number of these privatised corporations, while privatisation was not accompanied by an adequate competitive framework. Indeed the state presence has actually expanded in some spheres, including the energy sector, such as in GAZPROM, Russia's energy giant and the world's largest gas enterprise. A historic legacy of intimate state involvement in the development of the national economy has profoundly influenced economic thinking in Russia. This tradition helps explain many of the current trends in Russia, such as a shift towards state capitalism and corruption in government circles (both curbed by the 'logic' of globalisation), the need to stimulate inward FDI whilst eliminating obstacles to outward FDI, and the establishment of a competitive environment. This chapter aims to analyse these major counteracting trends by focusing in particular on the transformation of GAZPROM.

This chapter is organised into six parts. Firstly, the history of ownership in Russia is briefly presented. In section two the principal legal foundations of privatisation are described. Sections three and four deal with the main features of network reform and the role of the natural gas industry in general and GAZPROM in particular in the national and the European economy. Section five considers overall FDI flows and the internationalisation efforts of GAZPROM. Conclusions follow.

I. Ownership in Russia

Cooperation between the state and private capital is not new in Russia, particularly in the network industries. Economic growth around the turn of the twentieth century gave rise to rapid development of the railways. Fifty years after the abolition of serfdom (1861) Russia became the world's fifth most important industrial producer.[2] The active policy of the state was reflected in significant investments in railway construction.[3] By the beginning of the twentieth century two thirds of the network was state-owned. After the First World War all private property apart from agriculture was nationalised. The Bolsheviks, who seized power in 1917, tried to introduce communism by expropriating private enterprise. As a result, by autumn 1918 industry, including the networks, was paralysed. The subsequent collapse of the economic system, famine and mass revolts forced the Bolsheviks to switch economic policy.

The New Economic Policy (NEP) started by reprivatisating enterprises. Increased competition stimulated economic progress.[4] The market economic system, however, was extinguished soon after 1929 and the monopoly of state and cooperative property continued until the end of the 1980s.[5] Sixty years of centralised planning put the skills needed in a market economy soundly to sleep. Russia presents a unique situation in world economic history since in the other Central and Eastern European countries (CEE) such a situation lasted only one generation or about 30 years.

Decades of absolute state domination over the economy gave rise to a particular kind of state-owned enterprise (SOE). Public enterprises in the West were expected to break even financially with their purchases of inputs and sales of outputs conducted in fairly open markets. They were therefore subject to the market, unlike Russian SOEs where inputs and outputs were part of the command economy.

A market economy inherits from a planned economy 'resources, but not the institutional organization of the public sector'.[6] The state has proved incapable of managing property effectively in all formerly centrally-planned economies.[7] Thus low levels of efficiency were an integral feature of SOEs in the countries with command-administrative systems. This contrasts sharply with public enterprises in western European countries, which could compete favorably with private ones.[8]

Many analysts have convincingly argued that efficiency depends on competition,[9] as well as 'on the quality of ... management ... rather than on ownership *per se*'.[10] Moreover, 'privatisation ... and ... liberalisation are logically quite distinct concepts'[11] that should not be confused. 'It is not the private ownership in itself that makes the market behave in a competitive way',[12] because 'it is possible (and regrettably common) to privatize without liberalizing'.[13] These statements are pertinent to the market reforms in Russia since privatisation failed to create an effective competitive environment: too often, private monopolies replaced state monopolies, whilst company management was poor by Western standards. One of the key problems in Russia remains how to properly regulate the network industries in the market economy without restoring direct state control.

II. Legal Foundations of Privatisation

Privatisation in Russia began after the passage of the privatisation law in July 1991 which outlined the definition, procedure and responsible institutions.[14]

According to Berelovitch and Radvaniji the privatisation of state property began 'when the technocrats who ruled the economy decided to prepare for retirement by realising the scenario of spontaneous privatisation of the state'.[15] Six years later this law was amended, marking the end of the first phase of rapid, mass privatisation. The new law further defined privatisation procedures, offered more methods of privatisation and regulated the transformation of enterprises into joint-stock companies, as well as the state use of the 'golden share'.[16] In December 2001 a new privatisation law stated that the privatisation of enterprises included in the list of strategic state firms could be executed once their removal from this list was approved by the President of the Russian Federation.[17]

Network industries, mostly represented by large monopolies, have a special place in the Russian economy and are generally understood as constituting natural monopolies which play an important role in the economic and social stability of the country. For these reasons they have been regulated by special laws. The transportation through pipelines of oil, oil products and gas, as well as electricity supply and rail transport were defined as enjoying the status of a natural monopoly.[18]

The reform of these natural monopolies was set out in various Presidential Edicts from 1992. The first step was to transform the SOEs into joint-stock companies.[19] Their privatisation could be carried out only according to these Edicts and presidential approval was needed before their transformation to joint-stock companies. In the case of electricity an Edict allowed for the creation of the RJSC UES (Russian joint-stock company for Unified Energy System of Russia, Russian acronym RAO EES – nearly 53 per cent of equity capital belongs to the state) in order to secure the energy supply.[20] Another edict permitted the transformation of state-owned natural gas monopoly GAZPROM into a joint-stock company.[21]

III. Competition and Network Reform

With the aim of fostering a competitive market economy and the regulation of natural monopolies a competition authority was created in the early 1990s by Presidential Edict. It has since been reorganised on various occasions, most importantly in 2003 when it was renamed and reorganised as the Federal Antimonopoly Service (FAS).[22]

Hypothetically one can conceive of reform by splitting up natural monopolies. However, this method is fraught with economic and social costs. The West European and American reform experiences do not suggest unconditional advantages for this approach. 'Imperfect restructuring could result in social losses', as Newbury has shown.[23] The privatisation of well-functioning services that are financially viable is particularly dubious.[24]

It is widely believed in Russia that the privatisation of network industries is not the main priority and the establishment of a competitive environment 'is connected with large costs and a possible deterioration in service conditions'.[25] Moreover according to the Accounts Chamber of the Russian Federation 'privatisation of a significant part of property in the fuel and energy complex has not produced the expected increase in efficiency yet'.[26]

The electric power holding RJSC UES proposed a plan for a comprehensive reform to render the company transparent and attractive to investors by dividing the electric power industry into competitive (generation and market) and monopolistic (transport and distribution) activities. This plan, however, was vigorously opposed by those interested in the continuity of its vertically integrated structure (where generation, distribution and marketing are carried out by one body). The European experience calls for reflection: electricity supply in most European countries technically worked quite well under the previous vertically integrated, largely state-owned structure.[27]

Of course there are other ways of creating competition. It has been argued that technological progress and globalisation make competition in networks possible without restructuring. For example, in the energy market, competition emerges from the development of alternative sources of power supply, forcing companies supplying oil, gas and nuclear energy to compete. Another method is to facilitate foreign capital access to the domestic market.

In natural monopolies economies of scale are paramount due to the capital intensity of network services and most utilities. For these reasons the Russian authorities have been cautious about the regulatory reform of networks by way of restructuring natural monopolies. Russian scholars of the Institute of World Economy and International Relations of the Russian Academy of Sciences (IMEMO RAN) have highlighted the comparative efficiency and stability of large public energy enterprises.[28]

In all East European countries privatisation was associated with deeply unpopular price hikes.[29] In Russia, however, this was exacerbated by the lopsided income stratification caused by the particular methods of privatisation. Privatisation produced 'an asymmetrical allocation of costs and benefits'. State resources 'were used by persons and groups, whose interests were different from the interests of ... the general public'.[30]

The government must regulate these activities in order to guarantee a reliable supply of resources and services for acceptable consumer prices. Since 2002 prices of electric energy, gas, oil and petroleum products, as well as rail transportation tariffs have been regulated by the Federal Energy Commission (FEC). FEC became the Unified Tariff Organ (ETO) for natural monopolies. To protect consumers against adverse pricing by natural monopolies it is essential to reform the state system of regulating tariffs for energy resources.[31] The administration of tariffs is to be replaced by regulation through taxes and credit rates. The administration of tariffs does not provide for a favourable investment climate.

Energy in Russia is a major factor affecting living standards because of its long, cold winters.[32] Besides, the taxes payed by energy companies constitute an important source of state budget revenue. It would take a long time to plan and perform an adequate liberalisation of the internal energy market in Russia that did not end up having negative consequences for living standards and the state budget.[33]

IV. The Natural Gas Industry and GAZPROM

The natural gas network is regulated by Federal Law No. 69-FZ (31 March 1999) 'On Natural Gas Industry Supplies in the Russian Federation'. Activities in the natural gas sector are dominated by the leading national champion GAZPROM, the most important Russian TNC, whose origins are rooted in the Soviet era. Initially GAZPROM functioned as a Ministry, after which it was transformed into a concern and later into a joint-stock company. Its shares were allocated mostly to the top management of the former Ministry, whilst the state secured overall control by retaining a decisive packet of shares.

GAZPROM, the largest gas company in the world, enjoys 16 per cent of the world's proven gas resources and nearly 60 per cent of Russia's gas reserves, and accounts for 25 per cent of world gas exports (with supplies to the Commonwealth of Independent States and the Baltic States). According to GAZPROM's deputy CEO A. Medvedev his company's share of Europe's market will climb to 33 per cent by 2010–15.[34] Minister of Industry and Energy V. Khristenko has stated that full state control of GAZPROM, a vitally important enterprise for Russia, would ease the sale of its share sales and raise its capitalisation as well as its credit rating.[35] This programme announced by Khristenko was realised. The state share in the equity capital of GAZPROM was increased from 39.27 per cent to 50.01 per cent by the end of 2005.[36] At the same time, the law amendments were adopted which provided for the free sale of the rest of GAZPROM's shares. As a result, GAZPROM's capitalisation immediately increased by 21 per cent (that is, by US$ 40 billion) making GAZPROM the seventh largest company in the world at that time.[37] Four months later GAZPROM became the world's second biggest energy company by market value and the world's fourth biggest publicly traded company after ExxonMobil, General Electric and Microsoft.

The state is extending its control over other segments of the energy sector via GAZPROM. For instance, GAZPROM owns 10 per cent of the shares in RJSC UES, 25 per cent of MOSENERGO (the regional power company of Moscow), and has recently bought 76 per cent of the equity capital in the large private oil firm SIBNEFT (later renamed GAZPROMNEFT).

The government currently regulates GAZPROM's gas wholesale prices, tariff rates for gas transportation over trunk pipelines for independent companies and gas retail prices for the population. The prospects of the gas industry in Russia for the first two decades of the current century are presented in Table 12.1.

Despite the impressive forecasts of natural gas production and export volumes shown in Table 12.1 future cooperation between Russia and the EU in the gas industry is not secure for many reasons, including the gaps in Russian legislation. For instance, there is no law yet to regulate pipeline transportation.

Table 12.1   Long-Term Outlook for Russian Natural Gas
Industry (m³ billion)

Variables	Years		
	2000[1]	2010[2]	2020[2]
Production	584	635	710
	(595)	665	730
Exports	194	265	275
	(186)	250	280

Notes:
[1] Data for 2002 are in brackets.
[2] Moderate projections on top, best case projections below.
Source: Compiled by author based on *Vneshneekonomitcheski
bulleten* (Moscow, 2004) No. 6, p. 69.

Table 12.2   Dependence upon Russian Gas (%)

Country	%
Finland	100
Bulgaria	99
Slovakia	97
Greece	76
Czech Republic	74
Yugoslavia	74
Hungary	70
Austria	66
Slovenia	61
Poland	58
Germany	33
Romania	29
Italy	26
France	26
Netherlands	5

Source: Compiled by author based on
The Moscow Times (26 April 2006) No. 3401, p. 2.

Some analysts have argued that EU enlargement has further exacerbated
existing problems in Russian–EU relations.[38] In the EU there is a tendency to
reduce state participation and encourage competition within the European
natural gas industry. Directive 98/30/EC (22 June 1998) concerning common
rules for the internal natural gas market was replaced by Directive 2003/55/EC
that provides for an early opening of national gas markets to competition.

It is a problem to create a competitive gas market where gas is imported (as in
the EU) from few sources and/or from monopoly suppliers, as Newbery claims.[39]
Table 12.2 shows the dependence of a number of European countries on Russian
gas supplies.

Some CEE countries have appealed to the EU to reduce their dependence on Russian gas supplies. This was probably provoked by the Russia–Ukraine gas dispute over prices when in January 2006 GAZPROM cut off gas shipments to Ukraine because the Kiev authorities refused to pay for the gas at market prices. Gas destined for Europe runs through the same pipeline as for Ukraine. Ukraine found it possible to use transit gas destined to the EU for its home needs. Therefore the Russian view is that Ukraine was to blame when some EU countries (including Italy, Hungary and France) did not get their quota of gas supplies.

Barysh has drawn attention to the fact that GAZPROM controls the access of Russian private oil companies that produce natural gas to export pipelines. Moreover private companies and foreign investors are forbidden (by the government) to build new pipelines.[40] Meanwhile huge investments in Russian infrastructure are necessary to increase gas exports from 130 billion m^3 in 2005 to 160–5 billion m^3 by 2020.[41] According to available estimates the EU will need annual purchases of gas to the tune of 300 billion m^3 by 2020,[42] and new investment in the Russian gas industry by 2020 will grow to US$ 170–80 billion.[43]

The European Commission's proposal to cooperate with Russia in the energy sector over the next 20 years, approved in October 2000 (Paris), implies considerable investments in the Russian fuel and energy complex, transfer of technologies, the doubling of European gas imports and a substantial increase in oil and electric power imports. In the framework of the Russia–European Union Energy Dialogue a technical working group has been created to study the problems of unifying continental European and Russian power grids. Both the EU and Russia foresee the need for infrastructural development to connect their energy markets. The EU–Russia summit in October 2001 in Brussels approved measures to secure FDI in Russia.

Russia's 'Energy Strategy' adopted in 2003 for the period up to 2020 is compatible with the EU Green Paper 'Towards a European Strategy for Security of Energy Supply'. However, as before, the lack of a stable legal basis impedes foreign investment in Russia. Despite the current difficulties the Commission considers that the systematic and continuously reliable energy supply from Russia is an encouraging factor.

V. FDI and the Transnationalisation of GAZPROM

According to Rosstat (government statistical agency, formerly Goskomstat) FDI includes investor's cash resources, material stocks and capital equipment brought to the enterprise (machinery, equipment, technologies and licences) and services (building and assembly costs) when the total share in equity stock is at least ten per cent.

FDI is the most effective means of economic cooperation because it provides for the transfer of management skills, commercial experience and technology capabilities. However, according to the UN Economic Commission for Europe 'symptoms of "Dutch Disease" are becoming quite visible in Russia'. Though economic diversification has long been declared the aim of Russian policy, so far very little has actually been achieved. Changes can only come about as a result of considerable private investment in sectors other than those related to oil and natural gas.[44]

Until quite recently, Russian FDI outflows substantially exceeded FDI inflows. In 2003 FDI outflows totalled US$ 9.73 billion and FDI inflows were about US$ 8 billion. In 2004 the trend changed: after two years of growth (2002–3) FDI outflows declined to US$ 9.60 billion, while FDI inflows increased to US$ 12 billion.[45] Russian FDI assets as a percentage of GDP in 2004 were 17.9 per cent according to the IMF and 16.9 per cent according to UNCTAD. FDI liabilities of Russia were correspondingly 19.8 and 14.0 per cent respectively.[46] In Russia the main FDI inflows and outflows are concentrated in natural resources.[47]

The integration of Russia in the world economy is taking the form of transnational investments in networks. By some estimates, 80 out of 100 world's largest TNCs have business in Russia.[48] The scale of FDI in Russia is, however, not only lower than in developed countries, but also lower than in many transition economies.[49] Foreign investors are hesitant because of a lack of transparency in Russian energy enterprises.[50] OECD General Secretary D. Johnstone declared that, even by Russian standards, GAZPROM is exceptionally non-transparent.[51] At the same time GAZPROM Deputy Chairman S. Ushakow claims that his company leads in information transparency among Russia's 11 largest companies according to the S&P Report on Information Transparency in 2005.[52]

In recent years Russia and the EU have successfully collaborated in a number of important investment projects (in 2004 GAZPROM obtained US$ 5.5 billion of foreign credits and European loans).[53] Among these are investments in gas export pipelines including: the 'Blue Stream' (Russia–Turkey); the Yamal–Europe (through Belarus bypassing Ukraine); and the North European Gas Pipeline (NEGP) – through the Baltic Sea bypassing transit countries.

Since 1999 natural gas has flowed to Poland and Germany through the first section of the gas pipeline Yamal–Europe. Participants in the Yamal–Europe project include GAZPROM, Beltransgaz (gas transportation company of Belarus), PGNiG (gas transportation concern of Poland) and Wintershall (BASF's oil and gas subsidiary company). The line allows the interconnection of large European gas mains, including Megal (Mittel-Europäische-Gasleitungsgesellschaft – joint-venture of Gaz de France and Ruhrgas, Germany), TENP (Trans-Europa-Naturgas-Pipeline – joint venture of Ruhrgas and SNAM, Italy), Gasunie (gas company of Netherlands) and Transgaz (Romania).

The project to construct a gas pipeline along the bottom of the Baltic Sea should increase the reliability of supplies and reduce the quantity of intermediaries, thus weakening the monopoly position of transit countries which often set very high tariffs for gas transportation. GAZPROM would retain control over this pipeline. A framework agreement (signed in September 2005) between GAZPROM, BASF and E.ON foresees the establishment of the joint-venture NEGP, in which GAZPROM has 51 per cent of the shares, and Germany's BASF

Figure 12.1 The Route of the North European Gas Pipeline (NEGP)

and E.ON split the rest (24.5 per cent each). Two parallel lines of 1189 km each will supply 55 billion m³ gas annually. It is planned to build outlet lines for gas supply to Sweden and Kaliningrad. The first NEGP line should be operational by 2010. Figure 12.1 shows the NEGP route.

Wintershall has become the first German enterprise to take part in an investment project to produce gas in Russia. In 2006 it was agreed that BASF/ Wintershall would obtain 25 per cent minus one share. Additionally, BASF/ Wintershall will get 10 per cent of non-voting shares in OAO Severnefte GAZPROM, which holds the license for the development of the South Russian field, the main source of gas for NEGP. So BASF/Wintershall will own 35 per cent minus one share of this field, while GAZPROM increases its interest in Wingas GmbH (a joint-venture of GAZPROM and Wintershall for gas transportation and distribution) to 50 per cent minus one share. Moreover GAZPROM and BASF intend to establish joint-ventures for natural gas trading in West European markets.[54]

The development of the Shtokman gas-field in the Barents Sea is a major Russian and European investment project with GAZPROM participation. Among the expected partners are ConocoPhilips, Chevron, Norsk Hydro, Statoil and Total. The prospect of cooperation with Norwegian companies with state capital Norsk Hydro and Statoil fits the Norwegian strategy of expansion to other world regions in the gas sector because of a substantial decrease in oil production in Norway expected from 2009.

GAZPROM, alongside other Russian energy companies, is actively moving into foreign markets. About half of outward Russian FDI is in the EU.[55] Table 12.3 shows the FDI of the privatised oil company LUKOIL.

GAZPROM considers itself a 'guarantor' of Europe's energy security. However, CEE politicians and the general public remain concerned about Russian corporations' efforts to invest in their domestic energy sectors, especially natural gas distribution and retail companies delivering gas to European consumers,

Table 12.3   Selected Russian Oil and Gas Company Subsidiaries in CEE, 2004

Countries	Companies	Activities	Owners/investors	% owned
Bulgaria	Lukoil-Neftokhim	Oil refining and petrochemicals	Lukoil	93*
	Topenergy	Gas trading and engineering Investment	GAZPROM	100
	Overgas Incorporated	Gas distribution	GAZPROM	50**
	Overgas		GAZPROM	23**
Estonia	Eesti Gaas	Gas distribution	GAZPROM	37
Hungary	BorsodChem	Petrochemicals	GAZPROM	25
	Panrusgas	Gas importing	GAZPROM	40**
Latvia	Latvijas Gaze	Gas distribution	GAZPROM	34
	LatRos Trans	Oil export pipeline	Transnefteproduct	34
Lithuania	Lukoil Baltija	Fuel distribution and filling stations	Lukoil	100
	Lietuvos Dujos	Gas distribution	GAZPROM	34
	Mazeikiu Nafta	Oil refinery and export terminal	YUKOS	54
Poland	Europol Gaz	Gas distribution	GAZPROM	48
	Gas Trading	Gas imports	GAZPROM	16**
Romania	Petrotel-Lukoil	Oil refining	Lukoil	93
	Virom	Gas distribution	GAZPROM	25**
Slovakia	Slovrusgaz	Gas trading	GAZPROM	50
	SPP	Gas distribution	GAZPROM	up to 16.3***
	Transpetrol	Oil pipeline	YUKOS	49

Notes:
* *Mirovaya energetika* [World Energy], Moscow (2005), No. 2, p. 20.
** UNCTAD TD/B/Com.3/EM.26/2/ Add. 4, 2 November 2005, p. 14.
*** The consortium composed of GAZPROM, Gas de France and German Ruhrgas has won the tender to purchase 49 per cent of the shares.
Source: Compiled by author based on *The Economist* (2005).

particularly when the corporations have state participation. Some CEE leaders consider Russian FDI not as purely economic, but as a lever of Russian geopolitics. For instance, despite the huge investment required by CEE countries GAZPROM's effort to take over the major Hungarian chemical company BorsodChem provoked a furious defensive reaction by other Hungarian firms. Most CEE governments prefer Western investors when companies are privatised, even if bids are less financially advantageous. The same problem is now arising in other EU countries where GAZPROM has also met with opposition to its plans to purchase retail companies delivering gas to European consumers.

Thus the climate for Russian investment in the EU is unfavourable. Such a cold reception to Russian FDI seems to be one of the reasons for Russian fuel and electric energy corporations' 'turn to the East'. The state sector of the Russian fuel and energy complex will supply gas to the eastern regions of the country and build infrastructure to export gas to the Asian-Pacific Region. The construction of 12,000 km of pipelines and the gasification of 1120 localities is expected.[56]

GAZPROM is also moving into the American market. According to the US Department of Energy the demand for natural gas in the USA is set to increase by 43 per cent to 2025. GAZPROM is cooperating with the leading Mexican state-owned energy company PEMEX. There are also plans for GAZPROM to collaborate with Royal Dutch Shell to deliver Russian natural gas to Mexico from 2008.[57] After 2010 GAZPROM plans to export liquefied natural gas in large volumes. These plans are based on natural gas's increasing role as the most ecological source of energy among hydrocarbon fuels.

Conclusions

Network industries in Russia are being transformed in various ways. The role of the state in the Russian gas industry is expanding. Since the middle of 2003 there has been clear evidence that government policy is to have a controlling package of shares in GAZPROM, which remains the most powerful network monopoly in Russian industrial infrastructure. State control over GAZPROM is complemented by the sale of the rest of GAZPROM's shares. Moreover, the state has extended its control over other segments of the energy sector via GAZPROM investments in a number of Russian energy companies. This practice of developing and expanding direct state intervention, if pursued in other spheres, could have far-reaching consequences in the future, including the establishment of state capitalism.

Trends to foster state monopolies in Russia are counteracted by the processes of globalisation and FDI flows. Across the EU a major reason behind privatisation was to intensify the integration process. Similarly in Russia the privatisation of enterprises is important if Russia is to integrate more into the world system. The resistance to Russian FDI in the EU countries due to the possible influence of Russia on their domestic affairs will force the Russian government either to make energy companies private or to let foreign companies establish subsidiaries in the energy sector. The long-term government strategy is to develop international cooperation and integration in the world economy by means of participation in worldwide networks, especially in the energy sector whilst maintaining a careful balance of state–market influence at home.

Notes

1   Klinova (2004) pp. 749–51.
2   Sorokin (1997) p. 115.
3   Gaidar (2005) p. 279.

4   *Strana Sovetov za 50 let* (1967) pp. 26–7.
5   On the history of enterprise ownership in Russia see: Varnavsky (2005); Kulisher (2004); Mau (1993); Radygin (1994); *Sobstvennost' v XX stoletii* (2001); *Transformatsia otnoshenii sobstvennosti i sravnitelnii analiz rossiiskikh reguionov* (2001); *Ekonomika perekhodnogo perioda: Otcherki istorii ekonomicheskoi politiki postkommunisticheskoi Rossii. 1998–2002* (2003).
6   Demidova et al. (2001) p. 28.
7   Gaidar (2003) p. 411.
8   Klinova (1988) pp. 110–13.
9   Bizaguet (1993) p. 73.
10 Clifton, Comín and Díaz-Fuentes (2003) p. 36.
11 Vickers and Yarrow (1989) p. 45.
12 Clifton, Comín and Díaz-Fuentes (2003) p. 11.
13 Newbery (2004) p. 7.
14 Federal Law No. 1531-1 of 3 July 1991.
15 Berelovitch and Radvaniji (1999) p. 229.
16 Federal Law No. 123-FZ of 21 July 1997.
17 Federal Law No. 178-FZ of 21 December 2001.
18 Item 4, p. 1 of Federal Law No. 147-FZ.
19 See Presidential Edicts No. 922 of 14 August 1992 and No. 426 of 27 April 1997.
20 Owing to the urgency of the problem Presidential Edict No. 923 was passed on 15 August 1992.
21 Edict No. 1333 of 5 November 1992 'On Transforming State Concern "GAZPROM" into Russian Joint-Stock Company "GAZPROM" '.
22 GKAP was created by Presidential Edict No. 915 of 24 August 1992.
23 Newbury (2004) pp. 11, 20.
24 Kessler and Alexander (2004) p. 8.
25 Varnavsky (2005) p. 38.
26 Accounting Chamber of the Russian Federation (2003) p. 187.
27 Newbery (2004) p. 20.
28 Kurenkov et al. (2004) p. 129.
29 Newbery (2004) p. 31.
30 Demidova et al. (2001) p. 29. Some 15 per cent of the population received 92 per cent of privatisation income, which accounted for around 70 per cent of savings in Russia. See Lvov (2004) p. 15. Inequality continues to intensify. Y. Gaidar, Director of the Institute for Transition Economies, points out that the Gini coefficient, which defines the concentration of income, increased in 2004 to 0.406 compared with 0.398 in 2001–2 (http://www.iet.ru/news.php?category-id=12158news-id=5572).
31 Accounting Chamber of the Russian Federation (2003) p. 178.
32 Goritcheva (2003) p. 28.
33 Glagolev, Demin and Orlov (2003) p. 41.
34 Medvedev (2005) p. 239. http:/eng.GAZPROMquestions.ru/page6.shtml
35 *Neft i Kapital* (2005) p. 5.
36 *Izvestia* (26 April 2006) p. 7.
37 UNCTAD (2005) p. 78.
38 http://www.lenta.ru/articles/2006/01/13/GAZPROM/
39 Newbury (2004) p. 20.
40 Barysh (2004) p. 38.
41 *European Union–Russia Energy Dialogue* (2003) p. 39.
42 Barysh (2004) p. 38.
43 Glagolev, Demin and Orlov (2003) p. 47.

44 UN (2004) pp. 43, 17, 42.
45 UNCTAD (2003), pp. 76, 77, 307.
46 IMF (2006) pp. 810–12; UNCTAD (2005) p. 324.
47 Khesin et al. (2006) p. 221.
48 Liventsev et al. (2005) p. 329.
49 UNCTAD (2003).
50 Barysh (2004) p. 29.
51 Frumkin (2005) p. 10.
52 *Izvestia* (23 June 2005) p. 10.
53 Galukhina and Korotetski (2005) p. 49.
54 See Vin'kov, Koksharov and Rubanov (2005) pp. 21–4; *Kommersant* (2006) p. 1.
55 BIKI (2006) p. 3.
56 *Izvestia* (4 April 2006) p. 7.
57 Khudiakov (2005) p. 94.

References

Accounting Chamber of the Russian Federation (2003) 'Ob ekonomicheskom i finansovom sostoyanii estestvennikh monopoliy' (Analytical Note), *Bulleten Schetnoy Palaty Rossiyskoy Federatsii*, 68 (8). (2003, No. 8, 68).
Barysh, K. (2004) *EU i Rossiia: sosedi ponevole?* (Moscow: Committee 'Russia in a United Europe').
Berelovitch, A., and J. Radvaniji (1999) *Les 100 portes de la Russie. Le l'URSS à la CEI, les convulsions d'un géant* (Paris: Editions ouvrières).
BIKI (Bulletin of Foreign Commercial Information) (2006) No. 33 (8979) (25 March).
Bizaguet, A. (1993) *Le secteur public et les privatisations* (Paris: Presses universitaires de France).
Clifton J., F. Comín and D. Díaz-Fuentes (2003) *Privatisation in the European Union. Public Enterprises and Integration* (Boston: Kluwer Acad. Publishers).
Demidova, L.S., et al. (2001) *Gosudarstvo i otrasli infrastrukturi v sovremennoi rynochnoi ekonomike* (Moscow: Nauka).
Edict of the President of Russia No. 922 of 14 August 1992 'On the Peculiarities of Transforming State Enterprises, Associations and Organisations of Fuel and Energy Complex into Joint-Stock Companies'.
Edict of the President of Russia No. 923 of 15 August 1992 'On the Organisation of the Management of the Electric-Power Complex of the Russian Federation in the Context of Privatisation'.
Edict of the President of Russia No. 915 of 24 August 1992 'On the State Committee of the Russian Federation for Antimonopoly Policy and the Support of New Economic Structures' (GKAP).
Edict of the President of Russia No. 1333 of 5 November 1992 'On Transforming State Concern "GAZPROM" into Russian Joint-Stock Company "GAZPROM"'.
Edict of the President of Russia No. 426 of 27 April 1997 'On Fundamental Principles of Structural Reform for Natural Monopolies'.
Ekonomika perekhodnogo perioda: Otcherki istorii ekonomicheskoi politiki postkommunis- ticheskoi Rossii. 1998–2002 (2003) (Moscow: Delo).
European Union–Russia Energy Dialogue (2003) *Energeticheskaya politica*, No. 6.
Federal Law No. 1531-1 of 3 July 1991 'On the Privatisation of State and Municipal Enterprises in the RSFSR'.
Federal Law No. 147-FZ of 17 August 1995 'On Natural Monopolies'.

Federal Law No. 123-FZ of 21 July 1997 'On the Privatisation of State Property and Guidelines for the Privatisation of Municipal Property in the Russian Federation'.

Federal Law No. 178–FZ of 21 December 2001 'On the Privatisation of State and Municipal Property'.

Frumkin, K. (2005) 'OECD posovetovala Rosii zamenit' chinovnikov', *Izvestia*, No. 103 (21 June).

Gaidar, Y. (2000) *A Long Time. Russia and the World: Essays on Economic History* (Moscow: Delo).

Gaidar, Y. (2003) *The Economics of Transition* (Cambridge, MA: MIT Press).

Galukhina, Y., and Y. Korotetski (2005) 'Beliy Medved prishel', *Expert*, No. 9.

Glagolev A.I., S.S. Demin and Y.N. Orlov (2003) *Dolgosrochnoye prognozirovaniye gazovogo rynka* (Long-term gas market forecasting: the practice of scenario programming) (Moscow: East–West Energy Dialogue Institute).

Goritcheva, L.G. (2003) *Estestvenno-prirodnaya sostavliayushaya kulturno-istoricheskoy tselostnosti natsional'no-gosudarstvennikh khoziastv Rossii i Zapadnoy Evropi* (Moscow: MAXPRESS).

International Monetary Fund (2006) *International Financial Statistics* (Washington: IMF) (April).

Izvestia (2005) Interview with the Deputy Chairman of GAZPROM S. Ushakov, No. 105 (23 June).

Kessler, T., and N. Alexander (2004) *Assessing the Risks in the Private Provision of Essential Services* (NY–Geneva: UN).

Khesin, E.S. et al. (2006) *Evropeiskiye priamiye investitsii v Rossii* (Moscow: IMEMO RAN 2006).

Khudiakov, N. (2005) 'Mexika stanovitsia blije', *Mirovaya energitika* [World Energy] No. 2.

Klinova, M.V. (1988) *Gosudarstvennoye predprinimatel'stvo v stranah Evropeyskogo Soobshestva* (Moscow: Nauka).

Klinova, M.V. (2004) 'La privatisation en Russie', *La Revue du Trésor*, No. 12.

Klinova, M.V. (2005) 'Logika i ratsional'niye predeli privatizatsii: sovremenniy evrokontext', *Mirovaya ekonomika y mejdunarodnye otnosheniya*, No. 10.

Kommersant, (28 April 2006), No. 76 (3407).

Kulisher, I.M. (2004) *Istoria russkogo narodnogo khoziaïstva* (Moscow: Socium).

Kurenkov, Y.V. et al. (2004) *Strukturnaya i institutsional'naya modernizatsiya ekonomiki Rossii – sektoral'niy analiz* (Moscow: IMEMO RAN).

Liventsev, N. et al. (2005) *Mejdunarodniye ekonomicheskiye otnosheniya* (Moscow: Prospekt).

Lvov, D.S. (2004) *Ekonomichesiy rost i kachestvo ekonomiki* (Moscow: Gudok).

Mau, V. (1993) *Reformi i dogmi, 1914–1929* (Moscow: Delo).

Medvedev, A. (2005) *GAZPROMEXPORT: noviye proyekti/ God planeti 2005* (Moscow: Ekonomika).

Neft i Kapital (2005) Interview with the Minister of Industry and Energy of Russia V.B. Khristenko, No. 4 (113).

Newbery, D.M. (2004) *Privatizing Network Industries*, CESIFO Working Paper No. 1132, Category 9: Industrial Organisation (February).

Radygin, A.D. (1994) *Reforma sobstvennosti v Rossii: na puti iz proshlogo v boudoushee* (Moscow: Respublika).

Sobstvennost' v XX stoletii (2001) (Moscow: ROSSPEN).

Sorokin, A.K. (1997) *Predprinimatel'stvo i predprinimateli Rossii: ot istokov do nachala XX veka* (Moscow: ROSSPEN).

Strana Sovetov za 50 let. (1967) (Moscow: Statistika).

Transformatsia otnoshenii sobstvennosti i sravnitelnii analiz rossiïskikh reguionov (2001) (Moscow: CEPRA, CIDA).

UNCTAD (2003) *World Investment Report* (Geneva: UNCTAD).
UNCTAD (2005) *World Investment Report* (Geneva: UNCTAD).
United Nations (2004) *Economic Survey of Europe* (NY–Geneva: UN) No. 2.
Varnavsky, V. (2005) *Partnerstvo gosudarstvennogo i chastnogo sectora. Formi, proekti, riski* (Moscow: Nauka).
Vickers, J., and G. Yarrow (1989) *Privatisation. An Economic Analysis* (Cambridge, MA: MIT Press).
Vin'kov, A., A. Koksharov and I. Rubanov (2005) 'Vzrosloye reshenie', *Expert*, No. 35.

13
Taking Control: Transforming Telecommunications in Mexico

Judith Clifton, Daniel Díaz-Fuentes and Carlos Marichal

Introduction

The establishment and expansion of utility networks laid the foundations – literally, in the form of physical networks of transport, communications, energy and water – for socioeconomic development in modern Mexico, playing a central role throughout each different historical period of development. Continually there was a trade-off between the aim of developing network services to promote national business, on the one hand, and the need to attract technological and business capabilities to sustain higher rates of growth through Foreign Direct Investment (FDI), on the other. During the Porfiriato (1876–1910) network services were essential for the emerging export-led growth strategy, financed in large measure through the accumulation of foreign debt (particularly Mexican National Railways). They were also key during the so-called 'economic miracle' between the 1940s and the late 1960s. From the 1970s to the 1980s Mexico's accumulating debt, headed by some of the largest networks – including oil and gas giant state-owned enterprise (SOE) Petróleos Mexicanos (PEMEX) – contributed significantly to highly cyclical economic trends and also generated what would be the deepest and most prolonged debt crisis in Latin American history. Networks were important also during the 1990s in the passage from a relatively inward-looking economic strategy to a more open, privatised economy, particularly the former national telephone monopoly Teléfonos de México (TELMEX) which was used as a symbol to increase the visibility and attractiveness of the privatisation programme to foreign investors.[1] As the newly privatised TELMEX exploited its privileges, becoming a 'national champion', strategic shareholder Mexican entrepreneur Carlos Slim consolidated his business activities to become a leading force in the internationalising ambitions of Mexican enterprise from the end of the 1990s.

This chapter focuses on the transformation of the telecommunications sector in Mexico during the twentieth century, selected because of its emergence from the 1970s at the heart of a new technological paradigm,[2] which provides the architecture for the information society[3] and is increasingly subject to intensified global competition and mergers and acquisitions. The role of the telecommunications sector is examined at four critical stages of transition: Mexicanisation, nationalisation, privatisation and transnationalisation. What emerges from this analysis is that post-revolutionary Mexican governments have continuously sought to bring telecommunications under their wing – and away from foreign control – though this development has been gradual. Ownership and control variants are arrayed along twin axes: public–private and domestic–foreign. In this light the government has repeatedly sought to use Mexican private investment when state ownership was either undesirable or unfeasible. Although ownership of other strategic networks – particularly railways, electricity, petroleum, gas and water – is only mentioned briefly to enable comparison there is a common trend to protect networks from foreign control and this despite Mexico's turn to open markets, the signing of the North American Free Trade Agreement (NAFTA) and the inward FDI boom in Latin America in the 1990s. This differentiates Mexico from many large Southern American countries that have opened up more to FDI inflows in these sectors.

Mexican SOEs have broadly evolved in the following way: (1) a relatively prolonged emergence from 1920 to 1960; (2) a dramatic expansion between 1960 and 1982; and (3) an equally dramatic decline from 1983 to 2000. The various reasons for setting up SOEs or nationalising private companies have been forgotten or distorted over time. In Mexico nationalisation was often used in order to keep foreigners out of the military, technology, energy, transport and telecommunications sectors. The state also nationalised by default to bail out companies in financial trouble, however, particularly during the 1930s and 1970s.[4] FDI played an important role in business transformation in each phase of economic development, though this was fraught with contradictions since, whilst FDI was a critical means of attracting technological capabilities and access to international standards, the Mexican governments sought to control or at least restrict foreign ownership of business. Inward FDI into infrastructure and network services was considered necessary for the export-led growth model of the late nineteenth and early twentieth century. During the period of 'stabilising development' inward FDI into manufacturing Transnational Corporations (TNCs) was considered a 'necessary evil' that would permit Mexico to leap from the second stage of import substitution industrialisation in the 1950s to a more complex phase of intermediate industrialisation in the 1960s and 1970s. In the 1960s a large number of TNCs moved into chemicals, pharmaceuticals and the automobile sector. In the following decade the development strategy was heavily oriented toward the promotion of intermediate industrial goods and energy, including the development of steel companies, petrochemicals, the nuclear industry and transport and further expansion of the (transnationalised) automobile sector (including automobile parts which began their export boom in the 1980s), and communications networks in general. Unfortunately, however, the jump to production of advanced capital goods did not work: for instance, production of industrial machinery. The industrial transformation was therefore incomplete and contributed to the shift to *maquiladoras* in the late 1980s and early 1990s, which did not require much new technology. The liberalisation of FDI as of the late 1980s was a clear requirement of the so-called 'Washington Consensus' and the privatisation of TELMEX was used as the flagship of the Salinas administration (named the 'Thatcher of Latin America' by *The Economist*) to attract FDI. Finally, outward FDI by companies, including TELMEX, heralds a new phase whereby the 'national champion' has come of age and can compete aggressively in regional telecoms markets.

The rest of this chapter is organised into five sections that roughly correspond to the historical phases of telecommunications transformation. In the first section the transformation of telecommunications from foreign, private TNCs to Mexicanisation is discussed. The era of nationalisation is analysed up to the 1982 debt crisis in section two. TELMEX's role in the privatisation process follows in section three showing how the option of creating a prominent national champion was selected. TELMEX's transformation into Latin America's largest Trans-Latin American telecom company follows in section four. Conclusions follow.

I. The Prolonged Emergence of Nationalised Enterprise

Telecommunications were not nationalised until 1972, later than railways, electricity, oil and gas. In order to put this nationalisation into perspective we shall first briefly consider the origins of SOE in Mexico and the nationalisation of other key networks.

The origins of public enterprise in Mexico were the creation of fiscal monopolies during the empire – particularly during the Bourbon period – in tobacco, mercury, salt, gunpowder and military activities, following similar patterns to Europe.[5] A few enterprises were established during the Porfiriato, namely Mexican National Railways (1908) and Caja de Préstamos para Irrigación y Fomento (1908), both with mixed public and private capital. This brought Mexico closer into line with a number of other Latin American countries, such as Argentina, Brazil, Chile and Peru, which had created state enterprises in banking and other activities from the 1860s and 1870s. However, after the crisis of 1890 they were largely privatised in Argentina and Peru, while in Brazil state railways and banks continued to flourish. During the Mexican Revolution the state played a more decisive role in the economy: from 1915 it effectively took over the tram system in Mexico City, most regional banks and many *haciendas*. The Mexican Revolution heralded change, one important consequence being the inclusion of Article 27 in the 1917 Mexican Constitution which invested the state with legitimate and inalienable ownership of key natural resources and infrastructure.

It was from the mid-1920s that a more modern concept of SOE came into play. Over the following few decades – and until the late 1970s – many enterprises (including electricity, railways, telegraphs and telephones) were incorporated into the so-called parastatal (public) sector, in general because of their perceived importance for Mexico's economic and social development, national independence and their strategic role. The nationalisation of these networks was often slow and complex, evolving over many decades. The main exception to this was the administration of Lázaro Cárdenas (1934–40) which saw an intensification of activity, climaxing with the nationalisation of the railways in 1937 and, in particular, with the dramatic expropriation of 17 American and British oil firms and the creation of the state monopoly PEMEX in 1938 (which is still celebrated in Mexico as a national holiday).

American and European FDI had played an important role in the Mexican economy during the Porfiriato, being largely destined for mining, petroleum, railway expansion, electric power, banking and textiles. However, in the key sector of transport the state early on took a major share and, at the beginning of the twentieth century, Mexican National Railways was the largest enterprise in Mexico. Half of its capital, however, was still held by foreign investors as shares or bonds. In 1914, in the face of fully-fledged revolutionary struggle, the Mexican government declared a moratorium on its foreign debt, including its railway debt. In post-revolutionary Mexico railways were in a poor state – destroyed, underfunded, overstaffed and increasingly subject to competition from roads. In 1937 Cárdenas declared the railways nationalised and the negotiations over their control and debt were not resolved until the mid-1940s, when foreign shareholders were paid back one tenth of the shares' original value.[6]

Foreign interests that had dominated the extraction of crude oil and natural gas started to clash over rising taxes with the Mexican government as it stabilised from 1920. Tensions further escalated after the passing of the Petroleum Law in 1925 which put restrictions on the foreign exploitation of oil and gas via concessions and, in the eyes of TNC owners, threatened their property rights.[7] The expropriation of foreign oil interests in 1938 has attracted the attention of many historians: the traditional view is that this was an act of anti-imperialism, marking the apex of revolutionary economic nationalism.[8] Revisionist historians, such as Knight, argue that the expropriation was not the result of pre-planned revolution ideology, but rather a case where the Mexican government's hand was forced due to a number of factors, including declining reserves in Mexico and newly discovered oil fields in Venezuela, the intransigent – sometimes arrogant – behaviour of TNC managers that still treated Mexico as a colony and an intractable labour dispute with a powerful trade union. In short, the government acted to save face.[9] Debate among historians continues as to whether the assertion that the PEMEX expropriation was, as Knight claimed, a 'spectacular exception' to an otherwise moderate and pragmatic approach to FDI,[10] or whether the Cárdenas administration represented the climax of a genuinely revolutionary industrial policy.[11]

In contrast, nationalisation in the electricity and telecommunications sectors was slow, unfolding over decades. The origins of electricity in Mexico are during the Porfiriato when foreign TNCs became involved in generation and distribution. Tensions, however, between the Mexican government and the TNCs gave rise to disputes about pricing, interconnection of networks and infrastructure development beyond the main cities. In 1937 the Mexican government established the CFE (Federal Electricity Commission) in order to increase pressure on TNCs gradually. By the late 1950s the Mexican government was in charge of plants providing nearly half the total national generating capacity (in many cases thanks to World Bank loans).[12] By 1960 the only remaining foreign interests were Belgian Mexican Light and Power and the American Foreign Power Company, which were mainly involved in electricity distribution. The Mexican government bought both in 1960 while Article 27 of the Constitution was amended to reserve electricity services for the Mexican state.

The incorporation of telecommunications into the public sector was particularly long-drawn-out, with the firm only becoming fully nationalised in 1972.[13] As in the case of electricity TNCs established telephone services in Mexico City during the Porfiriato. Fierce competition, non-cooperation and a lack of regulation characterised the industry which, by 1925, had been consolidated into two TNCs: Ericsson of Sweden and ITT of the USA.[14] The Great Depression forced the two TNCs to start negotiating a merger, whilst pressure grew during the Cárdenas administration to interconnect their systems. While both foreign companies were in favour of a merger each was determined to set the conditions and both were vehemently opposed to accepting the conditions laid down by the government, which tried to reign in their privileges. Correspondence between the directors of the foreign firms and the Secretary of Communications and Public Works, Múgica, reveals that tensions were high during this period. This mutual distrust was exacerbated when Múgica was offered bribes if the foreigners could have their way, and – infuriated – cut off correspondence. The vehemence of the correspondence between Múgica and the foreign TNCs was such that it has been suggested expropriation could not have been entirely ruled out.[15] However, the oil expropriation acted as a shock wave: both the Mexican government and the foreign companies moderated their behaviour from 1938, whilst the Cárdenas administration ended in 1940 and was followed by a more conservative administration.[16]

From the 1940s the government opted to gradually 'Mexicanise' telecommunications. Mexicanisation is a loose, flexible notion describing a range of different policies, from wholesale nationalisation to a more incremental shift in ownership away from foreign interests and towards Mexican private investors, allowing foreigners to regain significant, though less visible, privileges once out of the limelight.[17] The rationale was to attempt to channel FDI into priority areas for Mexico rather than in the interests of foreigners. The Mexicanisation of telecommunications occurred in two phases: first, the Mexican government negotiated with Ericsson to create TELMEX in 1947, to be jointly owned by Mexican and Swedish interests with a majority Mexican board.[18] Next, the government negotiated the acquisition of the ITT-owned firm. By 1957 TELMEX controlled 96 per cent of telephone services and the following year the Mexican government pressurised Ericsson and ITT to sell their remaining shares to Mexican private investors, thus consolidating its Mexicanisation. From this time the state gradually increased its ownership of TELMEX, obtaining revenues via taxes on local and international calls and a scheme whereby new subscribers would buy state-issued shares in the company (to dilute private Mexican interests) and then buy them back using telephone taxes. By 1970 the state controlled 48 per cent of the shares: when Echeverría's government bought a further 3 per cent in 1972 TELMEX was finally officially nationalised.[19]

II. Organisational Anarchy and Debt Crisis

In 1970 there were 272 SOEs, mostly in the transport, communications, banking and industrial sectors. From 1970, however, the public sector grew at a dizzying speed: in 12 years the number of enterprises more than quadrupled, peaking at 1155 in 1982. Nationalisation was implemented either via rescue operations or for politico-economic reasons and took in enterprises from all sectors, in any form, shape or size. Not only did this result in organisational anarchy, increasing bureaucracy and managerial problems, but it also contributed significantly to Mexico's rising external debt.

From the 1940s state promotion of enterprises in transport, communications and energy had largely been financed by utility profits whilst foreign credit played a minor role.[20] However, Mexico's foreign debt gradually rose, becoming notable in the 1960s but booming in the 1970s. Mexican consolidated foreign debt, set at US$ 7 billion in 1970, doubled by 1974, doubling again to reach US$ 29 billion by 1977. By 1982 it reached nearly US$ 80 billion.[21] The bulk of loans were destined for SOEs and banks that had required heavy financial support for their rapid expansion in the 1970s. PEMEX and the CFE absorbed most debt. While in 1970 PEMEX's foreign debt stood at barely US$ 367 million, by 1981 this surpassed US$ 11 billion, representing 27 per cent of total long-term Mexican public debt. The expansion of the electricity network, promoted by President Echeverría (1970–76) and López Portillo (1976–82), also led to massive accumulated debt, rising from US$ 990 million in 1970 to over US$ 8.2 billion in 1981 (see Figure 13.1).

Why did Mexican technocrats and bankers not smell danger with this dramatic escalation of foreign debt? From 1976 huge oil reserves had been discovered in the Gulf of Mexico and it was generally believed the debt could be paid off using 'black gold'. In a short period of time Mexico's debt had also internationalised: while most of the foreign loans during the 1960s and early 1970s were extended directly to the Mexican government by multilateral financial agencies, from the mid-1970s the international debt scenario changed dramatically as private American, European and Japanese banks aggressively sought out new clients in Latin America. Literally hundreds of American banks provided loans to Mexican public and private enterprises but

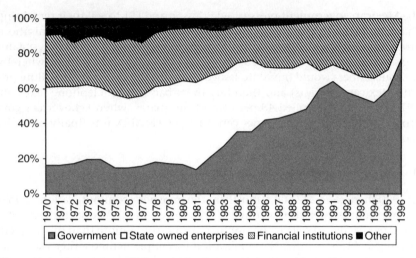

Figure 13.1   Proportion of Mexico's Net Foreign Debt Owed by Different Institutions 1970–1996
Source: Elaborated by authors based on Ibañez (2000).

by 1982 six large banking corporations led the pack: Citicorp (US\$ 2.8 billion in Mexican loans), Bank of America (US\$ 2.5 billion), Manufacturers Hanover (US\$ 1.9 billion), Chase Manhattan (US\$ 1.6 billion), Chemical Bank (US\$ 1.4 billion) and J.P. Morgan (US\$ 1.1 billion).[22] The 1982 crisis was also provoked by the financial strategy of Mexican private and public banks to obtain low cost loans from abroad and then re-loan domestically at higher rates.[23] State-owned banks such as Nacional Financiera increased its debt to US\$ 20 million in this period. This irresponsible strategy assumed international interest rates would not rise and that there would not be devaluation in Mexico. After the Federal Reserve Bank of the USA increased interest rates in the early 1980s most Latin American debtors had to find additional loans to bridge the costs provoked by the increase in interest payments. The huge debt service obligations went beyond the relatively limited budgetary possibilities of Latin American governments: financial globalisation and indebtedness had surpassed both expectations and fiscal realities. The first country to fall was Mexico, which declared a temporary suspension of payments in August 1982. Its total external debt at this point was US\$ 87 billion, of which almost US\$ 60 billion was public sector debt, US\$ 19 billion private sector debt and US\$ 8.5 billion commercial bank debt. Successive debt restructuring over the next few years consisted fundamentally of refinancing loans authorised by the international banks so the government did not declare a moratorium. Foreign creditors persuaded the Finance Ministry to assign profits from petroleum to cover interest on the debt. A large part of public sector debt was transferred to the government and the public banking sector, guaranteed by PEMEX.

Privatisation was part and parcel of the new policy recommendations by the World Bank and the IMF known in retrospect as the 'Washington Consensus'.

III. The Role of TELMEX in the New Neoliberal Consensus

Privatisation in Mexico has been analysed elsewhere,[24] so the focus here will be on the role TELMEX played. By 1982, 1155 SOEs were controlled by the Mexican government, accounting for 18.5 per cent of GDP and employing around 1 million workers. During the De la Madrid administration (1982–8) one half of these were divested, mostly small or medium-sized enterprises in non-priority areas where it was difficult to defend government ownership. Of these divestures 294 were closed down, 204 were sold, 72 merged and 25 transferred.[25] Even though the number of SOEs was slashed by half, there was little impact on government finances or government participation in the economy during this period. Revenue generated by sales in this period was US$ 500 million and had only a small microeconomic impact.[26] Moreover the number of public sector workers actually increased since, as some enterprises were divested, others from the private sector were incorporated. Only in 1988, in the last year of the De la Madrid administration, was the privatisation of a small number of large SOEs – including Aeroméxico and Mexicana, Mexico's two national airline – begun.

The Salinas administration, which came to power in December 1988, took dramatic and rapid steps to deepen and extend the opening up of the economy. In 1989 the financial system was liberalised and FDI restrictions softened in order to make new areas of the economy accessible to foreign investors. An ambitious privatisation programme was launched to sell off many of Mexico's largest firms. Between 1989 and 1994 TELMEX, Mexicana, steel mills including Altos Hornos and Sicartsa, dozens of sugar mills, automobile companies including Dina and mines including Cananea were all sold off. Between 1982 and 1994 the number of SOEs shrank from 1155 to 220.

As Newbery observes, governments face a range of options regarding corporate governance, stakeholder arrangements and overall transparency and openness when privatising.[27] What model of privatisation would Salinas opt for? Certainly the sale of TELMEX was the single most important instance of privatisation in Mexico for three principal reasons. Firstly, the revenue generated by the sale for the Mexican Treasury, which totalled around US$ 6 billion, was easily the largest sum obtained from the sale of any single firm at the time, constituting around 30 per cent of all proceeds generated during the Salinas administration. Secondly, TELMEX was chosen by Salinas as a 'launching pad' from which the rest of the sales were carried out. A successful sale would send a message to investors that the government was serious in its plans to privatise.[28] Thirdly, the sale of TELMEX was used for political ends. It should be remembered that Salinas came to power under suspicious circumstances, many sectors of society, including some of the main trade unions, having failed to support him.

A dramatic privatisation programme could engender resistance from the general public and the unions, who associated this with job losses, the 'flexibilisation' of labour contracts and the weakening of trade union power.[29] Salinas's objective, thus, was to guarantee a successful privatisation early on in his mandate, free from union conflict. In the run up to the TELMEX sale Salinas held meetings with the leader of the Trade Union of Mexican Telephone Workers (STRM) in order to pact a mutually satisfactory privatisation. He informed them of his plan to promote them as an example of 'vanguard, new unionism', promising them they would benefit from privatisation if they cooperated. Salinas inaugurated the STRM's annual meeting in 1989 and announced the privatisation of TELMEX to its workers before this had been made official. Six promises were made: (1) there would be no redundancies; (2) labour rights would be respected; (3) workers would get shares in the company; (4) the state would still be the regulator; (5) the new owner would be Mexican; (6) telecommunications services would improve. The workers were in general flattered by this personal attention: they were the union 'pets' of the President of Mexico and agreed to cooperate.

Prior to the sale the government modified TELMEX's ownership and corporate governance in an innovative way to *ensure that Mexican investors would end up with control of the private business*. Special controlling shares restricted to Mexicans were reduced and concentrated, so that, with only a relatively small amount, Mexican investors could afford to take control.[30] The sale was announced in August 1990: of the three offers made, the controlling 20.4 per cent share was awarded to Grupo Carso. This Mexican conglomerate owned by Carlos Slim bought 10.4 per cent of total capital stock (51 per cent of special controlling 'AA' shares reserved for Mexican investors). Its partners were Southwestern Bell (SBC) and France Telecom, each with 5 per cent of total capital stock.[31] Thus TELMEX passed from a public to a Mexican-controlled private monopoly in 1990, which would expire after six years and thereafter face competition. Moreover the STRM were also awarded shares in exchange for cooperating with the privatisation.[32]

In 1994 the Salinas administration ended in scandal and the entire privatisation programme came under scrutiny. Rumours abounded that Salinas had used Slim as a 'straw man' to buy TELMEX on his behalf, though this has not been proved. It is clear, however, that the new TELMEX owners were privileged, gaining a six-year period to enjoy a monopoly over national and international services. This gave them time to expand and modernise the network according to the targets set by the government and also to become consolidated as a national champion before competition got a look in. TELMEX also enjoyed a head start in new telecommunications markets, such as mobile telephones and internet services. When mobile telephone licences were awarded in 1998, TELMEX was awarded one licence to operate in each of the nine regions (under the name TELCEL), having to compete as a duopoly with a different operator in each region (TELCEL was the only operator with national coverage).

From 1995, as TELMEX's monopoly drew to a close, provisions were made to prepare for competition. The regulatory body, the Federal Commission of Telecommunications (COFETEL), was established and a new regulatory framework for telecommunications implemented. Institutional pressure increased further when, in 1993, FDI restrictions were loosened, allowing foreigners to buy more than 49 per cent of mobile telephone companies, subject to approval by the National Foreign Investment Commission, and in 1998, when, as a result of the new commitments Mexico agreed to at the WTO under the fourth protocol to GATS, TELMEX was forced to offer interconnection services to its rivals. Restrictions to 49 per cent of foreign ownership of TELMEX still stand in 2006.[33]

IV. The Return of Foreigners and the Rise of the Trans-Latin American Corporation

Deep privatisation of former national monopolies and other SOEs in most Latin American countries helped feed a boom in inward FDI flows to the region in the first half of the 1990s. This was the first wave of transnationalisation of the late twentieth century, characterised by TNCs, usually from the industrialised world, entering and taking advantage of newly privatised enterprises in the region. A second wave of transnationalisation started around 2000 and is still ongoing. Economic crisis, global (and regional) declines in global and regional FDI flows,[34] combined with a rise of investment dispute claims going to the GATS-WTO (Mexico was second only to Argentina in the number of claims presented), characterised this period.[35] As a result, as some disillusioned TNCs started to pull out of the region Latin American investors moved to fill the vacuum.

The Economic Commission for Latin America and the Caribbean (ECLAC) labels these new regional actors 'Trans Latins': these are (usually) private enterprises based in one Latin American country that cross borders by acquiring assets in other enterprises in the region, possibly as a springboard to international expansion. In order to distinguish Latin American companies from other 'Latin' companies, such as Spain and Portugal, which also seek to exploit the 'Latin' business world, they are referred to here as Trans Latin American Corporations (TLACs).

In Mexico between 1970 and 1993 inward FDI flows averaged around US$ 3 billion, and the proportional contribution to Gross Domestic Investment (GDI) was below 7 per cent. From 1994 onwards inward FDI flows increased fivefold while GDI contributions reached 15 per cent. Outward FDI also changed significantly, increasing from an annual average of US$ 100 million between 1970 and 1993 to over US$ 1.5 billion between 1994 and 2004. From 1997 outward FDI reached an average 1.5 per cent of GDI (see Figure 13.2): although this shows outward FDI is still much less important than inward FDI, as in many developing countries, there is increasing internationalisation by Mexican TNCs, as reflected in the number of cross-border mergers and acquisitions.[36]

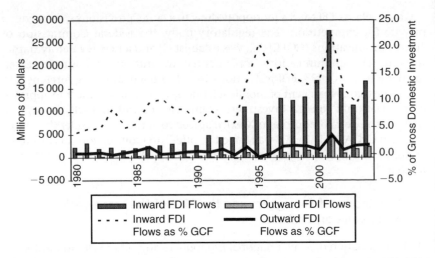

Figure 13.2   Mexico – Inward and Outward Foreign Direct Investment, 1980–2004 (millions of dollars and percentage of Gross Domestic Capital Formation)
Source: Elaborated by the authors based on UNCTAD (2000–2005).

By 2003, of the top 25 TLACs in the region half were Mexican-based. TELMEX and its spin-off América Móvil ranked second and third respectively, whilst Grupo Carso, Slim's industrial and commercial group, ranked eighth. The top five TLACs are composed either of telecommunications actors (TELMEX and América Móvil), extraction (Petrobras, CVRD) or cement (CEMEX). As can be seen in Table 13.1 TELMEX is a very recent TLAC because, until 2003, the bulk of its revenue originated from Mexico. Indeed it was with the acquisition of AT&T assets in 2004 that TELMEX became properly internationalised.[37] Comparing the transnationality index (TNI) of all five companies TELMEX has the lowest result.

The remainder of this section analyses the strategy of TELMEX and América Móvil during both waves of transnationalisation. In the case of Latin American telecommunications in general, in retrospect, the objectives sought through privatisation were to maximise inward FDI rather than to introduce competition, with the exception of Brazil.[38] Mexico was different in that the overriding objective was to nurture a national champion. At the global level telecommunications in the 1990s was characterised by rapid technological change, increased competition and mergers and acquisitions. Latin America became a playground for operators, mostly from the industrialised world, which saw its underdeveloped networks and unexploited technologies as offering attractive ways to extend their markets. Thus the first wave of transnationalisation involved European enterprises, particularly Telefonica, France Telecom, Telecom Italia and Portugal Telecom, and American enterprises

Table 13.1 Top Five Trans-Latin American Corporations in Leading Non-Financial TNCs, 1999–2004

Corporation	Home country	Industry	Revenues*		Transnationality Index*						Main countries of operation
			2003	2004	1999	2000	2001	2002	2003	2004	
Petrobras	Brazil	Oil	42.7	48.3	7.2	5.8	4.3	6.1	15.6	14.9	Brazil, Argentina, Bolivia, Colombia, USA
Telmex	Mexico	Telecoms	10.8	12.1	0	0	0	0	0.8	11.8	Mexico, Brazil, Argentina, Chile, Colombia, Peru, USA
América Móvil	Mexico	Telecoms	7.2	11.2	9.9	22.7	30.7	30.6	35.9	44.1	Mexico, Argentina, Colombia, Ecuador, Guatemala, Venezuela, Nicaragua, Brazil, USA
CEMEX	Mexico	Building materials	7.6	8.1	54.6	54.8	70.4	67.9	72.3	71.9	Mexico, USA, Spain, Venezuela, Colombia, Egypt, Finland, Indonesia, Thailand, Barhein, Costa Rica, Chile, Jamaica, Nicaragua
CVRD (Compania Vale do Rio Doce)	Brazil	Mining	7	8.5	34	28.9	32	35.9	40.5	41.9	Brazil, USA, Argentina, Chile, Norway, France, Bahrain

Notes: * gross revenues in millions of dollars.
**TNI (UNCTAD's definition) is calculated as the average of the following three ratios: foreign assets to total assets, foreign sales to total sales and foreign employment to total employment.

Source: Elaborated by the authors based on company annual reports and UNCTAD (2001–2005).

such as Verizon and Bell South gaining new markets via the acquisition of former telecoms SOEs.[39] Telefonica emerged as the leader: by 1999 it was the largest TNC in the region by consolidated sales, with coverage in most segments and most countries.[40] Most early efforts focused on gaining access to fixed-line telephony in South America via privatisation, whilst in the latter part of the 1990s TNCs strengthened their positions and entered new segments, such as Internet, mobile telephony and multimedia services.

Two foreign TNCs, SBC and France Telecom, entered the Mexican market with the privatisation of TELMEX (France Telecom was to sell its shares in 2000 in order to withdraw to European markets). Gradually, as TELMEX's monopoly came to an end in 1996 and institutions for competition were established, more TNCs entered to compete with TELMEX. In the late 1990s local telephony was gradually opened up, and concessions were granted to new companies (Axtel, SPC and Amaritel). In the mobile telephone sector, new licences were awarded: as had happened in the previous round TELMEX's TELCEL successfully won a licence to operate in each of the nine regions. The difference was that this time TELMEX was not alone; Pegaso (a partnership between a local group and Leap Wireless of the US, subsequently bought by Telefonica in 2002)[41] also gained national coverage. Long-distance services were also opened up: new players with foreign and Mexican capital quickly snapped up one quarter of TELMEX's market share.[42]

Despite these encroaching challenges TELMEX still enjoyed very large market shares: in 2000 it held 95 per cent of local telephony, 66 per cent of long-distance, 72 per cent of mobile and 60 per cent of data/Internet services. ECLAC is critical of the development of Mexican telecommunications since privatisation, arguing that although the privatised TELMEX has expanded and modernised its network, other privatised Latin American telecommunications operators have developed at much better rates.[43] Moreover prices remain high in Mexico, even when compared to OECD members, and the disparity between penetration levels is increasing. Slowness in introducing competition, reinforced by the policy of protecting the national champion and a weak regulatory capacity, and TELMEX's application of high interconnection fees and cross-subsidisation policies (lowering prices in exposed activities and raising them in protected ones such as local calls) in order to fend off competition are all noted as the causes.[44] The regulatory body COFETEL has been criticised for being too dependent on the executive, lacking transparency and failing to regulate TELMEX properly. When the newly established Federal Commission of Competition warned COFETEL that TELMEX had a dominant position in all key telecommunications markets COFETEL seemed incapable of correcting this: when COFETEL took TELMEX to court in 1999 TELMEX won. The American FCC fined a TELMEX subsidiary in the USA because TELMEX headquarters would not allow two competing joint ventures, Alestra (AT&T) and Avantel (WorldCom), to connect to its network. A complaint was also lodged at the WTO against the Mexican government for failing to regulate TELMEX over practices such as refusing to resell long-distance calls and charging high interconnection fees (this was suspended in 2001 with the election of a new president).

While TELMEX has been criticised for blocking competition at home, it has at the same time emerged as one of the leading TLACs. TELMEX announced its strategy to internationalise from 1998, stating that its natural market was Spanish speakers across the Americas. In 1998 it firstly bought 18.9 per cent of Prodigy, the American Internet service provider and the next year agreed with Microsoft to design a portal for Spanish speakers, and secondly signed an agreement with Telecomunicaciones de Guatemala that involved TELMEX managing the company restructuring with an option to buy 49 per cent over the next five years. The following year TELMEX acquired an American company that supplied prepaid fixed telephony and, together with SBC, Cellular Communications of Puerto Rico. In 2000 TELMEX restructured, keeping basic telephony, data and Internet, and spun off TELCEL, television interests and international assets to América Móvil. The newly established América Móvil formed an alliance with SBC and Bell Canada International to expand their platform across the continent for mobile telephone, Internet and data service provision, and profited from their experience diversifying risk outside Mexico. The aim of Telecom Américas was to integrate systems and establish a large digital footprint in the region.

Between 2000 and 2002 Telecom Américas bought four Brazilian mobile telephone companies. Due to different strategic approaches América Móvil bought the shares in both of its foreign partners and restructured in order to initially focus on the Brazilian market. At the end of 2003 América Móvil unified its regional operators under a single brand, Claro, and by 2005 had a solid position in this country, though Telefonica was still leader. As foreign investors abandoned the region América Móvil stepped in, buying Argentine CTI Móvil from Verizon, Compañía de Telecomunicaciones El Salvador from France Telecom, Telecom Italia's Peruvian subsidiary and Chilean Smartcom from Spain's Endesa. By the end of 2005 América Móvil was neck and neck with its competitor Telefonica. So TELMEX is a recent TLAC: until 2003 its aim was to 'provide telecommunications services, primarily in Mexico' but most recently it has been transformed into a regional powerhouse.[45] Between 2003 and 2005 it invested US$ 4750 million in Latin America, and this was reflected in the 2004 annual report which paid much more attention to its regional operators in Argentina, Brazil, Chile, Colombia and Peru (see Table 13.2).

Conclusions

According to Latin American FDI specialist Michael Mortimore, the inward FDI boom to Latin America and the Caribbean in the 1990s resulted in two broad patterns. From the point of view of international business strategy American firms seeking efficiency, mostly in the manufacturing sector (in order to compete with Asian imports) dominated investment into Mexico and Central America. FDI inflows largely resulted in the creation of new assets, which

Table 13.2   TELMEX International Subsidiaries and Affiliated Companies, 2005

Subsidiary company	Country	Acquisition		
		Equity*	Value**	Date
Telmex Argentina ***	Argentina	100		Feb. 04
Telmex do Brazil ***	Brazil	100		
Telmex Chile Holding ***	Chile	100	196	
Telmex Colombia***	Colombia	100		
Telmex Perú***	Peru	100		
Embratel	Brazil	90.3	672	Jul.–Dec. 04
Telmex Corp. (Chilesat)	Chile	99.3	114	Apr. 04
Techtel	Argentina/Uruguay	83.4	100	Jun. 04
Metrored	Argentina/Uruguay	83.4	12	Jun. 04
Latam Telecom	US	100	n.a.	before 2003
Affiliated companies				
Televista	US	45	34	before 2003
Technology and Internet LLC	US	50	17	before 2003
Net	Brazil	36.6	311	Feb.–Mar. 05

Notes: * Percentage corresponds to controlling interest in 2005.
      ** All acquisition values from 2003 were recorded at the purchase price for the net asset in millions of dollars.
      *** Assets of AT&T Latin American Corp.

Source: Elaborated by the authors based on TELMEX *Annual Report* (various years).

increased export capacity and international competitiveness. In the case of South America, international business, mainly from Europe (especially Spain) sought access to markets and services and was mainly concerned with the purchase of existing assets through acquisitions and privatisation, which tended to strengthen systemic competitiveness.[46]

Within these broad trends, and taking a perspective from Mexico, the general observation is that attempts to open up networks to (foreign) private capital have been significantly hampered. There has been some privatisation, such as of the railways (through concessions), and in oil and gas (through supply and building contracts for PEMEX), whilst competition has been introduced into electricity supply. Some of the benefits of these processes have been channeled towards Mexican economic groups but many others have gone to foreign firms.[47] In general, however, the networks are still majority state-owned. Vicente Fox rejected the privatisation of PEMEX and CFE when he came to power in 2000.[48] Barriers to foreign capital continue to apply, such as restrictions on TELMEX's ownership. In contrast to other large Latin American countries, therefore, Mexico has experienced low FDI inflows into its main networks, with the exception of mobile telephony. Meanwhile TELMEX has been dynamic and is the only clear competitor to Telefonica in the region. The two giants will largely dominate telecommunications in the future. The increased stock value of Slim's companies was reflected in his being named by Forbes as the world's third richest man (after Gates and Buffet) in 2006. In the case of telecommunications a lack of competition at home has helped TELMEX fund its international spree.

Notes

1 Ramamurti (1996); Clifton (2000).
2 Freeman and Soete (1994).
3 Castells (1996).
4 Clifton, Comín and Díaz-Fuentes (2003).
5 Comín and Díaz-Fuentes (2004); Comín and Díaz-Fuentes (2006).
6 The original agreements of 1942 and 1946 are in Secretaría de Hacienda y Crédito Público (1958) pp. 195–578.
7 Maddison et al. (1989) pp. 35, 55.
8 Meyer (1968).
9 Knight (1994).
10 Knight (1994).
11 Grunstein Dickter (2005).
12 Glade and Anderson (1968) p. 81.
13 For an official but detailed historical description of the evolution of the telephone industry in Mexico see Teléfonos de México (1991).
14 For the official story of Ericsson in Mexico see Gabriel Szekely (2000).
15 Grunstein Dickter (2005).
16 Grunstein Dickter (2005).
17 For further analysis of Mexicanisation see Adler Hellman (1988).
18 Telmex was owned by: Mexicana Corporación Continental S.A., Ericsson, Bruno Pagliai, Octavio Fernández Reynosa and José Joaquín César (Petrazinni 1994) p. 107. TELMEX would allow Ericsson to consolidate its business in Mexico whilst enjoying the protection of Mexican laws behind the guise of a Mexican company.
19 See Petrazzini (1994). This turn to Mexicanisation was explained by President Echeverría's (1970–76) new economic policy towards foreign investment and Mexicanisation. In 1973 Echeverría introduced the first serious piece of legislation that regulated foreign direct investment. See Lewis (2005).
20 See Green (1978).
21 For an analysis of debt in the 1970s see Green (1998).
22 Quijano (1985) p. 85.
23 Green (1998) p. 104.
24 Aspe Armella (1993); Baer and Conroy (1994); Bazdresch and Elizondo (1994); Clifton (2000); Ramamurti (1996); Rogozinski (1997); Sánchez and Corona (1993); Tandon (1992); and Teichman (1995).
25 Aspe (1993).
26 Galal (1994).
27 Newbury (2003).
28 Ramamurti (1996).
29 See Clifton (2000).
30 For more details on how the shares were restructured see Clifton (2000).
31 Clifton (2000).
32 Clifton (2000).
33 OECD (2005).

34 ECLAC (2003).
35 UNCTAD (2005).
36 A recent study of the internationalisation of Mexican firms is de los Angeles Pozas (2002).
37 UNCTAD (2005) Annex, Table A.1.100, p. 271.
38 ECLAC (2000).
39 ECLAC (2000), Table IV.6.
40 ECLAC (2000) p. 213.
41 ECLAC (2003) p. 56.
42 Mexican Alfa and Bancomer group which formed Alestra with AT&T, and Banamex-Accival which joined MCI WorldCom to create Avantel.
43 ECLAC (2000).
44 ECLAC (2000) p. 193.
45 In August 2005 Peruvian telephone enterprise TIM Peru was acquired by TELMEX from Telecom Italia for US$ 500 million; and in April 2006 TELMEX and América Móvil bought the stock of Verizon Communications in telephone firms in Puerto Rico, Venezuela and the Dominican Republic for US$ 3700 million.
46 Mortimore (2005).
47 Lewis (2005) p. 35.
48 ECLAC (2000) p. 43.

References

Adler Hellman, J. (1988) *Mexico in Crisis* (New York/London: Holmes & Meier).
Aspe Armella, P. (1993) *El camino mexicano de la transformación económica* (Mexico: Fondo de Cultura Económica).
Baer, W., and M. Conroy (eds) (1994) 'Latin America: Privatization, Property Rights, and Deregulation I and II', *The Quarterly Review of Economics and Finance*, vols 33 and 34, Special Issues.
Bazdresch, C., and C. Elizondo (1994) 'Privatization: The Mexican Case', in Baer and Conroy (1994) pp. 45–66.
Castells, M. (1996) *The Rise of the Network Society* (Oxford: Blackwells).
Clifton, J. (2000) *The Politics of Telecommunications in Mexico* (Basingstoke/New York: Macmillan).
Clifton, J., F. Comín and D. Díaz-Fuentes (2003) *Privatisation in the European Union: Public Enterprises and Integration* (Dordrecht/Boston: Kluwer Academic Publishers).
COFETEL: 'Historia de las telecomunicaciones en México', http://204.153.24.194/html/la_era/info_tel2/hist1.shtml, last accessed 23 July 2006.
Comín, F., and D. Díaz-Fuentes (2004) *La empresa pública en Europa* (Madrid: Síntesis).
Comín, F., and D. Díaz-Fuentes (2006) 'De una Hacienda imperial a dos Haciendas nacionales: las reformas tributarias en México y España durante el siglo XIX', in R. Dobado, Al Gómez Galvarriato and G. Márquez (eds), *España y México: ¿Historia económicas paralelas?* (México: Fondo de Cultura Económica).
De los Angeles Pozas, M. (2002) *Estrategia internacional de la gran empresa mexicana en la década de los noventa* (Mexico: El Colegio de México).
ECLAC (various years) *Foreign Investment in Latin America and the Caribbean* (annual reports 1985–2005).
Freeman, C., and L. Soete (1994) *Work for All or Mass Unemployment?* (London: Pinter).
Galal, A., et al. (1994) *Welfare Consequences of Selling Public Enterprises: An Empirical Analysis* (New York: World Bank/Oxford University Press).

Glade, W., and C. Anderson (1968) *The Political Economy of Mexico* (Madison: University of Wisconsin Press).

Green, R. (1998) *Lecciones de la deuda externa mexicana de 1973 a 1997: de abundancias y escaceses*, (Mexico: Fondo de Cultura Económica, 1998).

Grunstein Dickter, A. (2005) 'In the Shadow of Oil', *Mexican Studies* (Winter).

Ibañez, J.A. *Subdesarrollo, mercado y deuda externa* (2000).

Knight, A. (1994) 'Cardenismo: Juggernaut or Jalopy?', *Journal of Latin American Studies*, 26 (1).

Kuntz Flicher, S., and P. Riguzzi (eds) (1996) *Ferrocarriles y vida económica en México, 1850–1950* (Mexico: UAM, El Colegio Mexiquense y Ferrocarriles Nacionales de México).

Lewis, C. (2005) 'States and Markets in Latin America. The Political Economy of Interventionism', Working Paper 09–05 (London: LSE): http://www.lse.ac.uk/collections/economicHistory/GEHN/GEHNPDF/WorkingPape r09CML.pdf

Maddison, A. et al. (1993) *La economía política de la pobreza, la equidad y el crecimiento: Brasil y México* (Mexico: Fondo de Cultura Económica).

Meyer, L. (1968) *México y los Estados Unidos en el conflicto petrolero* (Mexico: El Colegio de México).

Mortimore, M. (2005) 'The Policy Framework for Investment in Latin America and the Caribbean (UN-ECLAC)' http://www.oecd.org/dataoecd/59/41/35623939.pdf (accessed October 2005).

Newbery, D.M. (2003) 'Privatizing Network Industries', CESIFO Working Paper No. 1132 (November).

OECD (2005) *Communications Outlook* (OECD).

Petrazzini, B.A. (1994) 'Telecomunicaciones en México ante la integración económica regional', in Ibarra Yuñez et al. (eds), *Telecomunicaciones en México ante el reto de la integración* (Mexico: University of California at San Diego/ITESM).

Quijano, J.-M., H. Sánchez and F. Antía (1985) *Finanzas, desarrollo económico y penetración extranjera* (Puebla: UAP).

Ramamurti, R. (ed.) (1996) *Privatizing Monopolies: Lessons from the Telecommunications and Transport Sectors in Latin America* (Baltimore/London: Johns Hopkins University Press).

Rogozinski Schtulman, J. (1993) *La privatización de las empresas paraestatales* (Mexico: Fondo de Cultura Económica).

Rogozinski Schtulman, J. (1997) *La privatización en México: razones e impactos* (Mexico: Trillas).

Sánchez, M., and R. Corona (1993) *Privatization in Latin America* (Washington DC: ITAM/IADB).

Secretaría de Hacienda y Crédito Público (1958) *Legislación sobre deuda pública* (México: SHCP).

Szekely, Gabriel (2000) *Ericsson en el tercer milenio: 95 años en México* (Mexico: Planeta).

Tandon, P. (1992) 'Welfare Consequences of Selling Public Enterprises: Mexico', paper presented at the World Bank Conference, 11–12 June.

Teichman, J. (1995) *Privatization and Political Change in Mexico* (Pittsburgh/London: University of Pittsburgh Press).

Teléfonos de México S.A. (1991) *Historia de la telefonía en México, 1878–1991* (Mexico: Scripta).

TELMEX *Informe Annual* (1990–2005) (Mexico: TELMEX).

UNCTAD (2005) *World Investment Report* (UNCTAD).

Vega Navarro, Angel de la (1999) *La evolución del componente petrolero en el desarrollo y la transición de México* (México: UNAM).

14
Internationalising Electricity Companies in Canada

Pierre Lanthier

Introduction

Free trade development in North America changed the profile not only of the industrial and commercial world, but of the utilities as well. To be sure, the signing of the North American Free Trade Agreement (NAFTA) did not signal immediate change: the sale of electricity from Canada to the USA is a long-established activity, and in fact this diminished during the years immediately following the signing the treaty. By the middle of the 1990s, however, as deregulation was implemented across the USA the volume of energy crossing the border increased and electrical companies all over the continent underwent major structural changes in order to comply with the new rules of the Federal Energy Regulatory Commission (FERC).[1] Meanwhile in the rest of the world, and especially in developing countries, utilities were being privatised. Electrical networks became objects of intense financial speculation. Once again the Canadian electrical companies were favoured by these transformations since over the years they had built up solid expertise in the long-distance transportation of electricity and enjoyed significant financial surpluses. The combination of these two developments helped promote an international dimension to Canadian electrical companies. In itself this observation is not very original. However, if we add to this the fact that these companies were state-owned then important questions start to emerge. How can a nationalised company become a multinational? How does a nationalised company deal with deregulation in a neighbouring country? As multinationals, are these companies performing like private enterprises? And finally, by becoming multinational would these companies not be eventually forced (or tempted) to dilute their mission as nationalised entities?

To deal with these questions, three cases have been selected: British Columbia Hydro, Manitoba Hydro and Hydro-Québec. Very different in size and located at considerable distance from each other they simultaneously adopted similar structural changes and confronted similar challenges in their international ventures. After a brief presentation of these companies their sales activities in the USA and their participation in projects outside the North American continent will be examined. The Conclusions attempt to provide answers to the questions posed above.

I. Company Background

The three companies under study share many characteristics. Firstly, they are wholly owned by Provincial States.[2] Hydro-Québec is the result of a two-step nationalisation in 1944 and 1963. This enterprise produces electricity and sells it all over Québec, excepting a few middle-sized cities such as Sherbrooke. Until 1997 there was no institution in charge of regulating Hydro-Québec. However, on 2 June 1997 a *Régie de l'Énergie* came into existence with the mission of keeping an eye on price fixing, transportation and distribution of energy.[3] Manitoba Hydro was created in 1949 and produces and distributes electricity throughout Manitoba except for downtown Winnipeg.[4] Since 1988 price fixing has been under the surveillance of the Public Service Board of Manitoba. Finally, British Columbia Hydro and Power Authority (BC Hydro) was established in 1962. This enterprise provides energy to the entire Province excluding the central southern region. Price fixing is overseen by the British Columbia Utilities Commission.

Secondly, these companies represent some of the most important of their kind in Canada, along with Ontario Hydro and its successors,[5] and the TransAlta Utilities Corp. (Alberta). Table 14.1 gives the basic statistics for each company for 2000.

Hydro-Québec leads with an installed capacity over double that of the other two enterprises put together; BC Hydro follows in distant second place with a capacity twice that of Manitoba Hydro. The three companies benefit from impressive hydraulic capacities.[6] In 1998, 95.6 per cent of Québec's production originated from hydro-electricity; in British Columbia hydro represented 89.3 per cent; and in Manitoba it was 97 per cent. Production is mainly concentrated in powerful hydro-electrical plants, the other plants being complementary or providing energy to remote areas. In 2000 Hydro-Québec had 49 hydro-electrical plants, while BC Hydro had 30 and Manitoba Hydro 14.[7]

Table 14.1 Production Capacity of the Three Canadian Companies, 2000

	Manitoba Hydro	*BC Hydro*	*Hydro-Québec*
Installed capacity (MW)	5,210	11,133	31,512
Sales (GWh)	28,717	72,031	190,080
Employees (no.)	4,701	5,952	20,676
Fixed assets (million CAN$)	12,575	14,617	59,038

Source: Compiled by author based on annual reports.

Finally, these companies enjoy favourable conditions for exporting their energy. Their local markets consist of small but highly concentrated populations located in a few cities. In 2004 Québec had 7.5 million inhabitants, nearly half of whom lived in the Montreal area; 52 per cent of the 4.2 million British Columbians are concentrated in Vancouver, while 60 per cent of the 1.2 million Manitobans live in Winnipeg. The companies have moreover developed expertise in long-distance electricity transportation. In 1999 Manitoba Hydro had 18,300 km of transportation lines, BC Hydro 17,800 and Hydro-Québec 32,200.[8] Most of their plants are located at a significant distance from the consuming centres. Added to harsh climatic conditions this factor gives them considerable know-how in high voltage transportation and consequently in exporting electricity.

The companies' capacity to export, however, suffers from specific limitations. To begin with, their plants are victims of an irregular hydraulic system. Manitoba Hydro and BC Hydro, once every seven to eight years, suffer from droughts which force them to import electricity. Hydro-Québec does not undergo drought per se, but the irregularity of its hydraulic capacity plays a significant role in the amount of energy exported, as was the case in 2003. Moreover if the local population is not large its consumption is very high (despite efforts made to encourage clients to reduce their level of consumption – the so-called 'power smart' programmes). In 2003 the average amount of KWh per residential subscriber was 10,672.3 for BC Hydro, 14,138.5 for Manitoba Hydro and 17,114.1 for Hydro-Québec.[9] This level of consumption reduces significantly the capacity to export. To this should be added a very militant environmental conscience in Canada and the rising territorial demands from the Aboriginal Nations.[10]

Despite these obstacles, exporting electricity is not only a permanent part of the three companies' activities; it has changed them thoroughly over the last decade.

II. Exporting to the United States

Exporting electricity to the USA is not new for Canada: the first electrical line between the two countries dates from 1901. Canada is favoured by its cheap hydro-electricity and by the fact that the peak load in the two countries does not occur at the same time (in winter for Canada, in summer for the USA). However, exporting electricity to the USA is subject to regulation from both sides of the border. Canada's National Energy Board ensures that electricity exports are not carried out at the expense of national consumption. Thus it insists that export prices should not be significantly lower than those prevailing in the targeted market in the USA. On the USA side there is no authorisation to be requested for importing electricity.[11] However, there are regulating institutions: FERC, which is responsible for the regulation of wholesale electricity throughout the USA;[12] and the North American Electric Reliability

Council (NERC), a continental organisation created in 1968 which presides over regional coordinating councils such as the Northeast Power Coordinating Council (NPCC), the Mid-Continent Area Power Pool (MAPP) and the Western Electricity Coordinating Council (WECC). These regional councils provide guidelines on the networks' reliability. They overlap the American–Canadian border with the purpose of harmonising the transmission activities of both countries.[13]

The signing of NAFTA and the adoption of deregulation in electricity impacted energy exports. As far as electricity is concerned NAFTA[14] imposed the rules of the GATT. Article 902, among others, forbids the imposition of any minimum price or export taxes by one country on the energy sold to another country. Article 904 stipulates that, in case of supply shortage, there should not be any discrimination on the part of one country that would be prejudicial to the customers of the other. And finally, Annex 905.2 of Article 905 specifies that both countries must make efforts to get rid of or to strongly attenuate the existing regulation of electricity so that there should be neither price increases in energy exports nor prohibition of access to neighbouring markets. In the years that followed Annex 905.2 would open electricity to major changes known as deregulation.[15]

Deregulation has been the object of a massive literature in recent years.[16] In the American context this concept is used to describe the changes that occurred during the 1990s in the structural reorganisation of the electrical industry. The old structure, based on the vertical integration of production, transportation and distribution of energy, providing a 'natural monopoly' over a region or a state, was deemed to be out of touch with the new reality. From the mid-1970s the growth of electrical consumption slowed down, making any new investment in heavy (and in particular thermal) production plants highly risky. Over-investment was denounced as very expensive for consumers (especially for the industrial sectors consuming high amounts of electricity). Instead, a new structure was proposed which separated production, transport and distribution. Transport and distribution activities would then have the opportunity to select their sources of production among competitors. Of even more benefit to customers was the fact that gas propelled turbines had experienced recent technological breakthroughs in the field: the traditional economies of scale provided by huge integrated plants was reduced by smaller gas plants, which were cheaper to build and operate, as well as being more efficient. These changes would bring serious competition to the existing (and very expensive) dinosaurs dominating the market. Consequently in 1992 the USA passed the Energy Policy Act to stimulate greater competition in the electricity industry through free access to transmission lines all over the country. At the same time, the Government asked FERC to establish an access system to wholesale electricity throughout the nation. FERC, after a long consultation period, set up an 'open access order' in May 1996 (Order 888) requesting all electricity companies to allow undiscriminating access to their networks and encouraged the formation of Regional Transmission Groups.[17] In December 1999 (Order 2000), following difficulties relating to the organisation of energy transmission, FERC established the Regional Transmission Operators (RTO), to which it gave precise goals and functions, including control over the transmission networks of companies operating in the same region, the fixing of a common policy to avoid overloading and the implementation of inter-connecting mechanisms with other regions.[18] This would be of enormous importance for the Canadian companies.

During the 1990s the three firms dismantled their vertical organisation and reassembled into three separate entities: production, transmission and distribution of energy. Although they remained state-owned, each division had separate policies and accounts. Companies were allowed to transmit electricity from many sources (not only from their own plants), according to the best price available. This would force them to produce energy as cheaply as possible.

BC Hydro was the first to react: by 1988, with the advent of NAFTA, it had already privatised part of its gas and railway activities in order to focus more on electricity and surrounded itself with a number of subsidiaries, including British Columbia Power Export Corporation (Powerex), a company that bought energy from BC Hydro and other Canadian producers (such as Alcan) and exported it to the west of the USA, with, from February 1996, the help of the BC Hydro transport network.[19]

The most significant change occurred in 1995, however, when FERC authorised Powerex to become a member of two Regional Transmission Groups and consequently to buy electricity from any source and sell it directly to distributors. Powerex thus acted as an electricity broker on the American market. In 2001, for instance, Powerex bought 25,893 GWh from producers other than BC Hydro and sold 23,900 GWh outside British Columbia.[20] This change led BC Hydro to restructure its activities according to Power Supply, Transmission, Distribution, and Customer Services.[21] As one commentator put it in 1997: 'The so-called crown jewel of B.C.'s Crown Corporations is now an unashamedly commercial enterprise'.[22] BC Hydro postponed mega projects in order to benefit from short-term contracts all over the continent. On the whole, the new structure proved to be beneficial. In 2004 Powerex had more than 150 companies as customers and sold energy as far away as Mexico from 1997. This activity south of the border encouraged other BC Hydro subsidiaries to do business in the USA. Westech, for instance, sold licences relating to emergency medical systems to over 50 American institutions in 1996.[23]

Powerex, however, got involved in the Californian electricity crisis. The company is said to have bought from BC Hydro electricity for about US$ 5.50 per MWh and to have sold it for up to US$ 425 per MWh to the Californians. Over a nine-month period between 2000 and 2001 it made profits of CAN$ 1 billion.[24] All this led to a legal suit in 2002 that ended in October 2003 in a settlement whereby 'Powerex will be returning [US]$ 1,300,000 the total revenues (…) from Powerex's participation in alleged gaming practice'.[25] In its

2004 annual report BC Hydro explained that 'as part of the settlement agreement, Powerex agreed to pay US$ 1.3 million to avoid the burden, costs and uncertainty associated with the litigation process and to achieve closure of the FERC proceedings'.[26] But BC Hydro was itself directly involved in a lawsuit relating to this issue. Although a US Federal court gave immunity to the company there is still a possibility this judgment could be reversed, just as there is a possibility of further enquiries and proceedings against Powerex. BC Hydro has consequently increased its provisions for legal costs.[27]

Alongside these events BC Hydro underwent other structural changes. First in 2002 it adopted the Generation, Transmission and Distribution 'Lines of Business', with the addition of two services, Field and Engineering.[28] The most significant change, however, occurred in April 2003, involving the outsourcing for ten years of services worth CAN$ 1.27 billion (including customer services, financial services and Westech) in favour of a subsidiary of Accenture, Accenture Business Services for Utilities (ABSU). BC Hydro claimed it would save CAN$ 250 million.[29] Moreover another company was created: the British Columbia Transmission Corporation (BCTC), responsible for the transportation division of BC Hydro. BCTC is not a subsidiary of BC Hydro; it is a distinct Crown corporation and has to submit itself to BC Utilities Commission regulation. BC Hydro and Powerex must henceforth be treated on equal terms with their competitors when using BCTC's lines. This separation of activities was necessary in order to comply with FERC Order 888 and to 'return to regulation'.[30]

Hydro-Québec also underwent dramatic changes in its commercial relations with the USA. During the 1970s and the 1980s, through its subsidiary the Société d'énergie de la Baie James (SEBJ), the company started to develop James Bay's enormous hydro-electrical potential (10,282 MW). This project was largely dependent upon the growth of sales to the USA. In that respect the first years following the signature of NAFTA did not favour Hydro-Québec. In 1992 the New York Power Authority terminated the 1000 MW contract it had signed with Hydro-Québec in 1989.[31] This, together with the strong opposition shown by the Cree[32] and by environmental groups led to the abandonment, two years later, of the second phase (3200 MW) of the James Bay project.[33] Nevertheless the situation improved. While putting aside its mega projects Hydro-Québec reinforced its commercial relations with its neighbours. In 1997 its newly created subsidiary Hydro-Québec Energy Services (USA) was awarded by FERC the same status as Powerex, that of energy broker in the American market, buying and selling directly to wholesalers. This new possibility was very interesting since Hydro-Québec had an export capacity of 3080 MW to the USA. It led to a first restructuring in the same year. Transmission became the responsibility of a new division, Transénergie, whose mission was to give non-discriminatory access to its network.[34] Hydro-Québec Energy Service was made a subsidiary of Transénergie under the name of Transénergie US.[35]

This change would be followed by others. In 2001, in compliance with 'the new regulatory setting guiding the electrical industry in North America', Hydro-Québec reorganised its activities into four divisions, each of which headed by a president: Hydro-Québec Distribution, Hydro-Québec Transénergie, Hydro-Québec Production and Hydro-Québec Ingénierie, Approvisionnement et Construction. Each of these divisions heads a series of subsidiaries in Canada and elsewhere (in association with Hydro-Québec International). Moreover in 2002–3, restructuring was completed with the splitting of the last division into three: Hydro-Québec Équipement (for future projects to be materialised in association with SEBJ), Hydro-Québec Technologie et Développement Industriel (technology and risk investment) and Hydro-Québec Pétrole et Gaz (oil and gas, in association with a subsidiary, Noverco).[36] This reorganisation (with Hydro-Québec Transénergie at the core of exporting activities), gives more permanency to the international activities of Hydro-Québec. In that respect, Hydro-Québec became a multinational group during the 1990s.

Manitoba Hydro adopted a somewhat different pattern. In 1996 it participated in the Mid-Continent Area Power Pool (MAPP) and had access to the American wholesale electricity market whilst opening its network to neighbouring utility companies. In the following year, like the others, it restructured its activities according to three autonomous units, but with a different content: Power Supply, Transmission and Distribution, and Customer Service. Putting together distribution and transmission can be explained by the fact that retailing energy in Winnipeg was not its responsibility before 2002.

Manitoba Hydro suffered from drought in 1988, forcing the reduction of its exportations by 42 per cent, and again in 2004, resulting in a net loss of CAN$ 436 million. This situation incited the company to pursue investments in mega projects in order to diversify its sources of energy[37] and to sign a coordination agreement, by 2002, with the Midwest Independent System Operator (MISO).[38] Collaborating with MISO could be seen as a decisive step towards continental integration. However, Manitoba Hydro did manage to keep control over its network.

On the whole, the three companies adjusted to the new set of rules prevailing in the electricity market all over North America. How did these changes translate into electricity sales to the USA? Figure 14.1 shows total exports to the US of the three companies from 1988 to 2003. The results are not dramatic: in 1985, for instance, Canada exported 41,441 GWh to the USA as compared to 42,911 in 1999.[39] It is worth noting that the exports were more dynamic before NAFTA than during the years immediately following its implementation. Only from the mid-1990s did a significant rise occur, but briefly, since sales were again reduced after 2000. Such fluctuations do not depend only on the market situation. Climatic conditions are also important. Figure 14.2 shows that imports increased significantly after 1995 for BC Hydro and after 2000 for Hydro-Québec and more so for Manitoba Hydro. However, the overall increase

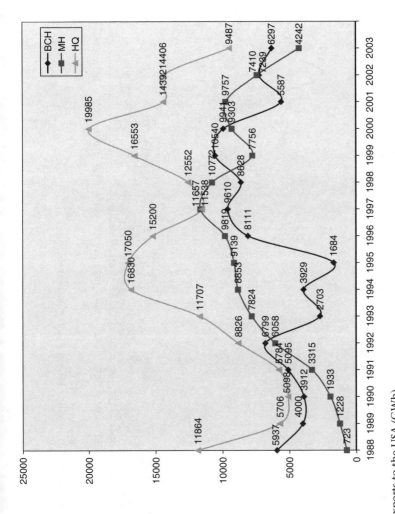

Figure 14.1 Exports to the USA (GWh)
Source: Compiled by author based on National Energy Board, annual reports.

198

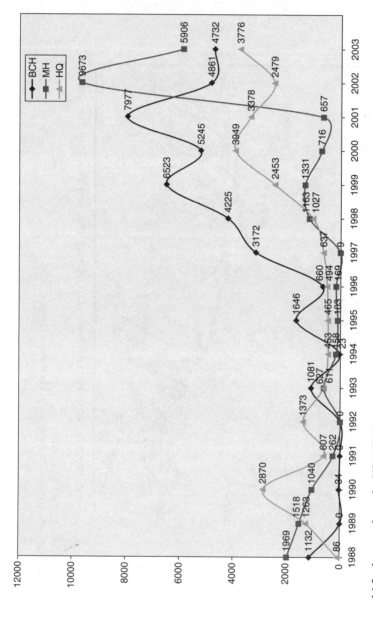

Figure 14.2 Imports from the USA (GWh)
Source: Compiled by author based on National Energy Board, annual reports.

Table 14.2   Average Revenues from Exports (CAN$ million)

	BC Hydro	Manitoba Hydro	Hydro-Québec
1988–1992	135	64	353
1993–1997	125	228	562
1998–2003	2027	422	2012

Note: These revenues include exports to both neighbouring provinces and to the USA.
Source: Elaborated by author based on annual reports of the three companies.

in imports is not superior to exports: the commercial balance favours the Canadian companies.

These two figures actually suggest a more intensive use of the transmission lines crossing the border and this has proven to be very advantageous to the companies. First, the intensification of sales prevented them from investing in huge generating plants. From the 1990s to 2002 Hydro-Québec added only 820 MW to its capacity; BC Hydro increased by 300 MW; only Manitoba Hydro built a 1300 MW plant at Limestone. Moreover the trade permitted the companies to maintain their tariffs as among the lowest in North America: in Québec the price of electricity in 2002 was 3.2 cents US per KWh; in Manitoba 3 cents and in British Colombia 3.1 cents. In the USA most of the rates varied from 4.5 to 8 cents, and in New England and California this reached 10 cents.[40] Manitoba Hydro admitted exports helped maintain its rate at 30 per cent lower than it should be.[41] As Table 14.2 shows, average revenues from exports increased sharply, especially after 1997.

However, such sales will bring the companies to an uncomfortable situation. Firstly, what was seen as an opportunity is now becoming a dependency: such an advantageous market will require significant investment from the companies to build new production and transmission facilities. This possibility is even more real now that the companies have achieved successful relations with members of the First Nations by making it possible for them to participate in the benefits of new development. Secondly, the companies will have little choice but to collaborate closely with the Regional Transmission Operators which are being established all over the continent; consequently they will have to negotiate a special status for their transmission networks and eventually expose themselves more to American rules and supervision. They have already adopted US accounting and statistical methods. In 1997–8, Manitoba Hydro shifted to the Uniform Rating of Generating Equipment (URGE) in order to be in conformity with MAPP system control.[42] This involvement in international activities is enhanced by the business the companies have outside the continent.

III. Becoming International

The three companies did not limit their activities abroad to the USA. Investment went beyond the North American continent, once again with differing results. They had incentives to do so. First, they have made important efforts in R&D related to hydro-electricity and long-distance transportation. In association with major electrical manufacturers (such as ABB, GE and Siemens) and other nationalised electrical companies (such as Électricité de France), and sometimes with the help of the Canadian government, the three Hydros have exported their expertise throughout the world and helped private consultants from their respective provinces to do business abroad. Asia (particularly China) and South America (Chile, Venezuela and Brazil, to name but a few) are the most frequently mentioned areas of activity.

This led to the creation of entities specialising in international activities. Hydro-Québec as early as 1978 was the first to launch a subsidiary, Hydro-Québec International (HQI), in order to exploit the research of the Institut de recherche en électricité (IREQ), Hydro-Québec's R&D subsidiary. This became a success story. Soon, however, HQI and IREQ would take separate paths. IREQ went international on its own, signing research contracts with institutions such as Chicago-based Argon National Laboratories. HQI offered professional services relating to engineering, operating, planning and development, and high technology.

In 1997 HQI was given a ten-year mission to exploit the world's electrical potential (estimated at 665,000 MW). Under the supervision of a newly created branch, the 'Projets et affaires internationales', and with the assistance of the Société de développement de la Baie James, HQI was instructed to make direct investments up to CAN$ 1.2 billion in the world, alone or as a joint venture. Consequently it invested in projects to be brought to maturity and to be sold at a profit. For instance, in July 2004 the company sold its investments in Meiya Power Co. Ltd (China) to Darby Asia Investors Ltd (Hong Kong) for US$ 84.6 million (making a profit of US$ 12.9 million). HQI has also created subsidiaries in order to build or rebuild networks. In many respects HQI benefited from the privatisation and deregulation policies in other countries to position itself as a major provider of services and consulting, and as an investor. To take a few examples, in 1998–2000 HQI became involved in the construction of a transmission line between Mantaro and Socabaya in Peru. Besides putting money in the project the company required the services of 80 Hydro-Québec employees and involved some 30 Québec firms. In Australia, along with the Fonds de solidarité of Fédération des Travailleurs du Québec (a major labour union in Québec), Country Energy and Transénergie Australia in 2000 HQI built a 65 km interconnection cable which would be exploited by Transénergie Australia as a 'market line', transmitting electricity according to the market price. In the same year HQI bought from Endesa the biggest transmission network in Chile, Transelec. In

2003, while receiving an investment of around US$ 60 million from a financial subsidiary of the World Bank, Transelec acquired the Northern electricity network of Chile for US$ 107 million. As a consequence its total network measured 8234 km and provided energy to 98 per cent of the population. Its assets are worth almost CAN$ 1.6 billion. This is a major investment; in comparison, Hydro-Québec has invested CAN$ 745 million elsewhere in the world (half of it in the USA).[43]

British Columbia Hydro International Ltd (BCHIL) was created in 1988, at the same time as Powerex. Its mission was to sell its consulting engineering expertise in Canada and abroad. For instance, it developed a generator airgap monitoring system for a hydroelectric power plant in Venezuela in 1989. BCHIL was helped by other BC Hydro subsidiaries like Powertech Labs and Westech.[44] BCHIL gave itself a very enterprising image; according to BC Hydro's 1995 annual report it 'has been aggressively marketing our exceptional expertise in developing power plants and transmission networks around the world'. The company was using the BOO (Build, Own, Operate) strategy, notably in Asia and South America.

In Pakistan BCHIL got involved in a US$ 120 million thermal power plant project in 1995, with the assistance of Kilhorn Engineering. In China, in the same year, it signed a contract to build small and medium sized plants with a total capacity of 1100 MW. In 1997 the company implemented a US$ 2 million electricity demand reduction programme in Brazil. However, the Pakistani project turned sour. BCHIL, directly and with partners, managed to invest US$ 9 million and get 33 per cent of the shares of Southern Electric Power Co. Ltd (SEPCOL), a company designed to set up and operate the project. The next year, however, the Pakistani government accused the owners of SEPCOL of 'corrupt business practices' and demanded the project be cancelled. Eventually the issue became political in both Canada and Pakistan. BC Hydro had to make a CAN$ 5 million provision for investment loss. In 2002 it was forced to close BCHIL down, and consequently to end its international venture. Without getting in to the details, it seems clear that this related less to corruption than to mismanagement by directors unfamiliar with international business.[45]

Manitoba Hydro International (MHI) is a latecomer. Before its creation in 1999 it was only Manitoba Hydro's export services department, launched in 1985. MHI and its predecessor, from 1985 to 2001, participated in over 80 projects in 45 countries, including Tanzania, Uganda and, especially, South China. It exported its know-how in high voltage direct current (HVDC) transportation technology, and more specifically in HVDC converter stations. To that end, in 1999 Manitoba Hydro created the Manitoba HVDC Research Centre. In 2003 MHI favoured the participation of other Manitoban enterprises in its international activities, with the formation of the Energy Services Alliance of Manitoba (ESAM). It also sold its patents to or participated in joint ventures with multinationals such as SNC Lavalin, AMEC and Siemens AG. However, compared to those of Hydro-Québec International and British

Columbia Hydro International Ltd, the international activities of Manitoba Hydro remained modest.[46]

Conclusions

The international activities of nationalised utilities may raise many questions; even more so if they take an active part in other countries' deregulation and denationalisation processes. First, *how can a nationalised company become a multinational?* Three factors may be put forward. In the first place, since Canada is an important producer of cheap and renewable energy it could be expected that electricity would be sold across borders. Indeed this is an old practice. NAFTA and deregulation opened the gates to the next step: the creation of selling divisions or subsidiaries operating in the USA. The scale economies generated by large hydro-electric plants still constitute a commercial advantage, despite recent technical innovation. The second factor is the technological know-how in both hydro-electricity and long-distance energy transmission, which has attracted many customers outside Canada. The third factor is the financial capacities available resulting from their monopoly status in Canada. This has facilitated significant investment abroad.

Next, *how does a nationalised company deal with the deregulatory rules of a neighbouring country?* All three companies dismantled their vertical integration (their 'natural monopoly') and opened their transmission networks to competition. However, it is significant to see how, despite their similar status and advantages, different results were obtained. Hydro-Québec and BC Hydro created subsidiaries intervening directly in the American wholesale market. This proved to be a success; however, in the second case, the implication of Powerex in the Californian crisis brought about an uneasy legal and financial situation. Moreover BC Hydro outsourced part of its activities to an American multinational, a sign that there are difficulties in the company's management. As far as Manitoba Hydro is concerned the company dealt directly with the American market and even went further by collaborating with MISO, a Regional Transmission Operator (RTO). In all cases it is clear that the three companies were attracted by the lucrative American market. In return, they became increasingly subject to its influence: a clear dependency pattern is emerging. Moreover the formation of RTOs in the USA will certainly present strategic and statutory dilemmas.

Third, *as multinationals, are these companies as efficient as private enterprises?* By investing abroad the three companies are behaving like any private concern, acting according to their perceived best interests. It is significant that most partnerships have been with private companies. Joint ventures would be established in order to realise projects and later they would either sell their shares for profit or exploit what had been constructed. Major differences divide the companies, however, while Hydro-Québec has made large investments involving human and technical participation, BC Hydro by trying to do the same put itself in a delicate situation in Pakistan which ultimately forced the company to shut down its international subsidiary, while Manitoba Hydro chose to remain modest, privileging partnership and patent selling.[47]

Finally, *by becoming multinational will these companies not eventually be forced to (or tempted to) diminish their mission as nationalised entities?* All these companies have published an 'ethical code' to ensure their guidance by the same conduct (relating to social policy, sustainable development, and so on) inside and outside Canada.[48] Moreover they all justify their international ventures as a way of protecting the (financial) interests of their local consumers. And yet, as the case of BC Hydro has shown, 'aggressive' policies can seriously call into question the structure and even the survival of the company. In the near future pressure will be put on the companies to further develop their productive capacity to meet increasing demands south of the border.

In that respect, the fact that the three companies are under the surveillance of regulating institutions in Canada could be seen as a way of preserving their mission as nationalised entities. If this is the case it is paradoxical to impose regulatory mechanisms on nationalised entities, but it reveals the point at which being a public enterprise no longer guards against behaviour normally associated with private concerns. It is equally paradoxical to see how ready these companies are to comply with American rules, as if the Canadian ones are of less importance. The major restructuring which began in the 1990s is not a result of changes in the Canadian market. Not is it attributable to investments made outside North America, however big (as in the case of Hydro-Québec). It follows the implementation of deregulation in the USA (or more accurately, the replacement of one set of rules by a more complex set). The size, stability and buying capacity of the American market remain the priority for these companies, despite setbacks such as the Californian crisis and the blackout that paralysed the north-eastern part of the Continent in 2003. Yet it is not impossible to imagine that investing outside the continent will soon become inevitable and have major effects on the companies' policies and status. After all, for the countries receiving the investments does it matter whether these enterprises are nationalised or not?

Notes

1 On its website FERC defines itself as 'an independent agency that regulates the interstate transmission of electricity, natural gas, and oil.' In 1993 the American government gave FERC the mission of increasing the performance of energy production and transmission by setting up the best conditions for 'effective competition' (http://www.ferc.gov/about/ferc-does.asp).

2 In Canada electricity is under the jurisdiction of the Provinces, with the exception of the nuclear industry and the export of energy, for which the Federal Government set up a National Energy Board in 1959 (Association canadienne de l'électricité (2001) p. 25).

3 Association canadienne de l'électricité (2001) p. 27.

4   That is, until September 2002 when downtown Winnipeg was included in Manitoba Hydro's distribution network.

5   In 1999 Ontario Hydro gave way to various companies, including Ontario Power Generation and Hydro One Networks Inc.

6   In 1999 the hydraulic capacity of Canada was 66,954 MW and its gross non-developed capacity was estimated at 183,635 MW (Association canadienne de l'électricité, (2001) p. 64).

7   Association canadienne de l'électricité (2001) pp. 3, 5 and 52.

8   Annual reports of the three companies for 1999 and Association canadienne de l'électricité (2001) p. 79.

9   Annual reports of the three companies for 2003.

10 In 1982 the Canadian constitution underwent major changes, among which came the recognition of 'ancestral rights' for the First Nations over a vast amount of territory.

11 Bernard (1988).

12 The regulation of electricity retailing is the responsibility of each state; consequently the situation varies enormously from one state to another. See Finon and Serrato (2000).

13 See http://www.nerc.com

14 This paragraph coincides with the summary made by Philip K. Verleger (1988) pp. 96–7.

15 Tussing (1988) p. 116–17.

16 Among the many studies on the subject, see Hirsh (1999); Zaccour (1998); Audigier (2004); Ayoub (1998).

17 These groups are 'voluntary associations of transmission owners and users which are developing in the U.S. to implement open-access transmission on a co-operative basis' (BC Hydro, 1995, p. 8).

18 Hydro-Québec (2003) pp. 4–6.

19 'BC Hydro subsidiaries', a ten-page pamphlet attached to the 1989 annual report of BC Hydro; Association canadienne de l'électricité (2001) pp. 5 and 29.

20 BC Hydro Annual Report (2001).

21 http://www.canadianencyclopedia.ca, article on BC Hydro; BC Hydro *Annual Report* (1995), p. 4.

22 Ferry (1997) p. 34.

23 BC Hydro *Annual Reports* (1996, 1998 and 2004). http://www.powerex.com, accessed 25 August 2004.

24 Baldrey (2001) p. 23; Sweeney (2002) p. 156. See also Faruqui (2001) and Woo (1997).

25 106 FERC no. 61, 304, Docket nos. EL03-166-000 and EL03-199-000.

26 BC Hydro, *Annual Report* (2004) p. 6.

27 Ibid. pp. 91 and 121.

28 http://www.bchydro.com/info/history last accessed 26 August 2004.

29 BC Hydro, *Annual Report* (2004). 'A number of back-office functions, representing approximately 1600 employees, became the responsibility of BC Hydro's partner, Accenture Business Services of British Columbia (ABS), under a contractual agreement for services' (*Annual Report*, 2003). See also *Annual Report* (2004), pp. 4 and 12. According to Tony Wanless ABSU 'would first service the utility's administrative chores and then attack the larger administrative outsourcing market all over North America. Right out of the gate, the new company will have a solid core customer with specific industry knowledge, which can then be leveraged into servicing other businesses'. See Wanless (2003) p. 124.

30 BC Hydro, *Annual Report* (2004), p. 4. http://www.powerex.com/special/special_features.html accessed 26 August 2004.
31 Hydro-Québec, *Annual Report* (1992) p. 21.
32 The Cree are one of the Aboriginal people in Canada. Most of them live around James Bay.
33 Nadeau (2004) pp. 39–49.
34 In 2001, 20 customers used Transénergie's network (Hydro-Québec *Annual Report* (2001) p. 18.
35 Hydro-Québec, *Annual Report* (1997) pp. 4–6, 14, 18–19. See also Bernard (1998).
36 Hydro-Québec, *Annual Report* (2001), p. 4 and (2003) p. 2.
37 For instance, in 2003 Manitoba Hydro negotiated with the Nisichawayasihk Cree Nation to build a 200 MW generating station at Wuskatin in order 'to maintain and increase export revenues' (Manitoba Hydro, *Annual Report* (2004) pp. 7 and 23).
38 'MISO is the first Regional Transmission Operator (RTO) in North America and consists of 23 transmission-owning members in 15 USA states and Manitoba. Manitoba Hydro is the only Canadian utility participating in an international RTO' (Manitoba Hydro, *Annual Report* (2002) p. 27).
39 Association canadienne de l'électricité (2001) p. 68.
40 Hydro-Québec, *Profil financier 2003–2008*, p. 12.
41 Manitoba Hydro, *Annual Report* (1996) p. 17.
42 Manitoba Hydro, *Annual Report* (1999) p. 87.
43 http://www.hydroquebec.com/hqi last accessed 26 August 2004; http://www.can-elect.ca/francais/news2004/hydro-quebec31.html; Hydro-Québec, *Annual Report* (1997) pp. 5–6, 20, 25; (2001) pp. 3, 20, 27, 38, 54–9; (2003) pp. 6, 15, 22, 60, 71, 104. Hydro-Québec (2003) p. 17.
44 Association canadienne de l'électricité, (2001) p. 5.
45 BC Hydro Subsidiaries (see note 19 for reference) p. 2 and 6; BC Hydro, *Annual Report* (1994) p. 23; (1995) p. 5; (1996) p. 31; (1997) p. 46; (1997) (report on the environment) p. 39; (1998) p. 29, 57–8; (1999) p. 61; (2002) p. 82. BC Hydro (1995); Ferry (1997) pp. 35 and 39; http://www.legis.govt.bc.ca/1998-99.
46 http://www.mhi.mb.ca accessed 26 August 2004; Manitoba Hydro, *Annual Report* (1996) p. 23; (1999) p. 35; (2003) pp. 56–7; (2004) pp. 52–3.
47 These differences both in the American market and outside North America require explanations that would be too long to present in this chapter. However, one should look at the background and behaviour of each company's CEO and chairmen: BCH has been led by public officers and ex-politicians. For its part Manitoba Hydro has been managed by university professors or individuals who made their career within the company. Hydro-Québec has a tradition of hiring businessmen with experience in both the private and the public sector to manage its activities.
48 See, for instance, the *Code d'éthique* of Hydro-Québec International at http://www.hydroquebec.com/hqi/fr/code_ethique.html accessed August 2005.

References

Association canadienne de l'électricité (2001) *L'électricité au Canada 1998–1999* (Ottawa: Division de l'énergie renouvelable et électrique, Ressources naturelles Canada).

Audigier, P. (2004) 'Regards critiques sur quinze années de libéralisation des marchés de l'électricité', *Revue de l'Énergie*, no. 555 (March–April) pp. 171–8.

Ayoub, A. (1998) 'La libéralisation des marchés de l'énergie: utopie, théories et pragmatisme', *Revue de l'Énergie*, no. 499 (July–September) pp. 477–83.

Baldrey, K. (2001) 'California Calling', *BC Business* (May) pp. 19–25.

BC Hydro (1988–2004) *Annual Report.*

BC Hydro (1995) *Change, the Evolution of Efficiency*: *Corporate Review.*

Bernard, J.T. (1988) 'Canadian Electricity', *The Energy Journal*, 9 (4) (October) pp. 127–30.

Bernard, J.T. (1998) 'L'ouverture du marché d'exportation d'électricité québécoise: réalité ou mirage à l'horizon?', *Revue de l'énergie*, no. 499, (July–September) pp. 384–90.

Carpentier, J.-M. (2001) 'La mutation profonde d'Hydro-Québec', *Forces*, no. 132 (October) pp. 36–8.

Faruqui, A., H.-P. Chao, V. Niemeyer, J. Platt and K. Stahlkopf (2001), 'Analyzing California's Power Crisis', *The Energy Journal*, 22, (4) pp. 29–52.

Ferry, J. (1997) 'Power Surge', *BC Business* (December) pp. 33–9.

Finon, D., and G. Serrato (2000)'La diversité des stratégies des entreprises électriques américaines face à la libéralisation du marché électrique', *Revue de l'énergie*, no. 513 (January) pp. 5–19.

Hirsh, R.F. (1999) *Power Loss. The Origins of Deregulation and Restructuring in the American Electric Utility System* (Cambridge MA: The MIT Press).

Hydro-Québec (2003) *Profil financier 2003–2008* (Montreal).

Hydro-Québec (1988–2004) *Rapports annuels.*

Hydro-Québec (2003) *Le secteur de l'électricité au Canada. Exportations et importations; évaluation du marché de l'énergie* (Ottawa: Office National de l'Énergie).

Manitoba Hydro (1988–2004) *Annual Report.*

Nadeau, J.-B. (2004) 'Le retour des grands barrages', *L'Actualité* (February) pp. 39–49.

National Energy Board (Canada), Ottawa (1988–2004) *Annual Report.*

Sweeney, J.L. (2002) *The California Electricity Crisis* (Stanford: Hoover Institution Press, Stanford Institute for Economic Policy Research).

Tussing, A.R. (1988) 'Electricity and Gas: The US West', *The Energy Journal*, 9 (4) (October) pp. 111–9.

Verleger, P.K. (1988) 'Background and Summary of Energy Provisions', *The Energy Journal*, 9 (4) (October) pp. 95–9.

Wanless, T. (2003) 'The Big Bang', *BC Business* (July) pp. 120–31.

Woo, C.-K., D. Lloyd-Zannetti and I. Horowitz (1997) 'Electricity Market Integration in the Pacific Northwest', *The Energy Journal*, 18 (3) pp. 75–101.

Zaccour, G. (ed.) (1998) *Deregulation of Electric Utilities* (Boston/Dordrecht/London: Kluwer Academic Publishers).

Websites

Association canadienne de l'électricité: http://www.canelect.ca
BC Hydro: http://www.bchydro.com
British Columbia Government: http://www.legis.govt.bc.ca/1998-99
Canadian Encyclopedia: http://www.canadianencyclopedia.ca
FERC: http://www.ferc.gov
Hydro-Québec: http://www.hydroquebec.com
Manitoba Hydro: http://www.hydro.mb.ca and http://www.manitobawaterpower.com
Manitoba Hydro International: http://www.mhi.mb.ca
NERC: http://www.nerc.com
Powerex: http://www.powerex.com

15
Privatisation and Public Enterprises in the USA

Candra S. Chahyadi, William L. Megginson and Jesus M. Salas

Introduction

In general, governments privatise state-owned enterprises (SOEs) in order to improve their performance and profitability. Governments sell state enterprises to private investors in order to expose the SOEs to market discipline that will force them to improve their performance. Empirical research shows that when privatisation is done properly it usually accomplishes this goal.[1] In addition to improving the performance and profitability of SOEs a government may choose to privatise for other purposes, including raising revenue for the state, reducing public outlays to sustain uneconomic public enterprises, reducing the power of public sector unions and other government employees, promoting economic efficiency, reducing government interference in the economy, promoting popular capitalism through wider share ownership, reducing the size and scope of government, providing the opportunity to introduce competition and developing the nation's capital markets.[2]

Privatisation means something quite different in the USA than it does elsewhere in the world. In the American context privatisation refers primarily to the contracting out of public services to the private sector. Government provides public services in two ways, through internal and external provision. With internal provision government provides services using its own resources, while in external provision government contracts out service provision to private contractors, which are deemed to be more cost-effective and efficient. Though still less common than internal provision, contracting out of public services to the private sector is becoming more popular in many American cities because of its cost effectiveness and the improvement in quality of public services.

It is not surprising that privatisation in the USA differs from other parts of the world, given the minimal state ownership of economic assets and the fact that capital markets in the USA are highly developed and share ownership is widely dispersed. Despite the fact that there are very few SOEs American governments (including federal, state and local governments) still own many valuable assets that could be privatised. However, there is still pressure for government to intervene in economic activities to change economic outcomes from what they would be under pure market competition. One such condition that often attracts government intervention is when there are significant increasing returns to scale in production, so that only one producer can be efficient.[3]

Potential assets that the American government could privatise include commercial infrastructure, broadcast spectrum, land and mineral/timber resources, military bases, and many others. There are some security concerns regarding privatising some of the assets, such as prisons, air traffic control and military bases. However, research has shown that privatising does not imply loss of security. For example, prison privatisation has successfully improved the quality of correctional facilities and reduced the cost. Using data from 28 studies that compare the cost of government prisons to that of their private counterparts Moore and Segal find that contracting out correctional facilities to the private sector can save taxpayers, on average, 15 per cent of what the state facilities cost.[4] Segal also finds that in terms of quality of care, private prisons rank as high as or higher than their state-run counterparts in eight out of nine cases.[5]

I. The State-Owned Enterprise Sector Is Traditionally Small in the USA

Galambos explains that, historically, there were two phases of development of SOEs in the USA.[6] The first phase, called the developmental period, took place during the first half of the nineteenth century. It was widely believed that stimulating economic growth was the main force for establishing SOEs. That brief developmental phase was followed by the second phase, the planning phase, from the late nineteenth century until today. During the first phase the development of SOEs was comparable to that of other industrial countries, while during the planning phase the United States lagged behind other industrial countries in term of reliance on state enterprises. Since then the American economy has relied more on regulated private ownership and private litigation rather than on SOEs.

Prior to 1980 regulation in the USA was often extreme. Even then, however, economic reliance on private ownership and private litigation was strong. After the deregulation of many sectors, such as securities trading, airlines, trucking, oil and gas distribution, railroads, telecommunications, banking and, most recently, the electricity supply industry (ESI), economic reliance on the private sector became even more dominant. MacAvoy shows that deregulation dramatically reduced costs and created significant economic gains.[7] Because of deregulation commission rates in the brokerage industry dropped by 16 per cent and prices fell by 14.3 per cent in the rail freight business, by 7.2 per cent in the trucking industry and by 7 per cent in the passenger airline industry. Furthermore prices for petroleum products fell by 6.7 per cent following the removal of well-head price controls.

In contrast to deregulation there have been very few large privatisations in the USA. This very short list includes sales of Conrail in 1987, the Domain Name System (DNS) in 1995 and US Enrichment Corporation in 1999. In 1987 the government sold Conrail for a less than expected price of US$ 1.9 billion. The stock price then rose from $13 to $115 per share ten years after privatisation. The DNS sale was severely underpriced when it was sold to Network Solution Inc. for US$ 3.9 million in 1995. Unsurprisingly, because of the underpricing the market capital of DNS increased to US$ 2 billion soon after the sale. Kesan and Shah conclude that the government's strategy for privatising DNS was flawed.[8]

II. What Assets and State Enterprises Do American State and Local Governments Own?

Logue documents that the American federal government runs at least 50 major enterprises, employing more than 800,000 people and generating annual revenues of more than US$ 50 billion.[9] MacAvoy and McIsaac, analysing several of those large enterprises, find that their performance is inferior to the performance of their private counterparts.[10] Considering the research showing that privatisation can improve firm performance it is surprising that the government has not privatised the underperforming federal enterprises yet. In addition to SOEs the federal government still owns a large variety of valuable assets that could be privatised. The electricity production and distribution network is one obvious example. This asset has substantial value (estimated between US$ 40 and US$ 70 billion). However, Logue and MacAvoy argue that one of the assets, TVA, is near insolvency.[11] Despite Logue and MacAvoy's argument, the potential value of the state-owned power sector is significant, especially considering that these businesses are often poorly managed. The latest incident of electricity blackout in northeastern USA in August 2003 showed this very clearly. The power sector is both inefficient and overly reliant on taxpayer subsidies, and the need for improvement in management quality in the power sector is obvious.

Other assets still owned by the federal government include the USA Postal Service (USPS), Amtrak, infrastructure assets such as railways, roads and ports, portions of the broadcast spectrum that have not been fully privatised, as well as vast tracts of raw land and natural resources. The holdings also include 'sponsorship' of mortgages through the Federal National Mortgage Association (FNMA) and the Federal Home Loan Mortgage Corporation (FHLMC). In short, the potential revenue and economic payoff from privatising these assets is enormous.

Other important and potentially valuable sectors that could be divested include military bases, national laboratories and R&D centres. These sectors, however, are considered to be vital and strategic, which makes their privatisation extremely problematic politically, and the federal government shows no interest in their divestment.

In many cases American governments have opted to contract out the administration of state-owned businesses instead of selling the assets in order to reduce the negotiation burdens of privatisation. The problem with contracting the assets out instead of selling them is that the speculation and controversy regarding government intervention cannot stop when the government still owns the assets. However, it seems that even contracting out is better than no privatisation at all, as evidence does seem to indicate significant improvements in efficiency and costs.

Perhaps the best example of the problems involved with convincing entrepreneurs into investing in the public sector comes from electricity companies owned by state and local governments. While municipal electric companies are small (with few exceptions), they are quite numerous. With 2000 municipal electric companies, or 'munis', state and local governments still operate nine times as many companies as the private sector. On the other hand, investor-owned utilities (IOUs) control 78 per cent of the market, clearly suggesting that most munis are uneconomically tiny. As Moore and Woerner noted, the municipal utilities often retain many of the benefits the government used to provide, making it more difficult for private companies to compete.[12] For example, municipal utilities do not pay taxes, have lower cost and tax-exempt debt, and have preferential access to cheap power generated by federal hydropower facilities.

It is therefore surprising that even with the extreme benefits munis receive, some people suspect that munis will not survive the exposure to competition that will result from imminent deregulation of the American ESI. The reason: poor management. As documented by Moore and Woerner munis are almost twice as leveraged as IOUs and charge higher rates in order to pay off debt that was used to buy inefficient assets. In addition, since the state will not be allowed to bail them out after deregulation many observers believe the munis will not be able to survive the entry of competition.[13]

As we can see, the lack of incentives to run more efficiently does affect how munis are operated. Regarding investment, munis do not worry as much about the risks involved as do IOUs. Some munis will argue that IOUs care more about profits than they do about providing the service. Munis will argue that IOUs might stay away from investing in generating plants because of the risk that electricity prices may drop. In that case the consumer is negatively affected because there may be a situation in which the supply of electricity may not be enough. In a sense munis are often criticised for investing too much without considering the risks and IOUs are criticised for not investing enough because they are afraid of the free-rider problem.

Given these challenges it is unsurprising that munis are trying to avoid (or at least delay) competition. The munis would probably operate more efficiently if they were allowed to be more independent, at least in their day-to-day operations. Even stockholders of publicly owned corporations do not demand as much as the government when it comes to the administration of the business.

Perhaps it is not the employees of the munis that are blocking the competition. It may very well be that politicians do not want to let go of these munis because they provide important patronage benefits. It is no surprise that governments often prefer to contract out these services rather than sell them outright in order to avoid losing control of the businesses.

The ESI is not the only industry that the government still controls today. In fact it is not even the most controversial. The reason is that in most cases customers do not really know (or care) whether electricity is provided by public or private entities. When it comes to transit, on the other hand, it seems that every citizen of every town is very aware of what is happening. The most valuable state-owned transportation assets are airports, which in the USA are almost always government-owned because of tax and financing benefits open only to public sector borrowers. Ellet finds that user fees are too low, considering the costs involved with running airports, and thus governments receive much less revenue than they might.[14] The Federal Aviation Authority (FAA) is afraid that the airport user costs would have to increase if airports were privatised, causing air travel prices to rise. After a 1992 presidential executive order, however, this scenario became less probable. The executive order demanded that any federally aided assets to be privatised needed to repay the aid before they could be sold. As a consequence no state-owned airports have been sold to the public. It is very unlikely that any investor will be willing to repay the aid received by these airports. While Ellet argues that security concerns need to be taken into consideration before any privatisation takes place he also points out that the federal government seems to be stepping in beyond its authority to hurt consumers. Thankfully the current president has recently addressed this concern and expressed the need to find a way to encourage privatisation.[15]

Since the assets of the airports are difficult to sell the government has opted to contract out their administration. Once administration is contracted out it becomes easier to explore the contracting of other services within airports. For example, the government has explored contracting out air traffic control and security services. After the 11 September 2001 attacks the quality of airport security efforts came under intense scrutiny. At that point the federal government intervened and mandated government security provision, but the task was too large. In addition, evidence on privatisation seems to indicate that private security services are both more efficient and cheaper to provide. For example, Poole notes that an air traffic control operated by the FAA costs about US$ 1.344 million per year, while one operated by private contractors costs only $427,000.[16] That is, a tower operated privately costs a third of what one operated publicly does. With regard to airport security Poole points out that airport directors support the contracting out of airport security because of efficiency and flexibility.[17]

When governments do contract out a service they often select a for-profit firm to take over the administration of the service.[18] Some of the common areas contracted out include solid waste disposal, street construction, facilities operations, building repair, ambulance services, vehicle maintenance, engineering and architectural services, correctional services, airport air traffic control towers, and airport security. In most areas evidence has shown that the private company was much more efficient than the government.[19] However, since it is difficult to account for the bargaining costs of contracting it is difficult to give a definitive answer on the benefits of this procedure.

III. Prison Privatisation Is the Most Important Government Service Being Contracted Out

Privatising correctional facilities has recently become a very controversial topic because of the rising costs and increasing population. The incarcerated population in the USA has tripled since 1984 and spending has increased by 350 per cent.[20] It is well known that there are still pervasive overcrowding and poor conditions. The opponents of privatisation of correctional facilities argue that it is very risky as government tries to trade off cost saving with an escalated risk of jeopardising the safety of the general public. On the other hand, the proponents of privatisation argue that since private companies are trying to attract new customers and retain contracts they are more likely to provide high-quality service, a motivation government-run facilities do not have. In addition Moore and Segal find that the government is more efficient in monitoring private watchmen.[21] By shifting to private prison companies and putting the government in the role of independent monitor with the power to fire poorly-performing companies Moore and Segal note that states have more power to make significant improvements when necessary.[22] In another report Moore and Segal analysed 28 studies comparing the cost of government prisons with their private counterparts.[23] Twenty-two of the studies conclude that private prisons cost taxpayers an average of 15 per cent less than state facilities do.

In terms of quality of care, eight out of nine studies find that private prisons rate as high as or higher than their state-run counterparts. In addition, only ten per cent of the public correctional facilities are accredited by the American Correctional Association (ACA) compared to 45 per cent of their private counterparts.[24] Finally, Segal finds that private correctional facilities have better facilities, less overtime, better personnel management and less administration costs (29 per cent of total costs for public correctional facilities and 9 per cent for private ones).[25] It therefore seems likely that the trend toward privatising correctional facilities will continue in the future.

IV. Does Privatisation in the USA Have an Impact on Investment Abroad?

An important result of privatisation in countries other than the USA is the transformation of 'ugly ducklings' into 'new economic swans'. Companies in Europe invest abroad soon after they are privatised. Examples of such companies include France Telecom, Vodafone, Suez, EDF, Telmex, and so on. In contrast, companies that are privatised in the USA do not undergo such transformation. Companies that are privatised in the USA do not invest abroad. This is due to several factors: one, assets of privatised firms in the USA are not typically sold. With very few exceptions the American government maintains control of privatised companies. Since the function of American government 'companies' is to serve its own residents they will not get involved in any foreign investment. Two, many types of companies that are privatised outside the USA have always been privately owned (traded publicly) in the USA. For example, telephone companies in the USA have always been privately owned, whereas most companies abroad were government owned at one point. Others operate in industries that cannot legally operate abroad. For example, it is difficult to imagine USA prisons operating in Spain.

Another interesting point about privatisation outside the USA is that a large proportion of outward Foreign Direct Investment (FDI) in many industrialised countries comes from companies that were at one point publicly owned. In the case of the USA privatised firms do not play a role in FDI. As before, many of the types of privatised companies abroad which have a major role in FDI have never been owned by the government in the USA. In addition, firms in industries in which the American government contracts out do not typically invest abroad. Most outward FDI in the USA comes from privately owned but publicly traded firms that were never privatised.

V. Prospects for Further Privatisation in the USA

While the outlook for divesting prisons and airports seems quite positive, privatisation in other areas, such as the postal service, will probably never occur. Despite this, opportunities for privatisation seem to open up every day, particularly regarding contracts derived from the war in Iraq. In addition, the burgeoning federal deficit will probably encourage President George W. Bush to at least consider privatisation as a means to ameliorate the government's financial situation.

Most researchers would agree that privatising the postal service is improbable because of the large incentive not to provide as good a service to places where it may be less profitable. Although the parcel service is well served by competitive firms the day when regular mail will be picked up just around the corner in every city and town of the USA by a private firm will probably never arrive. This universal service obligation may not be as problematic for firms such as utilities where the marginal cost may not be large, but for postal firms, for which each pick-up involves additional man-hours, the costs can accumulate. As Crew and Kleindorfer note, the firm taking over the postal service would have to be so regulated (with price caps and universal service obligations), that possible efficiency gains would be very limited. This is not to say that the regulations are not necessary, but rather that the firms would not have much leeway to save costs.[26]

On the other hand, privatisation of other assets still seems to be possible. For example, as Boardman noted, electricity production and distribution is the current major asset of the United States federal government with a good chance of being privatised. While most distribution is still handled within the states the federal government has control of major generating facilities.[27]

Another company identified by Boardman as a possibility for asset divestiture is Amtrak.[28] Created in 1970 Amtrak may not technically be a public company since it is publicly traded, but since voting stock is owned by the government and the board is appointed by the President most would consider it to be publicly owned. While it was always intended for Amtrak to be privatised the bad earnings record (it had a loss of US$ 2.1 billion in 2001) makes the firm very uninteresting to investors. To attempt to solve the problem the Accountability Act of 1997 mandated that if Amtrak did not become financially self-sufficient by December 2002 it had to be restructured and liquidated. This obviously did not happen, although President George W. Bush did attempt to break up Amtrak in 2002. More recently (November 2003) the Senate approved funding Amtrak with US$ 1.2 billion for 2004. We will probably not see any privatisation efforts take place for Amtrak soon, but it may take place later on.

Other controversial firms which may lose government sponsorship in the near future are the Federal National Mortgage Association and the Federal Home Mortgage Corporation. As Boardman et al. note, these firms have been inefficient in delivering Federal subsidies because they retain nearly US$ 1 for each US$ 2 they pass through.[29] While these firms' stocks are publicly traded on the New York Stock Exchange they receive huge federal subsidies and operate with benefits not available to for-profit firms, including exemption from state and local income taxes and registration requirements of the Securities and Exchange Commission. Initially the companies were chosen because no other firm could provide the services Fannie Mae and Freddie Mac provided, but today there are many more firms that can provide the service, probably more efficiently.

At the state and local level Boardman et al. predict continuing privatisation of public transit.[30] Since we are talking about state- and county-level regulations, it takes less time to open up the market to outside investors. In addition, any debt that these firms might have would be smaller. In this sector gains in efficiency, costs and quality are the most notable.[31] However, labour laws and contracting restrictions are the biggest barriers to the contracting out of public transport. We expect to see the government address these concerns in the near future to increase transit privatisation.

Airports are another example of entities at the state and local level that will continue to be privatised in the near future. While airports themselves are rarely sold Poole identifies contracting out management for short periods of time (five years or less) and leasing as the most popular 'privatisation' strategies.[32] Obvious benefits in this area include efficiency from specialisation and savings from economies of scale. This would lead to a cheaper and more efficient service for those using airports. In the same area, privatisation of air traffic control has been extensively debated at the federal level. As Poole notes, people opposing privatisation point out job losses and possible loss in security as the major concerns.[33] On the other side, people supporting the privatisation of air traffic control speak of increased efficiency and passenger satisfaction. As security pressures go down we will probably see more pressure towards the privatisation of air traffic control. Electricity production and distribution is another area that will see continued growth in privatisation efforts, as Boardman et al. note.[34] First we had the California crisis. Then, just three years ago we saw a blackout in the northeastern states of the USA (14 August 2003). It is not surprising to see the government considering the privatisation of this sector.

An area which is much more relevant to the USA, given its bellicose nature, are the privatisation opportunities derived from war efforts, particularly in Iraq. Whether it is security efforts, rebuilding structures, educating the country or even feeding the people, the tasks involved in reconstructing a country are daunting. In the case of Iraq the process of contracting is so organised that it will probably provide the framework for future reconstructions, whether it involves the USA or not. In the privatisation efforts of Iraq two major differences come out. First, the contracting does not face political hurdles, since no loss of American jobs is involved. Second, the federal government and the military are the primary parties awarding the contracts. In addition, since the tasks are so far away from the USA it is difficult to evaluate the efficiency of the tasks.

While little empirical research has been published about prison privatisation, privatisation.org reports that local, state and federal government agencies are increasingly turning to the private sector for the construction and management of these facilities. Because of the nature of the task the only viable option at this point is contracting out through bidding, which eliminates leverage and federal support as objections to privatisation. Segal notes that savings is the most important reason for the privatising efforts, with averages around 10 per cent in Texas and Arizona. Segal predicts that as the economy recovers we should see a rise in the pressures for privatisation of correctional facilities.[35]

The corrections experience only accentuates the flexibility that the USA has when it comes to privatisation because this does not only mean the selling of facilities and assets. It is this fact that has allowed privatisation efforts to move smoothly in many different areas, thus avoiding the political problems that do not seem to have a solution in the near future. Over time the private sector's role in the American economy seems likely to increase even more.

Notes

1   See Megginson, Nash and Van Randenborgh (1994).
2   See Megginson and Netter (2001).
3   Logue (1995).

4   Moore and Segal (1998).
5   Segal (2003).
6   Galambos (2000).
7   MacAvoy (1993).
8   Kesan and Shah (2001).
9   Logue (1995).
10   MacAvoy and McIsaac (1995).
11   Logue and MacAvoy (2001).
12   Moore and Woerner (2000).
13   Moore and Woerner (2000).
14   Ellet (2003).
15   Ellet (2003).
16   Poole (2004).
17   The airline industry is much more dynamic than the government in their demand for security. This makes for a very inefficient administration of security staff that would be improved by contracting the service out. See Poole (2002).
18   Boardman et al. (2003) point out that some not-for-profit firms have won contracts (for example, social services such as nursing homes, hospices, welfare administration programmes, and so on) in recent years.
19   See, for example, Poole (2004) and Boardman et al. (2003).
20   Moore and Segal (1998).
21   Moore and Segal (2002).
22   Moore and Segal (2002).
23   Moore and Segal (1998).
24   Segal (2003).
25   Segal (2003).
26   Crew and Kleindorfer (2003).
27   Boardman et al. (2003).
28   Boardman et al. (2003).
29   Boardman et al. (2003).
30   Ibid.
31   See, for example, Love and Cox (1993).
32   Poole (1994).
33   Poole (2004).
34   Boardman et al. (2003).
35   Segal (2003).

References

Boardman, A.E., C. Laurin and A.R. Vining (2003) 'Privatisation in North America', in David Parker and David Saal (eds), *International Handbook on Privatisation* (Cheltenham: Edward Elgar) pp. 129–60.

Crew, M.A., and P.R. Kleindorfer (2003) 'Postal Privatisation in the United States', in David Parker and David Saal (eds), *International Handbook on Privatisation* (Cheltenham: Edward Elgar) pp. 187–205.

Ellet, T. (2003) 'Airport Privatisation after the Bush Executive Order', *Annual Privatisation Report 2003* (Reason Foundation) www.privatisation.org

Galambos, L. (2000) 'State-Owned Enterprises in a Hostile Environment', in Pier Toninelli (ed.), *The Rise and Fall of State-Owned Enterprise* (Cambridge University Press) pp. 273–302.

Kesan, J.P., and R.C. Shah (2001) 'Fool Us Once Shame On You – Fool Us Twice Shame On Us: What We Can Learn from the Privatisations of the Internet Backbone Network and the Domain Name System', *Washington University Law Quarterly*, 79, p. 89.

Logue, D. (1995) 'The Strategy for Privatisation in the United States', in Paul W. MacAvoy (ed.), *Deregulation and Privatisation in the United States* (Edinburgh University Press), pp. 88–108.

Logue, D., and P.W. MacAvoy (2001) 'The Tennessee Valley Authority: Competing in Markets for Capital and Electricity in Pursuit of Solvency', Yale SOM Working Paper no. OL-18.

Love, J., and W. Cox (2003) 'Competitive Contracting of Transit Services', *How To Guide No. 5* (Reason Foundation) www.privatisation.org

MacAvoy, P.W. (1993) 'Prices after Deregulation: The United States Experience', The Hume Papers on Public Policy 1, pp. 42–8.

MacAvoy, P.W., and G.S. McIsaac (1995) 'The Current File in the Case for Privatisation of the Federal Government Enterprises', in Paul W MacAvoy (ed.), *Deregulation and Privatisation in the United States* (Edinburgh University Press) pp. 88–108.

Megginson, W.L., R.C. Nash and M. van Randenborgh (1994) 'The Financial and Operating Performance of Newly-Privatized Firms: An International Empirical Analysis', *Journal of Finance*, 49, pp. 403–52.

Megginson, W.L., and J.M. Netter (2001) 'From State to Market: A Survey of Empirical Studies on Privatization', *Journal of Economic Literature*, 39, pp. 321–89.

Moore, A., and G. Segal (1998) 'Private Prisons: Quality Correction at a Lower Cost', Policy Study no. 240, (Reason Foundation) www.privatisation.org

Moore, A., and G. Segal (2002) 'Weighing the Watchmen: Evaluating the Costs and Benefits of Outsourcing Correctional Facilities', Policy Study no. 289 (Reason Foundation) www.privatisation.org

Moore, A., and J. Woerner (2000) 'Integrating Municipal Utilities into a Competitive Electricity Market', Policy Study no. 270, (Reason Foundation) www. privatisation.org.

Poole, R.W. (1994) 'Guidelines to Airport Privatisation: How to Guide', (Reason Foundation). www.privatisation.org

Poole, R.W. (2002) 'Improving Airport Passenger Screening', Policy Study no. 298 (Reason Foundation) www.privatisation.org

Poole, R.W. (2004) 'Contracting Air Traffic Control Towers: A Competitive Sourcing Success Story', Reason Foundation Study.

Segal, G. (2003) 'Privatisation Watch: Corrections Privatisation Outlook', No. 316 (April) (Reason Foundation) www.privatisation.org

Part III
Conclusion

16
Towards Understanding Network Service Transnationalisation

Judith Clifton, Francisco Comín and Daniel Díaz-Fuentes

At the heart of this book lie three main observations. Firstly, network services, focusing in particular on transport (railways, civil aviation and infrastructures, including roads, ports and airports), communications (telecommunications, post and broadcasting), energy (electricity and gas) and water, had – with important exceptions – been nationally or locally bound in terms of ownership and management for at least the second half of the twentieth century in Europe, North America and beyond. The USA was the most important overall exception to this trend which, as we have seen, organises its networks under mainly private but also public ownership. Secondly, this arrangement between the state and network services, which crystallised into a social settlement and economic regulatory framework, was changing and, in the face of privatisation, deregulation, liberalisation and regional integration policies, may be gradually unravelling. Insisting on the importance of these services for the quality of life of all citizens, organisations and societies, as well as the long-term importance assigned to these networks for welfare, security, economic development and technological progress, among other reasons, it was argued that attention was now due to the processes of their transformation.

A third observation was that during the 1980s one of the major debates, if not *the* major debate, surrounding public enterprises concerned ownership and management preferences, with the dominant trend being that many authors and institutions asserted the inherent superiority of the privately run and owned enterprise. According to this perspective it may be surprising that networks, some still largely publicly owned, others of private or mixed ownership have, in recent years, developed into the world's leading TNCs. Network 'giants' have emerged when formerly publicly-owned networks were privatised, but also where markets have been significantly liberalised and where ownership is still largely public, such as German, French and Swedish/Finnish telecommunications enterprises. They have also arisen in only partially liberalised markets, such as the electricity market, as the cases of EDF and E.ON show. Moreover they have emerged where domestic services are still characterised by monopolistic arrangements, such as post and the railways in most European countries.

The assumed superior efficiencies of private ownership and management alone cannot account for this transformation, for we have also witnessed the recent internationalisation of largely publicly-owned and run networks that do not fit the stereotype of sluggish, inward-looking rent seekers when they compete effectively with their private counterparts in markets overseas, as cases from Canada, Mexico, Belgium, France, Germany, Scandinavia, Spain and Portugal have shown, and to a lesser extent from the UK, Italy and Ireland. Moreover public and private dichotomies have questionable explanatory value for business behaviour when public enterprise goes abroad acting as aggressively as any other commercial enterprise in the pursuit of profit. In order to understand these transformations, in this final chapter we return to the original questions raised in the introduction relating to network transformation, before synthesising the findings of all chapters in an attempt to answer our questions.

First, and most generally, we wished to enquire *what kinds of transformation network service enterprises are undergoing*. We have seen how the recent wave of network internationalisation is not unprecedented in the sense that there were extensive cross-border flows across networks during the nineteenth century as countries built up and operated their infrastructure (as chapters here have shown in the case of Europe in general, and the case of railways in Belgium and Scandinavia in particular). In Europe, however, this was generally characterised by private enterprise from the most developed nations offering technology and technical and operational know-how to less-developed nations. This was followed by a period from the end of the nineteenth century onwards where host governments sought to gain control of the networks through nationalisation and the creation of SOEs, with technological change and the economics of networks being at least as important, and probably more important, than (socialist, Keynesian or Schumpeterian) ideology (see Millward 2005 and this volume). Greater deregulation of certain network services (deeper in telecommunications than electricity or postal services) and the liberalisation of FDI generated increased FDI flows to and from these services, particularly from the 1990s. This therefore constituted a sharp break from the past. Privatisation was, however, uneven according to sector and country despite the fact that network privatisation accounted for a significant volume of privatisation proceeds, States in many countries kept significant shares in these networks (see Clifton, Comín and Díaz-Fuentes 2003, and chapters by Schröter and Fridenson in this volume). Separate though interwoven policies affecting networks included deregulation and liberalisation in the consolidation of 'new' regional markets, such as the EU and NAFTA, the two integration zones under study here. Particularly from the end of the twentieth century we start to see the growth of international activities of many (recently privatised or state-owned) networks. This caused us to challenge the stereotypes and dichotomised categories of public and private enterprise, with the latter perceived as *inherently* more efficient, dynamic, entrepreneurial and so on. Sometimes the internationalisation activity of particular networks was largely unprecedented, but more often networks had been involved previously in one kind of internationalisation activity or another, whether this was offering expertise at the construction stage or agreeing technical norms, and so forth. For instance, Canadian electricity exports to the USA started from 1901, helped by the fact that peak loads in the two countries happen at different times and storage is not feasible. Decades later, NAFTA led to an intensification of electricity transmission between the two neighbours. Another example of early internationalisation was Belgian railways which commenced internationalisation almost immediately after it was built, from the 1830s, to become an international transit system a decade later, as a means of promoting that country's economic development. Decades of experience were relevant when, towards the end of the twentieth century, Belgium's railways were transformed into that country's largest TNC by staff in 2004, with hundreds of acquisitions in order to become an intermodal service. So, though there are important precedents of international activity from the nineteenth century, the recent surge of internationalisation – which we call the 'second wave' of internationalisation – is remarkable for its speed, reach and significance in terms of global FDI patterns.

This observation leads to many other questions. *Why did networks internationalise – or not – from the 1990s?* We have critiqued the tendency to dichotomise ownership and management into either private or public in the introduction and elsewhere.[1] It has not just been the recently privatised networks that have launched aggressive and successful campaigns to extend their networks abroad. To be sure, the internationalisation of some networks was facilitated by mixed ownership, such as the cases of SAS and Telefonica. In many other examples internationalisation followed privatisation, such as the cases of E.ON, RWE, Deutsche Post and Deutsche Telekom in Germany, Suez in France and TELMEX in Mexico. However, publicly-owned networks also embarked on aggressive internationalisation policies, as shown in the cases of Gaz de France and EDF, Hydro-Québec, BC Hydro and Manitoba Hydro in Canada, Aer Lingus, the Belgian railways NMBS and so on. There are many other instances not covered in this volume, such as, in the case of Spain, the Spanish Airport Authority AENA and the Spanish State Ports (which directly depend on the Ministry of Transport), which have ventured into Bolivia, Colombia and Cuba. In addition, though some networks were privatised they remained tightly linked to – or even partially controlled by – members of the political establishment. These networks, under political influence, also embarked on ambitious expansion programmes abroad, as in the case of GAZPROM in Russia, many of Europe's largest telecoms, energy and water companies and TELMEX in Mexico. Indeed the share of public ownership of an enterprise does not really matter in the case of France, as the government always kept full control of a company in which it had a share, as Fridenson argues (Chapter 5 this volume). Whether networks are public or private, political interference is sometimes inevitable. A case in point is German energy company E.ON's special relationship with Russian gas giant GAZPROM, in which Schroeder and Putin have been directly involved. Moreover, and perhaps even paradoxically, some SOEs continued to enjoy monopolies at home whilst they aggressively exploited new opportunities abroad opened up by integrated markets, such as EDF, Gaz de France, Deutsche Post and the Canadian electricity enterprises, as well as other enterprises such as European post companies. Janus-faced, they behaved as public entities at home and private ones abroad. If the private ownership and management of a network is not on its own a satisfactory variable to explain internationalisation which other variables can help us to understand the decision to internationalise?

A far more promising avenue to explain this phenomenon is *deregulation or, more accurately, re-regulation*. Ongoing regulatory reforms have played a central role in the transformation of TNC networks. This process, however, is complex: there is no single generalised deregulation process 'globalising' or homogenising networks around the world. Rather there are different patterns of business transformation in the face of regulatory reforms in sectors such as telecommunications, post, broadcasting, electricity, airlines and airport control, railways and so on. Rather than witnessing a generalised 'economic globalisation' (a universal and inevitable explanation of economic processes of deregulation, privatisation and transnationalisation), differentiated regional processes are emerging that are redefining the relationship between TNCs and governments at the national and supranational level, such as NAFTA, the EU, Scandinavia, and the transition economies, such as Russia. Regulatory change is not only affecting the exchange and provision of services (price, accessibility, investment) but also the expansion of new TNCs in terms of M&As (antitrust or competition policy).[2] Whilst some analysts, such as Schröter (Chapter 6 this volume), refer to these processes as the 'third wave' of an Americanisation of European life, in some ways the very opposite could be argued: that namely there are the beginnings of a consolidation of a 'European' way of life, exemplified in the provision of new, European regulations of public services, European sectoral regulations, a European single market, and even the emergence of 'European Economic Swans'.[3]

One factor requiring analysis is the *importance of economies of scale and scope in networks (despite the fact that some analysts claim technological change erodes economies of scale and scope)*. Findings here confirm that there are patterns of network enterprise transformation that could be attributed to the scale and scope of public enterprises in different activities. In activities such as railways and electrical systems national networks were tightly coupled and enjoyed long-term protection from deregulation and privatisation, as the case of Scandinavia shows. The notion of a public enterprise as the optimal way of organising industry remained very strong in many countries, particularly France, Sweden and Finland. Loosely coupled national networks, however, such as aviation, were easier to deregulate, at least from a technological point of view and therefore it was easier to introduce competition.

How important a factor was enterprise size or domestic market? While it seems that an enterprise of considerable size had an advantage when embarking on internationalisation this was not a necessary prerequisite. In the Canadian case British Columbia Hydro, Manitoba Hydro and Hydro-Québec were of different sizes but all three went abroad. The German case argues along similar lines: both large and small enterprises internationalised and there were success stories and failures in both categories. Spain's Telefonica was relatively small as it commenced internationalisation, but it grew rapidly into a large enterprise beyond the European market.

Another factor that explains some network internationalisation is the *policy of creating national champions.* When networks (public or private) have enjoyed strong market domination at home this has provided them with a firm base from which they have been able to 'leap' into new business abroad. TELMEX of Mexico is certainly an instance of this, as are Gaz de France and EDF in France, GAZPROM in Russia, Telefonica and Endesa in Spain and Deutsche Post, RWE, Deutsche Telekom and E.ON in Germany. Likewise, but in the opposite direction Toninelli and Vasta believe that Italy could have established other TNCs, apart from Telecom Italia and ENEL, in the world's top 100 if a policy of establishing a national champion had been pursued. The same could be said, perhaps, for the UK: here the government did not pursue a national champion policy nor did it restrict acquisitions and hostile takeovers in contrast to the French or the Spanish.

Another important explanation lies in the *rich experience* networks have accumulated over decades or even centuries in regard to technology, technical assistance and know-how which provided precedents and made them agile when confronting the challenges of their second internationalisation. This was certainly the case of the electricity networks in Canada, which exported these skills worldwide for over a century. The case of Belgium is similar: the railway network, Belgium's largest TNC in terms of staff in 2004, had decades of international experience. Internationalisation had been crucial for the country's economic development, establishing the transnational infrastructure required to export mining, industrial and agricultural goods, as well as to serve as a transit station for commerce between Britain, France and the Rhineland. In Scandinavia an early pooling of resources across borders to gain economies of scale and network economies, as a consequence of small domestic markets, as well as the influence of private business, was also important in the case of SAS, which commenced transatlantic traffic from the 1940s and is now one of the largest airlines in Europe and 15th largest in the world. SAS proved efficient in its confrontation of technological change and embracing of innovation, contrasting sharply with railways in Scandinavia that sought national solutions to public service problems.

Another useful explanation of network internationalisation has been the existence of a *geographical or cultural/linguistic comparative advantage.* In the case of Germany, for instance, Schröter argues that possibly one of the keys to their success was their intimate cultural, political and linguistic knowledge of the recently opened markets of Eastern Europe. The strategy of many German networks was largely to confine their market to Europe whilst focusing particularly on Eastern Europe, marketing their reputation, high technical standards and quality to secure access to these new markets. Though EDF's investment is worldwide the bulk is restricted to Europe. Portugal, Spain and Mexico are also cases where 'soft' criteria such as culture and language mattered. Portuguese networks such as EDP and PT expanded particularly in Portuguese-speaking countries including Brazil in the Americas and Cape Verde, Angola, Guinea-Bissau and Mozambique in Africa. Cross-border proximity to facilitate access to the centre of Europe was an additional factor that encouraged Portuguese strategic alliances with their Spanish neighbours. Spain's incursion into expansion abroad has also been important across Latin America, as in the case of Telefonica, Endesa and so on. TELMEX and its spin-off América Móvil management specifically stated they saw the Spanish speakers in the whole of the Americas ('latinos' in the USA and South America in general) as a natural market, and they exploited the Spanish speaking market across all telecommunications services. Cultural, linguistic and geopolitical affinity can, of course, also work the other way round. The case of GAZPROM is very clear. Here a highly ambitious programme to deliver gas to Europe, even the USA and Mexico, has been pursued by this company, but Russian outward FDI has been viewed with suspicion generally and by former members of the Soviet élite in particular, who preferred foreign capital from elsewhere. Resistance to Russian capital from Europe is such that GAZPROM has taken a turn to the East, pursuing markets in Asia.

Another, partially related factor that is sometimes important is *how favourably national enterprises are perceived by international markets*. Interestingly, the cases of French and Russian networks stress this the most. In the former case Fridenson argues that internationalisation weighed heavily in favour of privatisation as French public enterprises were unfavourably viewed by the international business community. In the Russian case, whilst all Russian business was viewed with suspicion Klinova argues Russian state enterprise was viewed with even more suspicion than its private counterpart. However, whether an enterprise was public or private was in other situations irrelevant, such as the case of Canada. Moreover one of the reasons provided for the success of German network internationalisation was their reputation for quality and tradition abroad, even though they were recently privatised SOEs.

A further explanation of successful internationalisation is *accumulated know-how and expertise in operations abroad*, providing networks with experience and boldness in this field. Hydro-Québec, BC Hydro and Manitoba Hydro, for instance, aggressively moved abroad, embracing risk and exploiting their accumulated know-how which they had internationalised from the beginning of the twentieth century. Long-term international experience was also a reason for the success of many French networks since they were eager to move abroad – agile operators indeed in comparison with their more cautious Japanese, counterparts.

Sometimes networks expanded abroad because they were *forced to by new competition* resulting from the formation of successful new, private companies in markets where they had previously enjoyed a monopoly. This is the case of Irish airlines. Ryanair was the first airline to exploit deregulation in Europe. Interestingly it is argued that some new incumbents – including Ryanair – have started to break up integrated network logic, replacing it by point-to-point travel. Other successful new entrants after network deregulation causing pressure to incumbents not covered in this volume include Vodafone, Tele2 and EasyJet. Ryanair took advantage of new organisational structures (low or non-unionisation, outsourcing, reduced services, higher load factors, Internet bookings, quicker turnarounds, reformulating products and so on) to pose a serious challenge to incumbent Aer Lingus, which saw its passenger market decline rapidly. Aer Lingus thus transformed itself into a successfully commercialised airline, adopting many of the practices of Ryanair, increasing its international operations and therefore reinventing itself, achieving the highest operating margins in Europe. Its privatisation was announced in 2005. New pressures have forced some airlines to fail, such as Sabena, or to transform their traditional business strategies in order to seek alliances, mergers, acquisitions, low-fare airlines and so on.

Finally, we have seen how some countries enjoy *a clear competitive sectoral advantage*. This is particularly clear in the case of natural resources, such as in France (water and other urban services), Russia (gas) and Canada, as a leading producer of cheap and renewable energy.

Given these observations, what, then, is the *consequence for the relation between network services and government regulation*, which had arrived at a settlement from at least the post-war period? Is this relationship untangling? This, of course, is a highly complex question and the evidence is quite mixed. The Canadian evidence shows how SOE electricity networks have gone abroad, aggressively seeking out new markets and usually choosing private partners. Some have almost run into trouble, such as Canadian BC Hydro subsidiary Powerex's involvement in the Californian electricity crisis. At home, however, they continue to be national and public enterprises, justifying their activities abroad in order to defend their services at home. It is fascinating that, behind this duality, their evolving configuration exhibits more dependence upon the American (or, more accurately, Federal state) regulation than the Canadian regulatory framework. This would seem to be evidence of a breaking away from the national Regulatory State (Majone 1996) towards a foreign state, or even towards a multinational one. The case of Russia is also illuminating. In the aftermath of privatisation the Russian government has actually sought to increase its participation in GAZPROM in recent years, amounting to the rise of state capitalism. Privatisation has not brought about a competitive framework in Russia nor has it improved the poor managerial skills inherited from decades of a non-market economy. Thus, its ambitious expansion abroad increases in parallel to the fortunes of its new owners. In other words, enterprises can be partially or wholly privatised formally, yet the government can find ways of maintaining or extending its grip on them by 'placing' directors on the board and forging government–business links. Mexico bears some similarities here to the Russian case. Mexico has behaved rather differently from other large Latin American countries, such as Argentina, Brazil and Chile, when reforming its networks. When TELMEX was privatised an explicit and personal promise was made by the President not to sell to foreigners but to Mexican private entrepreneurs. This promise was given both to the trade unions and to the public at large. It was an explicit concern to prioritise European or Canadian technological partners at the expense of US ones (Clifton 2000). Preference towards Mexican owners, whether public or private, has been constant over the long term. Networks and national resources, particularly PEMEX, are considered part of the national identity. So, though privatisation signals a formal rupture between state and business in Mexico and Russia the reality is more complex. In France from the 1980s, as in most of continental Europe such as Spain and Portugal, there is the tradition of the '*noyau dur*', whereby existing or new ties are sought with other large national enterprises in order to build up strategic alliances and cross-ownership to avoid hostile foreign takeovers (Morin 1998). In Portugal national private industrial groups linked to energy markets were prioritised during the privatisation of EDP and Petrogal.

What happens when foreigners own or control national or local networks? Does foreign ownership matter? First, some countries have been more stubborn in resisting foreign network ownership than others, signalling that foreign ownership is perceived to matter. The case of Mexico has been discussed. France has also sought to protect many of its networks. Britain has been more liberal than most countries in its opening up to FDI. Second, some countries prefer FDI from particular countries rather than others. The examples of aversion to Russian FDI or French public enterprise are two cases in point. But even between 'friendly' large countries, such as Germany and Italy (Deutsche Telecom and Telecom Italia) in 1999, Italy and France (Enel and Suez) or indeed Germany and Spain (E.ON and Endesa) in 2006, network ownership is sensitive. In the latter case the issue of Germans owning Spanish or Catalonian energy is still a contentious one, generating debates at the popular level about the national interest, despite regulatory guarantees. So, even in the era of regional integration and NAFTA the international trade of electricity does not correspond to capital liberalisation. Canadian and Mexican electricity companies fiercely guard corporate control. The perception that networks remain an important part of the national interest is still relevant, though perhaps to an uneven extent across countries. Geopolitics also still matter. Even in the USA, where network privatisation in terms of sales has been limited, restrictions are placed on inward FDI and justified by national security concerns. In the energy sector, for instance, in 2005 the unsolicited bid by CNOOC (Chinese National Offshore Oil Co.) to buy

Unocal, a US oil company, was rejected on the ground that CNOOC was a state-controlled company, thus not a free market enterprise and would challenge national security. In the same way, in 2006 US authorities blocked the acquisition of six US commercial ports previously owned by British P&O when P&O was taken over by Dubai Port World, an United Arab Emirates SOE. National interest is still a real issue despite regional integration and networks are still perceived as key to this in all countries, though to a different degree.

Finally, how are society and its citizens responding to these transformations? It is important to consider the role played by society in demanding technological change and network development. The production, implementation and organisation of networks have had to respond to public demand and support. The importance of society and technology pull has been visible in many of the chapters here, such as society's preference for public ownership and management of the Belgian railways in the nineteenth century for price, quality and safety reasons, as well as social protest and demands that networks provide for welfare and regional development across Europe. This was particularly visible in the Scandanavian case. Most likely the general public is more sensitive to the activities of publicly owned and run enterprises that go abroad (since they are paying for them with their taxes). Do they perceive the public service is diluted when publicly-owned enterprises become international commercial operators? In Europe, changes to national networks in terms of ownership and/or management are subject to national and supranational regulation. Despite this, possible takeover of part of the energy sector by German interests has sparked debate about what is and is not in the national or local public interest. This development is an interesting test of the countries' commitment to the integration process. Spain – seemingly one of the EU's most supportive members, as confirmed over the long term by public opinion polls and, most recently, with its support of the draft Constitution – is currently being tested. When publicly-owned and run networks go abroad they risk damaging their reputation at home. This is because their job changes: if at home they must comply as a public service provider, abroad their remit is freed up and may be driven to make money, resulting in a completely different managerial style. In Britain, the BBC has made huge legal, financial and managerial efforts to separate off its commercial and public service broadcasting activities so that its commercial global channel BBC World is perceived as a different, international and commercial product. Canadian BC Hydro subsidiary Powerex also ran risks when it chose to behave like any commercially driven concern. Seeking partnerships usually only with private companies, using more outsourcing, aggressive managerial styles and short-term profit opportunities they have become energy brokers. Like the BBC, these companies justify their commercial activity abroad by claiming the profits help shore up public services at home. Engaging in international commercial activities does not necessarily or directly dilute public service at home, especially when good regulation is in place. Clearly, however, though these activities are separate, a scandal abroad would indirectly wreak havoc on an enterprise's brand. Thus although it is perhaps too early to know yet, certainly publicly-owned and run networks do run new risks in their international adventures. On the other hand, many former SOEs which have accumulated decades of experience providing quality public services under social regulation in their home markets have finally profited from their experiences when bidding in privatisation processes in Latin America or Eastern Europe. Their capacities and reputation for providing universal, affordable, reliable and secure services have been their competitive advantage in the challenge of internationalisation.

By way of final conclusions, research on network transformation here has confirmed that, despite technological change and deep policy reforms, networks are still perceived as playing a special role in society, and governments are hesitant to relinquish too much control. Deregulation and increased international competition will bring further transnationalisation, though there remains a lot to be accomplished, as the TENs project for transport, energy and communications in the EU shows. Important advances include the effort to forge transnational regulation of public services in the EU (Clifton, Comín and Díaz Fuentes 2005), and the turn to focus on user satisfaction, as shown by Andersson-Skog and Pettersson in this volume (Chapter 10). The recent terrorist attacks, quite cheap to execute and asymmetric in damage caused – particularly from 11 September 2001 – on airlines, metros and trains in the USA, Spain and Britain, using mobile phones to activate bombs or the post to send anthrax, may well reinforce this trend. Additionally, if the cost of increasing security in telecommunications and transport traffic (both air or maritime) is to be assumed by industry, users or society at large, this would restrict further network service development and TNC expansion, whilst security concerns may also warn against the possible increased political risk involved in some network transnationalisation, as we have seen in the case of the EU and Russia, and the USA and the East. Networks differ from the average manufactured good, due to their role in society, politics and economics, as well as their various technological features. Though the organisation of networks has often been explained by ideology (whether nationalism, socialism or the influence of the New Right on national security), there are so many common trends in network organisation that explanations of changing institutional forms are better explained by technology and economic features, as well as societal and strategic concerns. The age of network globalisation may well come, but the nation remains a key player, at least for the moment, whilst the supranational players are slowly taking shape.

Notes

1   Clifton, Comín and Díaz-Fuentes (2003).
2   Grosse (2005).
3   Clifton, Comín and Díaz-Fuentes (forthcoming 2007).

References

Clifton, J. (2000) *The Politics of Telecommunications in Mexico: Privatisation and State–Labour Relations 1982–1995* (Palgrave-Macmillan).

Clifton, J., F. Comín and D. Díaz-Fuentes (2003) *Privatisation in the European Union: Public Enterprises and Integration* (Dordrecht/Boston: Kluwer Academic Publishers).

Clifton, J., F. Comín and D. Díaz-Fuentes (2005) 'Towards a Charter for Services of General Interest', *Public Management Review*, 7 (3) (September).

Clifton, J., F. Comín and D. Díaz-Fuentes (forthcoming 2007) 'On the Rise of European Network Economic Swans?', in H. Schröter (ed.), *In Search of the European Enterprise* (Springer).

Grosse, R. (ed.) (2005) *International Business and Government Relations in the 21st Century* (Cambridge University Press).

Majone, G. (1996) *Regulating Europe* (London: Routledge).

Millward, R. (2005) *Private and Public Enterprise in Europe: Energy, Telecommunications and Transport c. 1830–1990* (Cambridge University Press).

Morin, F. (1998) 'The Privatisation Process and Corporate Governance: the French Case', in OECD, *Corporate Governance, State-Owned Enterprises and Privatization* (Paris).

Index